Behavioural Science for Quality and Continuous Improvement

D0762991

This impactful volume demonstrates the application and power of psychology and behavioural economics in the pursuit of quality and continuous improvement.

It focusses on how the works of stalwarts such as Daniel Kahneman, Richard Thaler, Mihaly Csikszentmihalyi, and many others can be used to build an organisation that is known for quality products and flawless service delivery. The application of psychology and behavioural economics is still new to quality improvement, and in this book, Debashis Sarkar shares 25 lessons, featuring specific examples based on real life, that show how their application can increase the effectiveness of outcomes.

Behavioural Science for Quality and Continuous Improvement: 25 Lessons from Psychology and Behavioural Economics is ideal for business-improvement professionals of all hierarchies and across different functional areas and industries seeking to understand the potential of psychology and behavioural economics and their applications, as well as in training and executive development programmes and for scholars of operations management, quality management, and engineering.

Debashis Sarkar is a managing partner at Proliferator Advisory & Consulting, a firm focussed on customer centricity and operational excellence. A pioneer in the field of quality and organisational improvement, Debashis has authored several books, including *The Little Big Things in Operational Excellence*. He is the recipient of various recognitions such as the Phil Crosby Medal, the Simon Collier Award, and the first Quality Champion Platinum Award from the Quality Council of India – the highest award for quality from the Indian government. He is a fellow of the American Society for Quality.

Behavioural Science for Quality and Continuous Improvement

25 Lessons from Psychology and Behavioural Economics

Debashis Sarkar

Routledge
Taylor & Francis Group

LONDON AND NEW YORK

Cover image: © Getty Images

First published 2022
by Routledge
2 Park Square, Milton Park, Abingdon, Oxon OX14 4RN

and by Routledge
605 Third Avenue, New York, NY 10158

Routledge is an imprint of the Taylor & Francis Group, an informa business

British Library Cataloguing-in-Publication Data
A catalogue record for this book is available from the British
Library

Library of Congress Cataloging-in-Publication Data
A catalog record for this book has been requested

ISBN: 978-1-032-16839-5 (hbk)
ISBN: 978-1-032-16837-1 (pbk)
ISBN: 978-1-003-25051-7 (ebk)

DOI: 10.4324/9781003250517

Typeset in Bembo
by Apex CoVantage, LLC

This book is dedicated to my mother,
Malabika Sarkar,
With love.
Ma, we miss you every day since you left us on
April 10, 2020.

Contents

Notes to readers   ix
Preface   x

Introduction   1

Lesson: 1   Solidifying the business case   7

Lesson: 2   Cementing relationships   12

Lesson: 3   Gaining commitment   19

Lesson: 4   Getting across the message   25

Lesson: 5   Not always about people   33

Lesson: 6   What quality experts need to know   36

Lesson: 7   When facts are overlooked   42

Lesson: 8   The intricacies of change   48

Lesson: 9   The power of familiarity   58

Lesson: 10   The role of emotions   61

Lesson: 11   Engaging hearts and minds   68

Lesson: 12   The biases in problem-solving   75

Lesson: 13   Minimising cognitive overload   84

Lesson: 14   Five rules for customer solution design   92

Lesson: 15   Making quality issues known   98

Lesson: 16   The halo effect   103

Lesson: 17   Building psychological safety   110

Lesson: 18   The power of open-ended questions   119

Lesson: 19   The invisible gorillas   123

Lesson: 20   Goals, measurements, and targets   130

Lesson: 21   When employees are defensive   138

Lesson: 22   Blind optimism during eruptions   145

Lesson: 23   Communicating visually   151

Lesson: 24   Not-so-obvious tactics for solving problems   156

Lesson: 25   Taking employees on board   159

About the author   167
Bibliography   168
Index   179

Notes to readers

This book is an assorted set of lessons which have been written in such a way that you can start from any lesson.

While "he" has been used as a gender in the book, the words "he" and "she" have been used synonymously.

The term "quality professional" refers to someone who uses methods of quality for organisational improvement. It includes professionals engaged in continuous improvement, Lean manufacturing, business excellence, operational excellence and process improvement, intelligent automation, Six Sigma, and so on.

The words "quality professional", "quality-improvement professional", "continuous-improvement professional", "quality practitioner", "continuous-improvement practitioner", "Master Black Belt", "Lean Master", and "quality leader" all refer to a quality professional.

The words "quality improvement", "continuous improvement", and "quality transformation" have been used synonymously.

The terms "continuous-improvement programme", "quality-improvement programme", and "quality programme" refer to a journey of quality and continuous improvement, which is often an ongoing effort in an organisation.

The terms "company", "firm", "business", "organisation", "business-organisation", and "enterprise" all refer to an entity engaged in commercial or business activity.

The words "product" and "service" have been synonymously used.

When you read the book, I would recommend that you highlight the areas that you find important and see how you can apply them in the world of quality and continuous improvement.

The application of behavioural science to quality and continuous improvement is new. Over the next few years, I see more information and experience being added to the book of knowledge. Feel free to share with me your challenges and successes; it will help to take this practice forward. My email is in the preface.

Preface

My exploration of behavioural psychology started a decade ago, when I cata-lysed a business improvement at a leading service company. The project had been completed and all solutions had been implemented, yet the desired results were not seen. We had used the best data and analytics to arrive at our recommendation, but in vain. Down the road, however, we discovered almost by happenstance what we had missed. I realised during a conversa-tion with just one employee, almost six months after implementation, that our recommendations were perceived somehow to be in contradiction to employees' self-images. There were psychological elements we had never considered that prevented the staff from implementing the solutions we had recommended!

This experience taught me that psychology plays a big role in all quality and continuous-improvement efforts. It's up to us to look for those dimensions and proactively embed the right tactics as we go. Since the fiasco I just mentioned, I have been consciously trying to use the principles of psychology and behav-ioural economics in all of my consulting work. I am happy to share that, in most instances, strategies adopted from psychology and behavioural economics have surely helped me. Or they have given heft to solutions that were being proposed that we were otherwise unsure about.

Over the last couple of years, as I have been exploring and navigating where the worlds of psychology and behavioural economics meet with the world of quality, I've become fascinated by how much can be applied from one to the other and how much can be achieved when that happens.

Let me clarify that this is a book by a practitioner for a practitioner. It focusses on how the works of stalwarts such as Daniel Kahneman, Richard Thaler, Mihaly Csikszentmihalyi, and many others, whose names and books you will find in the bibliography at the end of this book, can be used in an effort to build an organisation that is known for quality and continuous improvement.

The concepts of behavioural science and their application to quality improve-ment are still evolving. I have just scratched the surface of this subject. Your feedback on what you read in the following pages will sharpen our thinking and add to our body of knowledge. I would love to hear your perspective and stories. Please reach me directly at: debashissarkar4@yahoo.com or debashis.sarkar@proliferator.net.

Happy reading.

– Debashis Sarkar
Founder & Managing Partner
Proliferator Advisory & Consulting
Mumbai, January 2022

Introduction

What is psychology?

The word "psychology" is derived from the Greek words *psyche*, which means soul or mind, and *logia*, which means study. Psychology is our scientific study of mind and behaviour.

The first experimental laboratory of psychology was established at the University of Leipzig in 1879 by Wilhelm Wundt. Thus began the journey of psychology research, opening up so many areas that had been previously unexplored. It also demonstrated that the study of the human mind and human behaviour is truly an area for scientific inquiry, one with a knowledge base to be built upon research and the work of successive generations.

For many, our introduction to psychology may have happened in school, when we learned about the 1890s experiments of Ivan Pavlov. He studied the salivation activity of dogs when they were being fed. He saw that dogs would salivate when food was placed in front of them, and he observed too that dogs would salivate when they heard the footsteps of his assistant who brought the food. What he then found was that any object or event that the dogs related to feeding triggered the same response. Pavlov proved that animals could be conditioned to produce a response. This sparked similar studies adapted for humans and investigating how our behaviours are shaped by the environment.

Since then, the study of psychology has never stopped developing and today covers the whole gamut of human and animal behaviour. Psychology has many streams, such as social psychology, developmental psychology, cognitive psychology, behavioural psychology, clinical psychology, biopsychology, comparative psychology, and so on. It is one gigantic subject that impacts each of us. I am not sure if there is any discipline that is not affected by psychology.

Its importance in the business world is evident in the many professionals spending time understanding the subject so that it can help them better understand the world around them, the people with whom they work, and why we humans do what we do.

DOI: 10.4324/9781003250517-1

What is traditional economics?

Traditional economics believes that the economic behaviour of human beings is rational. We humans apply reason and think through consequences before making every decision. And we do this while keeping in mind the objective of maximising benefits, whether for ourselves as individuals, for our families, or for a business. It assumes that we humans are always weighing the pros and cons, the costs and benefits of alternate paths, and selecting the option that provides maximal gain. To recap for emphasis: the belief here is that each decision is rational, meaning traditional economics assumes that (a) all people are rational, (b) individual choices are consistent with expected utility theory, and (c) people update their beliefs and opinions based on new information received.

Do I have to say it? In real life, things are very different. Many of the decisions that we make may not undergo rational evaluation and also may not be overly beneficial to us. We humans, most of the time, don't realise that most of our decisions are based on emotions and influenced by innate biases, things which often may not serve our best interests. While we may think that we are very rational, reasonable at least, in our decisions, in reality, we are quite irrational about the choices we make.

So, what is behavioural economics?

Behavioural economics is the study of the effects of people's psychological processes on their decision-making. It takes insights from psychology and economics to explain why we decide the way we decide and what we actually do as a result. It draws on both of these areas, often exploring our irrational decision-making and noting how our behaviours don't follow the predictions of classic economic models.

As Sendhil Mullainathan and Richard Thaler mentioned in a 2000 working paper,[1] there are three important ways in which humans deviate from standard economic theory.

- **Bounded rationality.** This is the idea that humans have limited cognitive abilities that constrain their problem-solving.
- **Bounded willpower.** This is the idea that humans make choices that are not in their long-run interest.
- **Bounded self-interest.** This idea captures the fact that humans are often willing to sacrifice their own interests to help others.

Behavioural economics tells us that human beings have cognitive limitations. They tend to have difficulty with self-control. Humans are inconsistent and often choose things that have immediate appeal and not long-term benefit. The basic takeaway is that humans tend to make errors in this idealised world of maximum rationality. They need to be nudged to make better decisions that are in their own interest.

Behavioural economics as we know it today developed because of the incredible work done by true thought leaders. I would fail in my duty if I don't mention the names of a few of these pioneers.

The psychologists Daniel Kahneman and Amos Tversky came first. Their 1979b paper, "Prospect Theory", demonstrated that people dislike losses more than they like equivalent gains. This idea continues to be a pillar of the field. Despite being a psychologist and never having taken an economics course, Kahneman was awarded the 2002 Nobel Memorial Prize in Economics. His book *Thinking, Fast and Slow* (2011) is a compendium of his work in behavioural economics.

Yale University's Robert Shiller updated efficient markets theory with his work in behavioural finance, for which he was awarded the Nobel Prize in 2013. Behavioural finance looks at all the psychological, cultural, and social reasons that humans and our institutions make economic decisions that disagree with classic economic theory.

And then comes the work of Richard Thaler of the Chicago Booth School of Business. His popular books *Nudge* (Thaler and Sunstein 2008) and *Misbehaving: The Making of Behavioral Economics* (Thaler 2015) join his other contributions to how psychology affects finance and economics. He received his Nobel Prize in 2017.

Scholars who have influenced me

As a practitioner of quality improvement and someone who is trying to take the learnings of psychology and behavioural economics to the domain of quality improvement, here are some of the scholars whose work has taught me a lot. While it's not possible to mention everyone's name, I wanted to specially name the following stalwarts who have influenced me immensely:

- Stanley Milgram (1933–1984): American social psychologist known for his obedience experiments.
- Leon Festinger (1919–1989): Social psychologist best known for his theory of cognitive dissonance.
- Aaron Beck (1921–): Best known for pioneering the use of cognitive behavioural therapy for treatment of clinical depression and anxiety disorders.
- Donald Broadbent (1926–1993): British cognitive psychologist known for his ground-breaking work on attention.
- Daniel Kahneman (1934–): Nobel Laureate known for his work on the psychology of decision-making and judgement; credited with having integrated psychological research into economics.

- Paul Ekman (1934–): Psychologist known for his work in emotions and their linkage to facial expressions.
- Mihaly Csikszentmihalyi (1934–2021): Hungarian-American psychologist known for his work on *flow*, a mental state conducive to maximum productivity.
- Martin Seligman (1942–): Famous for his contributions to positive psychology and well-being.
- Daniel Schacter (1952–): Harvard professor working in the space of cognitive neuroscience on memory, imagination, future thinking, creativity, and ageing.
- Kurt Lewin (1890–1947): Considered the founder of social psychology; did pioneering work in group dynamics and organisational psychology.
- Robert Zajonc (1923–2008): A leading expert on how people behave; his research was foundational to the field of social psychology as we know it today, as it explored the connections between how people feel and how they think.
- Roger Brown (1925–1997): Remembered for his work in social psychology and children's language development.
- Elliot Aronson (1932–): Known for his work in influence and attitude change, cognitive dissonance, and interpersonal attraction; inventor of the cooperative teaching technique called jigsaw classroom.
- Philip Zimbardo (1933–): Known for a now-famous prison experiment and his research on heroism.
- BF Skinner (1904–1990): Known for his pioneering work in advocacy of behaviourism and its application to all aspects of psychology and life.
- Robert J. Schiller (1946–): Nobel Laureate and Yale professor; he predicted the 2008 American housing crisis and has played a pioneering role in behavioural economics; credited for having applied the insights of psychology and other social sciences to the study of economic behaviour.
- Richard Thaler (1945–): Nobel Laureate known for his work in the space of behavioural economics; has used behavioural economics to argue for "nudging" people to make better decisions.

Relevance to quality and continuous improvement

Over the years, many tools and methodologies have emerged to help businesses perform better in providing customers the products and services they admire. We have successfully used these techniques, and they have delivered results. Why do we now need to include psychology and behavioural economics as a part of our repertoire? Well, let me share a few reasons:

- **People are the heart of quality efforts.**
  People are at the heart of quality improvement. Sustained advancements only happen when employees are fully involved in the journey and they willingly adopt what is being recommended. Business leaders often struggle

to understand what drives employee behaviour and what prevents them from taking action. Psychology and behavioural economics can provide answers to these issues.

- **Quality improvement is not just about technical solutions.**
The success of any quality improvement depends on the quality of the technical solutions *and* how effectively we have been able to bring about the desired behaviour and mindset changes that support those fixes. We have seen quality projects that are superb technically but aren't able to stick due to human factors. The required behaviour and mindset adaptations didn't happen to secure the improvement effort. Quite often, these are softer issues, and psychology and behavioural economics can come in handy here. My belief is that many quality and continuous improvements can be strengthened when we enmesh learnings from behavioural science and anthropology with quality tools and practices.
- **Data has limitations.**
Data is critical to quality efforts. As quality professionals, we are taught that nothing should get done without having a look at the data. William Deming, the father of quality, said, "In God we trust, all others bring data". What he was saying is that data should be at the core of all of our decision-making. It's very true that data is vital to what we do; it tells us a lot about what we need to do and what direction we should go. However, one thing data alone cannot explain is human psychology. Why don't employees in a food factory use sanitisers? Why aren't people buying a particular product despite a price reduction? In such instances, the principles of psychology and behavioural economics can provide answers.
- **It's the problem-solving.**
The fundamentals of psychology and behavioural economics can be a formidable collection of arrows in the quality professional's quiver. When solving a problem, together with the hard tools and methods of our trade (Lean, Six Sigma, Theory of Constraints, 7 QC tools, 8D, and all the rest), the tactics from psychology should also be used as tools and enablers to achieve the desired outcome. When you are optimising a process and removing waste as we traditionally understand it, for example, also take a look at ways to reduce cognitive effort.
- **Humans are irrational.**
Despite presenting solutions and recommendations that are in the best interest of the people and the companies we serve, we have seen them not adopt them. This is because humans are predictably irrational. They will make decisions that may not be in their best interest. They make decisions which defy logic. They operate with cognitive biases that lead them to do so. They rely on instincts or mental shortcuts instead of a thoughtful examination of all the details. Such things have a negative impact on the management of quality. Knowing the fundamentals of social psychology and behavioural economics can mitigate the influence of these habits. It

will also help us to understand our customers – who also are humans! – and their irrational choices. Being able to work with the basics of psychology can help us provide a value proposition to customers that they like and would be willing to buy.

My recommendation to all quality professionals is that they learn the basics of psychology and behavioural economics. Indeed, I think it should be built into the curriculum of future quality leaders. In the meantime, I offer you the following 25 lessons that I have gleaned from my research and found success in applying to my work.

Note

1   Mullainathan, Sendhil, and Thaler, Richard H., *Behavioral Economics*. MIT Department of Economics Working Paper No. 00–27, September 2000. SSRN. https://ssrn.com/abstract=245828 or http://dx.doi.org/10.2139/ssrn.245828.

Lesson: 1

Solidifying the business case

The newly hired chief operating officer of a bank was passionate about quality. He had seen the power of Lean Six Sigma practices at his previous company. They had not only made the processes more efficient, but the customers had become happier as well. Hence, he decided to set up a quality team here. Getting a headcount approved and setting up a team was the easier part. What was more difficult was getting the CEO and other members of the C-suite to adopt quality practices for business performance improvement. He decided to make a pitch to the entire top management on the history and benefits of quality methodologies such as Lean Six Sigma and how and where they could help the bank the most. He also projected the financial gains the bank could reap if it adopted the quality practices for about three years. The presentation was appreciated by all the C-level members. The CEO even complemented the COO on his deep research. The COO was very happy with the response. He came out beaming, thinking he had accomplished his mission and that the business leaders would willingly adopt quality starting the next day. In reality, nothing much happened. He reached out to management, but the response thereafter was lukewarm. As a result, nothing much happened. The presentation, in the end, had little impact.

Incidentally, such is the case many times when we try to sell the power of continuous improvement by communicating its benefits. Many of us have likely experienced this in our professional lives. Whether you are an external consultant or an internal change agent, selling quality just by sharing its many benefits simply does not work sometimes. This is especially true when those in the top tier don't see quality to be an enabler for business improvement. So, what should you do in these situations? Well, if you talk to a behavioural economist, he might tell you that a better way to motivate this crowd is by using the principles of loss aversion.

Loss aversion is a concept proposed by Daniel Kahneman and Amos Tversky (1979b). It says that losses loom larger than gains. What that means is that we don't like to lose the things that we already have – the typical person would be more upset about losing $100 than they would be happy about gaining $100. In fact, the pain of losing something is twice as strong as the feeling of enjoyment

DOI: 10.4324/9781003250517-2

that comes with gaining something. This truth resonates with the old saying, *A bird in the hand is worth two in a bush.*

It's not surprising, then, that we tend to avoid losses at all cost. When the stakes are high and the context is riskier, loss aversion plays an even bigger factor in our decision-making. People will stick to what they are doing or to what they own unless there are solid reasons behind it. This manifests in the workplace in various ways, such as:

- Being unwilling to change.
- Resisting changes in the process.
- Holding on to the practice of doing things in age-old ways.
- Resisting productivity initiatives, as they could reduce head count.
- Reluctance to revisit and revise a management system that you have led.
- Hesitancy to change suppliers despite a negative audit report.
- Little focus is given to the change of mindsets during transformations.

Quality improvement is inherently about change, and therefore, those affected could very well be focussing on what they might lose rather than what they might gain. Hence, the resistance. So, coming back to the point of selling quality improvement to a CEO or business leader: What should you do? Use the principles of loss aversion, penalty frames, and social proof (which we'll get to shortly).

In much the same vein as loss aversion, Gächter et al. (2009) found that penalty frames are more effective than rewards in motivating people. When looking at a given issue, it can be considered – framed – in a way that can highlight either its positive or negative aspects. These are the lenses through which the problem is interpreted. The frames could be risk based (gain/loss), attribute based (lean/fat), or goal based (discount/penalty). The way we frame a situation impacts others' motivation and, in general, emphasising negative consequences is more potent than stressing positive benefits. For example, Simon Gächter and his team (2009) found 93% of students registered early when a penalty fee frame was presented for not registering for a conference, compared with just over 67% when it was framed as a discount. We will talk more about framing in Lesson: 4 and Lesson: 20.

This can come in handy when selling ideas of quality to business leaders. Tell a reluctant manager what he stands to lose by not adopting the quality-improvement practices for which you are advocating. Share explicitly what the organisation could possibly lose and the resulting consequences for its strategic objectives. List all the losses that you foresee as a result of not implementing your suggested improvements. Make it visceral! Use arguments, expressions, imagery, props – whatever is needed so that the business leader can visualise and *feel* the impact of not committing to quality.

I recommend also using the principles of social proof. This concept was first elaborated in the 1984 book *Influence* by Robert Cialdini. Social proof is the influence that other people's behaviour has on our own behaviour. The idea is that in ambiguous situations when we are unsure how to decide on things, we look at others' actions to help decide what we should do. Social proof is enhanced under the following conditions:

- **Uncertainty.** When we don't know what to do, we refer to others for guidance; we look up to those around us before taking action.
- **Similarity.** When things are uncertain, we tend to adopt the behaviours of those who are similar to us, others with whom we are able to relate.
- **Expertise and Competence.** When those around us are considered to have greater expertise or competence than we have, we are more readily influenced by them.
- **Numbers.** As the number of people demonstrating an action or behaviour goes up, so does our likelihood of following in their footsteps.
- **Experience.** When someone who has used a product or service talks about it, it has a positive impact on social proof.
- **Authority.** When an authority figure engages in certain behaviours, we tend to place higher value on that example.
- **Stamps of Approval.** We value certifications, awards, Twitter likes . . . in general, the more the better.

How is this linked with selling quality to a business leader? In addition to talking about the negative outcomes of not adopting quality practices, you should also include one or more examples of social proof, such as:

- A success story about a competitor who has reaped the benefits of quality improvements.
- A statement by a CEO who is revered in the industry and has experienced the gains of quality principles would be compelling.
- The voice of an industry expert explains why he thinks quality practices add value.
- Details about the number of companies in one's field that have profited from committing to continuous improvement.
- The favourable numbers of a company that is admired by all, including the person to whom the story is being sold.

The other thing we need to keep in mind while selling the impact of quality improvement is that we need to avoid talking about benefits which are too far in the future. We humans give stronger preference to payoffs that are closer. The reason is called present bias (also discussed in Lesson: 25 and Lesson: 8). Given a choice between a payoff that can happen today and a payoff that will happen in the future, we tend to choose the payoff now. As O'Donoghue and Rabin shared in their 1999 research, people give stronger weight to payoffs that are closer to the present time when considering trade-offs between two future moments. As a result, short-term benefits seem to be disproportionately larger in our perception compared to similar or larger benefits in the future. This can have a huge influence on our decision processes. Clearly, while selling quality, benefits which will be gained sooner can be more compelling than larger benefits farther in the future. So, if a CEO was posed with a business case wherein he saw a benefit of $5 million from a quality-improvement project in six months versus $10 million in 18 months, which would he choose? In all likelihood, he will choose the former.

Quality professionals need to remember that when talking about benefits, the sooner it is to be delivered, the more compelling it will be. Hence, when talking about financial or non-financial benefits, make sure the results are shared that are expected in the immediate future. If your quality transformation is a multi-year effort wherein you see the final outcome coming in a couple of years, don't forget to share the benefits that you expect to see during the journey beginning in the next few months. For example, when Tod Henry, the chief quality officer at a manufacturing company, was selling a zero-defect programme to his top management, he not only mentioned when this would be achieved (5 years in this case) but also highlighted the dollar benefits that company would see in the first 3 months, 6 months, 9 months, 12 months, and even 18 months. This convinced the CEO, as he could see the immediate benefits. It also gave him an option to kill the initiative if it did not deliver the benefits in a year as promised and not wait till the end of 5 years.

To summarise our takeaway from behavioural economics on strengthening a business case for quality improvement:

- Discuss the problem or the opportunity that you are working on.
- Share the impact of the project or quality-improvement efforts on the strategic business objective. These could be metrics around revenue, customers, employees, operations, etc.
- Explain what the company stands to lose if the improvement efforts are not pursued. Summarise the loss, and make the impact visceral so that the person listening is able to visualise and feel the unfortunate results of passing up your offer.
- Describe the positive impact similar efforts have had on their competitors, the industry as a whole, or any other well-known company.
- If the quality improvement will take a long time, share information about the benefits that are expected in the immediate future. Make the time frames shorter with smaller but regular benefits.
- Do emphasise the short-term benefits over the longer-term ones.
- If there are costs associated with the quality improvement, try and make them more palatable by positioning them in the future. The near-term costs can also be reframed as an offset against future gains, thereby positioning the disadvantage in the future.

Meeting the C-suite

When you are meeting a CEO or a senior business leader, you may not get time to tell a big story. It's imperative that you do the following so that you're ready for opportunities:

1   Create an elevator speech that talks about the benefits of your suggestions on quality improvement and also what the company would tend to lose if they're not implemented. Include a few words on how it has been successfully applied in a competitor's company or a world-class enterprise. The following is an example of an elevator pitch the COO in our opening scenario could have prepared for the CEO and other members of top management:

> The plummeting productivity in retail banking can be addressed through a Lean transformation. My team has the capability to make it happen. If we don't address this, the business will be swimming in waste that will result not only in customer unhappiness and customer attrition but also have a terrible impact on cost–income ratio. Our competitor, Amaze Bank, had a similar problem two years back, and Lean transformation was their solution.

2   Give a detailed presentation that lasts between 15 and 30 minutes. Include all possible particulars and remove them as appropriate to use the same presentation in different contexts. Each version of the presentation include the following elements:

  • Description of the problem being solved
  • Impact of the problem on strategic objective of the firm
  • Broad time frame to implement solution/s
  • Critical success factors
  • Use of loss aversion: what could happen if the quality initiative is not deployed – and how awful that would be
  • Specifics: make explicit what sort of negative impact not going with quality would have on strategic objectives and business performance
  • Use of social proof: the success stories of others

Lesson: 2

Cementing relationships

Quality and continuous-improvement professionals focus a lot of their time on how their work can positively impact a business. They go all out to make this happen: They sharpen their subject knowledge and make it contextually relevant. They gather expertise on various tools and practices so that they are able to solve the myriad problems an organisation is facing. They dive deep into various standards and go to lengths to understand the explicit and implicit meanings of what they stand for. They look for every opportunity to apply what they know and make a meaningful difference. They want to know how and that their efforts are affecting a firm's strategic objectives.

While this is all well and good – and necessary – what certain quality professionals seem to overlook is the need to build solid relationships in addition to impressive technical skills. In fact, consciously building relationships and developing the skills to support them are now critical success factors in moving the agenda of quality forward.

Relationships can make or break a quality journey. My experience from the trenches is that sometimes the finest of quality efforts fail because the quality leader did not spend adequate time nurturing relationships. The failure came despite the fact that the quality leader had all the requisite skills and was qualified to do the job. What he missed was that he didn't invest time in people. Building workplace relationships is vital to making any quality project successful. For many, relationship skills do not come easily. If you are one of these people, realise that little steps can go a long way. Decide you can do it, and you will be on the right path. Relationship building can go a long way in getting difficult people on board and also in helping iron out issues that crop up along the way. The ability to relate to others also contributes to the development of a positive work culture, which is a critical component of workplace transformation.

There is a lot that psychology and behavioural economics can teach us that can be used to build workplace relationships. Here are some ideas you can pick from.

DOI: 10.4324/9781003250517-3

Use the power of reciprocity

The power of reciprocity is one of the key principles of influence proposed by Dr Robert B. Cialdini in his 1984 book *Influence: The Psychology of Persuasion*. We humans are wired to pay back debts; we don't like having a feeling of indebtedness to someone hanging over us. We also tend to treat others the way they treat us. People will help you if you have helped them advance their agenda or goals in the past. Reciprocity helps to build relationships and also enables the mending of relationships where they have broken. It's a brilliant tool that helps in achieving consensus, facilitating negotiation, and overcoming doubts and suspicions. I have even seen animosity towards others vanish through the power of reciprocity.

So how do you implement this tool? Look for every opportunity to be of service to others. A quality leader I know, Satish Kaul, has not only been an outstanding quality professional but is someone for whom helping others comes naturally. In the first two decades of his career, he spent a large amount of time catalysing quality and continuous improvement for a global beverage maker. Then, one fine day, he moved to a leading bank in the Middle East to be a part of their quality team. The team at the bank was initially not very welcoming. What was going on in the mind of the team members was something like, *What is this person from a consumer goods company doing in a bank?*

Satish took it upon himself to win by giving them more than he could receive. He said to himself that he would look for every opportunity to assist them and win their hearts. Having a solid understanding of business excellence models and ISO standards, he started helping his colleagues whenever they had any difficulty. Whether it was strategic planning or leadership or product development or processes, Satish became the go-to person for all their queries. Very soon, Satish, whom the team had initially viewed with lots of doubt about his capabilities, became a coach. And not just for office-related work. Satish also became the person teammates went to for solving personal problems. Given his practice of looking for every opening to help his colleagues, Satish very soon had built a solid network throughout the entire bank; there wasn't a department that had not been touched by his kindness.

Earlier, the quality team had struggled to take the bank through a TQM (total quality management) journey. But when Satish took over the responsibility of embedding TQM practices in the bank, it became a cakewalk. Leaders welcomed him with open arms and were willing to listen to what he had to offer. Not surprisingly, the bank was ultimately given a number of awards for excellent quality practices. This all happened because Satish assiduously worked to build relationships with all by giving, knowing full well that he would be repaid, if not by all, by at least a few for sure. What a great example of a quality leader winning hearts by helping others. His kindness and relationship building also encouraged reciprocal behaviour. When he went to them with his ideas on continuous improvement, his co-workers not only supported them but worked with him towards making them successful. People paid him back with cooperation. And when the benefits were visible, others willingly joined the rollout.

Be willing to be vulnerable

If you think demonstrating vulnerability is a weakness, think again. Many of us consider vulnerability to be a sign not only of weakness but even something shameful. We are taught since childhood to display confidence, competence, authority. But vulnerability doesn't mean you are giving in or being submissive; rather, it's a willingness to expose yourself to another person with greater honesty and transparency despite fears and misgivings.

When you pretend to be perfect or that you have all the answers, you end up alienating yourself from others. Instead, being openly vulnerable makes you more human to others, and people find it easier to relate to you. When you're able to share your insecurities and shortcomings as part of your relational repertoire, it can strengthen your stance as a leader. This sharing also sends out a signal that you value others' feedback and support. By demonstrating vulnerability, you are showing the other person that you trust them. And when you trust them, they automatically open up and become comfortable with you in return. All of this, naturally, supports the lesson of solidifying relationships for quality leaders.

Research work done by Alison Wood Brooks and Francesca Gino (Harvard Business School) and Maurice E. Schweitzer (Wharton School) (2015) found that when people show vulnerability at work, such as by asking for advice and help, they actually appear *more* competent to their supervisors. However, we also need to keep the pratfall effect in mind. This is a psychological phenomenon wherein people respond to another's vulnerability based on how they perceive them beforehand. When people appear capable and competent before showing vulnerability, they are considered more likeable, and people have greater sympathy for them. As a matter of fact, they may even find this vulnerability attractive. However, if people are perceived as less competent before showing vulnerability, they will come across as sloppy and even less likeable. That's something to keep in mind! Before you demonstrate vulnerability at work, it's important that you establish your competence.

Before Deb Cooper took over as the head of quality for a leading pharma company, he had already established his name as a thought leader. On assuming this new responsibility, he built trust through vulnerability and did a host of things that helped reveal him as a leader who carries his team along. He openly shared with his team his likes, dislikes, and challenges, and encouraged his teammates to likewise share theirs. Whenever there were instances of him not knowing something, Deb didn't shy away from telling his team that he didn't have the answer. He conveyed that he didn't always know and wanted to explore solutions with the participation of others. He readily took responsibility when a project failed and didn't mind coming in on weekends to aid his team members who had tasks to complete. He spent a lot of time listening and allowed others to take the driver's seat in meetings and deliberations. He was able to keep his ego out of it.

Collectively, such behaviour is a great propellant for building a quality culture. It's not surprising that Deb won everyone's trust and built some great relationships. He also created space for open conversation wherein people felt comfortable discussing their challenges and recovering from failures.

Be in touch

A key enabler for building good relationships is being in touch with those around you and those who matter to your work. You cannot expect to strengthen human bonds if you're off of people's radars. In today's world, being connected is much easier than before. You don't always need to meet people physically, in person. As someone who is responsible for quality, you have to be proactive in finding ways to stay in contact with not just your team members but all stakeholders.

In psychology, there is something called the propinquity effect. As per Merriam–Webster, *propinquity* means nearness in place or time, proximity. This is an easy-to-understand phenomenon that describes how people tend to form friendships and bonds with those with whom they come in contact quite often. When people come into contact often, the likelihood of them liking each other actually increases (Festinger, Schachter, and Back 1950). The more we come into contact with people, the more likely we are to become friends with them. And as we become more familiar with those with whom we are in touch, we tend to find things we like about them.

So, how does one take advantage of the propinquity effect on an ongoing basis? Here are a few ideas:

- Make a stakeholder map of all those who are important to your quality journey, and create a strategy for how you will engage each one of them with frequency.
- Create a go-to list of all the channels and methods that you can use to engage stakeholders.
- Make it a point to regularly meet with employees beyond your immediate team/s.
- Don't just have lunch with your team. Make it a point to lunch at least twice a week with those who don't belong to your team.
- Attend celebrations and events that have been organised by other departments.
- Observe people and see if there are matters of common interest you share with them. Connect with them around these common interests.
- Regularly send emails to all employees on what's happening in the domain of quality within the company and even outside.

- Share articles and ideas with all key stakeholders. The more they see your content, the better they will get to know your thinking and beliefs.
- For teams or colleagues who are in a different region or geography, don't underestimate the extra familiarity offered by video technologies.
- Be generous in sharing information with those around you.
- Create an online platform, and use it to interact with and listen to all employees.
- Try to hang out at the same places important stakeholders frequent.

One thing to keep in mind is that the more similar your opinions and interests are to those of others, the more likely you will be liked by them. Finding common ground is important!

Tim was a quality leader in an industrial goods company. He realised the power of staying in touch and looked for every chance to interact with all key stakeholders in his organisation. He made sure that he was in touch with all business heads. Since physical meetings were not always possible, he routinely sent emails or text messages on the latest developments in quality, what competitors were doing, the industry at large, etc. As a result, whenever there was a business problem, business leaders did not reach out to an external consultant. Instead, they reached out to Tim, asking him and his team for help resolving them. The CEO of this company loved golf. To make sure he could be in contact with the CEO, Tim learned how to golf and regularly met the top boss at the golf course. Here was a quality leader who was on the minds of all key stakeholders of the company. What a great enabler in taking the agenda of quality forward in the company.

Demonstrate reliability

Without reliability, you can't think of building solid relationships.

Reliability is about delivering what you promise. It is also about living up to the values you espouse to others. It's about having the laser-like focus to do what needs to be done by shutting off all the distraction.

Let's understand the psychology of reliability and how it impacts relationships. When you rely on someone, you are agreeing that the other person takes on the responsibility to work on something that you value. You are agreeing to be vulnerable to the other person. The reason you're vulnerable is that you know your success depends on their success. You also know that the outcome they produce may not be as desired. When someone performs reliably in such situations with you, not once but repeatedly, it builds trust.

Reliability is about trust. When you commit to something and don't follow through, it damages trust. A person who is reliable takes responsibility for what is entrusted to him and doesn't let the other person down. Reliability is not about the big proclamations you make in conversation, but little things that you do on an ongoing basis that show you have the best interests of your stakeholders in mind.

Reliability is about competence. It means you know what needs to be done and how it's to be done – and other people know they can count on you to do it right. You commit, you prepare, you consistently deliver. Your commitments are backed with meaningful action.

How do you demonstrate reliability while engaging in quality work? Here are a few suggestions:

- Spend more time listening and less time talking. When you are with someone, make sure you listen attentively.
- Respond to every query and email from your stakeholders as soon as possible, never going more than 24 hours without communicating.
- When working on a quality project, provide stakeholders with a detailed plan.
- Ensure that your work is reviewed on a regular basis with stakeholder participation.
- When you promise something to someone, make sure you follow through.
- Never miss appointments or reschedule them at the last minute.
- Don't make promises you can't keep.
- Plan ahead of time for any meeting or project discussion.
- Ensure that you are competent in your chosen area of work and well qualified for the projects you accept.

Create positive memories

Treat all individuals with whom you want to build relationships as your customers. They may be your "internal customers", but treating them as "external customers" adds the heightened sense of care that the relationship requires. This also forces us to make sure that we don't take these relationships for granted and constantly work towards improving them. This becomes more important for those relationships, those with leaders and influencers with whom you don't meet regularly yet they have an impact on your work. Since the interactions are fewer, each of them matters a lot in forming perceptions. Hence, look at each interaction as a moment of truth that can make or mar the perception. While you try and work to make these interactions flawless, this may not be sufficient. A conscious effort has to be made towards creating interactions which are memorable. We humans tend to remember events and encounters that have stirred our emotions. This is where Nobel Laureate Daniel Kahneman and Barbara Frederickson's (Kahneman et al. 1993) Peak-End Rule can come handy.

Our evaluation of an experience is based on this rule. The peak refers to the moments when an experience has had the strongest emotion (positive or negative), and the end is simply how it ended (positive or negative) (Doll 2020). Although in the ongoing relationship that we are talking about here, there may not be any end point. But what a quality professional should remember is that he has to work towards hatching a few interactions which create these positive emotions. The human brain prioritises interactions that are neutral and inconsequential, remembering only significant and intense moments. The duration and number of interactions don't matter. What matters are those intense moments. Our memories are not comprehensive pictures of experiences as we are limited by the amount of information we can hold. They only capture the highlights. Hence, when we recall an event, we tend to remember the highlights and extreme experiences. What this means is that recalling negative experiences helps us to avoid such moments in the future, while positive experiences push us to seek similar moments in the future.

What this means for a quality professional is that he has to create moments which his important relationships remember. This can be achieved in a number of ways, such as: helping to solve a chronic customer pain, going above and beyond to do things that were not expected, or coming up with an innovative solution to a business problem. While he focusses on creating positive memories, he should make sure that there are no negative encounters. The advantage of creating a positive memory is that next time the person has a problem, you will be at the top of his mind. Clearly, key relationships have to nurtured as you would do with an external customer.

Lesson: 3

Gaining commitment

Garnering commitment to a quality initiative can be a tall order. One thing that a quality leader has to constantly grapple with is how to get people on board – and what should be done so that they are consistently engaged during the entire initiative. Commitment can mean various things to various people.

Let me share some of the interpretations of this word:

- Dedication to a cause or initiative.
- Willingness to give time and energy to a cause that you believe in.
- Loyalty to a cause or an organisation.
- Make a promise to do something.
- Something that a person has agreed to do.

As you see, it may not mean the same to all.

But when it comes to quality improvement, we should be clear what commitment means to us. It has the following contours:

- **Intention:** Accepting that we are interested in something and declaring our intention to pursue it.
- **Purpose:** Sharing a vision about quality.
- **Objective:** Having specific goals that we intend to achieve in the pursuit of our purpose.
- **Action:** Taking specific steps to achieve our goals and purpose.
- **Investment:** Investing the necessary time and resources to achieve the larger purpose.

Alongside our traditional approaches, psychology and economics may have tactics that can be adopted.

Ask small questions

We humans can get intimidated by any new idea. When you talk about quality with someone who has not been involved in it before, their first

DOI: 10.4324/9781003250517-4

reaction will often be to treat it as a threat. A fight-or-flight response is triggered. Sometimes, this causes people to retreat into a shell; it can even paralyse them. Robert Maurer (2014), in his book *One Small Step Can Change Your Life: The Kaizen Way*, shares a technique that can come in handy here: Asking the small questions. Ask simple, non-threatening questions around the themes of quality and your proposed initiatives to trigger others' minds to think and self-discover. When we discover something on our own, we tend to own it better, more completely, than when someone else tells it to us. For example, if there is a customer issue being faced by a company and you want the teams to own it, you can ask questions such as the following:

- Have you all heard about the customer issue?
- How did you come to know this?
- What are your suggestions to address this problem?
- What should we do?
- How do you think we can avoid a recurrence?
- What do you think would be the impact of not taking any action?
- What are the few things we should do immediately?
- Would any one of you like to lead the effort?
- Who all would like to get involved?
- What short of review structure should we put in place?

Nudge to commit publicly

When you want to get the buy-in of others on a quality journey, one technique that works is securing a public commitment, based on the idea of behavioural consistency. Robert Cialdini (2008) also endorses this approach in his book, *Influence: Science and Practice*. It is about people's tendency to act in a manner that aligns with what they have decided and done in the past. This is especially true when one has made a commitment in public and would not like to do things contrary to what they have said. This is because behaving inconsistently with what they have said earlier can be seen as an undesirable trait, and the person can be less liked. It can also be seen as something deceitful and a sign of incompetence. It creates a lot of social pressure on the individual. Hence, people go all out to be consistent with their past behaviour and decisions. If they don't do this, it creates a lot of internal confusion and stress.

In the context of quality, this technique can be used to make an indifferent leader commit to the effort towards quality. Let's say you are a quality leader catalysing quality improvement in a company. There is a leader who pays lip service to quality effort and does not want to spend time reviewing the progress of the quality-improvement projects. How do you get him on board and also make sure that he reviews the projects on an ongoing basis? Organise a town hall and launch the projects with a bang! Invite a business leader to address the gathering and launch the projects. Encourage him to talk about the power of quality and how he believes in business improvement. Quality improvement is the sort of topic that no business leader can ever say shouldn't be done. Before he speaks, ask him to also talk about how *he* could be an enabler to the success of the projects. Urge him to talk about *his* involvement in toll gate reviews. (Perhaps someone on your team can even supply a draft of possible remarks to help him out.) Once he commits in public, it will be very difficult for him to not be a part of it later. Even if he doesn't like it, he will try to comply with his public proclamation. After all, as the idea of behavioural consistency predicts, he does not like to be viewed as a leader who appears inconsistent.

For another example, consider when you need the involvement of employees, some of whom may be reluctant, in a continuous-improvement effort. Ask them in a meeting, town hall, or other gathering about what they would each do to contribute to the journey of continuous improvement. Make sure these are not closed-door interactions, but gatherings that have a large number of people in attendance. Seek individual commitments in front of others. Once they have committed in public, they will later find it difficult to not follow through on what they have promised. Tell everyone that they'll be regrouping in a couple of weeks to report on the progress made. Not wanting to appear in front of everyone as someone who hasn't kept their word, people in general will try to accomplish what they committed. They want to comply with their promise for that sense of behavioural consistency, and they won't want to be embarrassed in front of their peers for not having done so.

Make people sign on to a charter

Another method that is quite powerful in getting leadership commitment to quality efforts is having leaders sign a charter. This is a document that details the contours of the quality initiative and includes things such as the business case, the critical success factors, the broad roadmap, etc. A charter can be drawn up for a project, an awareness drive, a process roll-out, a cultural transformation, any initiative. Require the involved leaders' signatures, whether they are sponsors, process owners, impacted persons, resource providers, or anyone whose direction is critical for its success. Whatever the role, when a person signs a charter with others, she will in all likelihood make the effort to understand what she is committing to, reading through every line carefully. She can no longer be involved on the surface. Having signed, she cannot deny involvement in the future. In my experience, I have noticed that once a leader signs a document, she is more serious about the work ahead and provides input and gets involved wherever required.

Us-versus-them approach

When a line divides two groups, it unites teams on each side. Have you not seen people connect over being an iPhone lover versus an Android lover? In India, during the 2019 elections, a similar thing happened. The Bharatiya Janata Party (BJP), to which PM Narendra Modi belongs, projected itself as the party that could not only take India towards economic prosperity but also keep the nation safe. This was so emotional for many citizens that the nation saw a division into two clear groups despite so many parties standing for the elections. The two groups were those who stood by Narendra Modi (who stood for India's progress and safety) and those who supported any of the others (who projected themselves as those who were fighting against the divisive politics of the BJP, as they said).

Steve Jobs, for example, employed us versus them effectively. He would rally his people by showing images of Apple's enemies (a.k.a. competitors). As Robert Sutton and Huggy Rao (2014) mention in their book *Scaling Up Excellence*, Jobs likened IBM to an evil dictatorship bent on taking over the world with its soulless wares. He made fun of Microsoft by saying, "The only problem with Microsoft is they have no taste."

This is a method leaders can use to seek people's commitment. One finance leader by the name Tim Howden (name changed for confidentiality), who led a shared service centre of a global company in India in 2017, wanted to address the issue of errors in finance processes. Quality as a concept, being new to finance operations, was taking time to settle in, and this was an industrywide problem. For those unaware, India has been a global hub for finance shared service centres. Many global companies have offshored their processes there, as talent is easily available and costs much less than what a company would pay in western markets. Shared services not only help in achieving cost savings, they also help in addressing issues around process inefficiencies and process standardisation. India has a large number of finance shared service centres, and there are forums where leaders of these shared service centres regularly meet to discuss their common issues.

One common problem faced by all of them was that of "errors". Tim found an opportunity here. He found that there was an opportunity to use the us-versus-them approach. He came back and gave a clarion call to his team members that they had to fight the menace of errors and not be like the other finance shared service centres. He further declared that this was the opportunity to be the best among the rest, and he launched a major quality-improvement programme around it. He asked in town halls if his employees would like to be like other shared service centres, whose work output was a disgrace for finance folks. When he mentioned all this, he dramatised quite a bit to stir people's emotions. He attempted to persuade them that they were all superior beings engaged in meaningful work represented by a finance professional.

This seems to have worked with the employees. It was heartening to see how people rallied around this challenge. Even those employees who were initially indifferent to quality came on board and started participating and contributing. Within six months, the error levels came down. Of course, it was backed with major capability development and problem-solving initiatives as well. But it was the call to be "not like the rest" that helped to galvanise everyone.

One thing to keep in mind here is to apply us versus them with care. Never, for instance, rally your people around fear. Fear can impede their cognitive ability and cause unnecessary worry. People tend to be paralysed by fear and lose their creativity in the face of it. It leads to behaviours such as maintaining the status quo and diverting attention from the real issues that are not optimal for continuous improvement.

Emphasise the importance of little changes

As a part of getting people on board on a quality journey, request that everyone make improvements, however small they may be. One of the reasons that employees do not join a quality-improvement effort is because they believe their small contribution would not make any difference to the larger enterprise. This is not a new concept; many companies have been focussing on small improvements to build a continuous-improvement culture. However, what needs to be stressed here is a change (however small) that makes the company or workplace better is welcome.

In the book *Yes! 50 Secrets from the Science of Persuasion* by Noah Goldstein, Steve Martin, and Robert Cialdini (2007), the authors talk about why people say *no* to small requests. Their hypothesis is that when people are asked to make a charitable donation, they say no because they can't afford much and assume their small contribution wouldn't help the cause. They performed an experiment wherein they informed people that even an extremely small amount of money would help the cause. When the research assistants went door to door, they added to their requests: "Even a penny will help". The outcome was that the number of people who donated almost doubled. That was the result of explicitly making a statement that every little contribution matters.

The focus on small improvements has been in manufacturing companies for a while, but I have noticed that it's not as prevalent in service companies. Rather, the focus in service companies tends to just be the big quality-improvement projects that have a direct impact on company performance. Organisations should focus on both big and small.

Keeping "even a penny will help" in mind, it's important to encourage people to carry out improvements, however small they may be. Leaders have to explicitly say that "every little improvement matters". Getting everyone involved is the goal. Of course, there also must be a framework in place to capture and recognise ideas of all sizes.

I have had the opportunity to use this concept in a global bank. The explicit communication that "even small improvements matter" made so much difference, not just in improving process performance but in our ability to get as many people as possible aboard the quality journey, especially those who weren't sure if their efforts would make a difference to their company.

Emphasising the little things is a brilliant tactic to recruit as much of the workforce as possible to a quality movement.

Lesson: 4

Getting across the message

One principle of behavioural economics is the power of clear messaging in any transformation. When communication is clear, it helps in easy adoption by those who need to be involved. It's imperative that the messaging is such that it is able to get the attention of all those people. It has to be precise, cogent, and sharp. It has to be bereft of jargon, and the words used are those that can be understood easily.

A message includes how you name the programme or the words you use to describe it. It should resonate with all the employees. They should feel emotionally connected with it.

A good message for quality should have the following attributes:

- It should only contain a few words – the fewer the better.
- It should encapsulate the larger purpose or the objective that you are trying to accomplish.
- It should be catchy.
- Even the uninitiated should be able to understand it.
- Make it contextually appropriate.
- The information is easy to remember.
- It should be in a language that is understood by all.
- The content of the messages should be backed with feelings expressed through body language, tone, gesture, voice modulation, and facial expression.

Short messages and slogans: the power of simple messages

As a part of your quality-improvement efforts, if you are planning to create a catchphrase or a short message to galvanise people around quality improvements, keep the following in mind.

Always keep the message short and simple. The strongest messages are the simplest. I always suggest that a good message results from taking out the unnecessary and sharing the essence. It focusses on what's important

DOI: 10.4324/9781003250517-5

and does not confuse people by providing too much information. Donald Trump's 2016 campaign slogan: "Make America Great Again" (Margolin 2016). When a message is clear and easy to understand, it is easy for people to act on it. This was a simple yet powerful message which emotionally resonated with many citizens who thought that America was on the decline.

Or, for that matter, let's look at the December 2019 British elections, in which Boris Johnson led the Conservative Party and gained a handsome majority. One reason attributed to this majority was the sharp slogan "Get Brexit Done", which was all over the place (Perrigo 2020). This was because the slogan appealed to leavers (or those who wanted the UK to exit the European Union) but also because it appealed to some remainers who were sick to the back teeth of Brexit and wanted to get it over with.

It is also recommended that the message should be crafted in such a way that people act on it. Nudge people into action by using the imperative form of the verb in the message. The message can be directive and yet friendly. Let me give you some examples:

- Just do it (the famous Nike tagline)
- Make Lean a part of our DNA (an in-house mantra of a leading banking operations company in the United Arab Emirates)
- Create flawless processes (a message adopted for quality improvement)
- Let's become world class.

Remember, short messages should be within 3 to 10 words.

Use culturally relevant names

We sometimes want to name our quality-improvement programme so that it has better acceptability and traction. If you decide to do this, it would help to keep in mind that it's imperative to use socially and culturally identifiable names that give a clear message of the programme's purpose.

For example, the Indian government has come up with various names for its development programmes which clearly communicate their objectives. These are three examples:

- *Namamai Gange* (Amrit 2019) ("Namamai Gange" is in Hindi and means "I pray to Ganga", as the river Ganga is revered in Indian culture) – This programme focusses on cleaning the Ganga, which is one of the major rivers in India and is even worshipped by the citizens.
- *Ayushman Bharat* ("Ayushman" is a Hindi word that means "being blessed with long life") – This programme focusses on providing holistic healthcare to Indians.

- *Jan Dhan Yojana* ("Jan Dhan" implies "money of the people") – This is a financial inclusion programme that aims to create affordable access to financial services such as banks, insurance, and pensions.

Let me give you other examples: One global business process outsourcing company launched a quality-improvement programme in India. To get traction, they asked the employees to come up with names which could signify what they were trying to do. Employees came up with various names, but the leaders wanted a name that was relevant in the South Asian context. Hence they named it *Unnati* (this is in Hindi and means "advancement"). This resonated very well with the employees, as "advancement" has been the focus of India at large, and there has been a lot of talk around it by the government, so it was very contextually relevant. Employees felt that quality improvement was needed not just for them but for the nation at large.

Acronyms

Using acronyms can be another way to communicate the essence of one's message. An acronym is an abbreviation using the first letter of each word. For example: NASA is an acronym for the National Aeronautics and Space Administration. What I like about acronyms is they help people remember the message easily.

India's prime minister is a brilliant orator and has this amazing ability to communicate messages in a simple yet clear manner (Doctor 2019). His messages are clear and connect with the masses very easily. He uses acronyms often.

For example, after assuming power in 2014, Narendra Modi stated

> Government is generally trapped in 'ABCD' culture from top to bottom. . . . A means Avoid, B – Bypass, C – Confuse, D – Delay. Our effort is to move from this culture to 'ROAD' where R stands for Responsibility, O – Ownership, A – Accountability, D – Discipline. We are committed to this roadmap.
>
> (Times of India News Item 2014)

In another instance, PM Modi mentioned that India should be a global manufacturing hub and should produce goods in the country with zero defects and to ensure that the goods have zero effect on the environment. Since then, a quality-improvement programme called ZED (short for Zero Defect Zero Effect) was launched by the Quality Council of India (India's apex quality body), and today, it's a successful programme being adopted by small enterprises. Not that the content of the ZED programme is new. It talks about quality-improvement practices which have been there for ages. One reason for its success is also the catchy acronym, which has played a big role in its adoption. Many owners of small enterprises have told me that earlier, they thought quality management to be complex stuff and were not sure of the impact. But now the acronym has made the benefits clearly explicit. The point here is that his simple messages connect with the citizens very well.

There are many such examples which one can learn from Narendra Modi's way of nudging people to adopt his ideas.

Let me give you an example from a customer-experience transformation that I catalysed for a leading global bank in East Africa. As a part of the rollout, we came up with a service intent. For those not familiar, a service intent is a short encapsulation of what customer experience is for a firm that would be demonstrated by the employees at a touchpoint. The service intent that we came up with was in Swahili (a lingua franca of Eastern Africa). The service intent was: "*Hapa Cas tu*" (This was in Swahili and meant focus on CAS only, where CAS stood for convenience, accuracy, and speed). Clearly, the clarity on what should be a customer experience was a key contributor to the enhanced Net Promotor Score (a measure of how likely it was that the customer would recommend the company). The phrase is simple yet captures the purpose that the quality rollout has set out to achieve.

Clearly, to increase the involvement of stakeholders in a quality-improvement effort, use simple and clear names that give a clear message of the objective that you plan to accomplish.

Giving life to communication through framing

The way a message on quality is framed does have an impact on its adoption. This is a very important behavioural economics principle. Frame your messages such that people clearly understand how they would gain by doing what you expect them to do and how they would lose if they don't do what they are expected to do.

This should be kept in mind while framing[1]* a message of quality or continuous improvement. Whatever message you craft, it should explain what one would gain by adopting practices of quality or what one would lose by not participating in quality efforts.

People make different choices when they go to the doctor based on what they are told. The doctor could tell them one of these:

• There is a 95% chance that the operation will be successful.
• There is a 5% chance that it could cause complications and major infections.

Clearly, the first message would clearly have a more positive impact than the second one.

Some of us may remember that in 1991, McDonald's came up with this advertisement which labelled the McLean Burger "91% fat free" rather than "9% fat" (McGrath 2008). Giving a positive spin made it much more appealing instead of saying it has fat.

We have read in Lesson: 1 about the principle of loss aversion, which says that losing hurts more than winning feels good. We humans try and avoid things that can cause loss. A loss could be financial, social, emotional, etc.

So, the question that is often asked is, should our messaging for quality have a positive or a negative orientation? Well, this is contextual. It depends on the type of objective you are trying to accomplish.

Irrespective of the frame that you use, it should be emotionally appealing and motivate an individual to take action. Don't send out messages that don't make an impact. Don't send out bland messages that don't get people's attention. Every message that you send out should have a gain or a loss frame. Let me give you an example.

Bland Message	Gain Frame	Loss Frame
It's time to adopt Lean manufacturing.	Let your processes become flawless, efficient, and deliver what the customer wants – adopt Lean manufacturing.	Do you want to miss the opportunity to create a waste-free operation through Lean manufacturing that only creates value for customers?
Our company needs a standard problem-solving approach.	A standard approach to problem-solving will help in bringing down the noise around the day-to-day issues in the company.	Not having a standard problem-solving approach hinders our ability to reduce customer and business pains.

Remember, the gains and losses for quality and continuous improvement can be one of these:

- Financial – This includes things like cost, profit, stock value, employee compensation, revenue and so on.
- Social – This refers to how it affects their position and status in comparison to others.
- Physical – This refers to an individual's physical well-being.
- Emotional – This pertains to people's feelings and psychological well-being.
- Customer – Everything related to customers, such as product quality, customer experience, and brand perception, falls under this category.
- SREC – SREC stands for shareholder, regulators, environment, and community. This relates to everything around them.

So which frame should one choose?

This depends on the audience and the people for whom it is meant. You have to understand the audience and their context. What is important to keep in mind is that if the audience sees potential for significant improvement in

Figure 4.1 Steps to framing a message for quality improvement

Table 4.1 Steps to framing a message for quality improvement

Steps	What it is	Details
State	State the objective.	What is the objective that you are trying to achieve through your message? What do you want the audience to do?
Understand	Understand the organisational context.	Understand the context. This is about delving deep in your business and ascertaining why quality-improvement practices are needed. Is it to make the organisation compete in the market, or is it to take the company to new level of performance, or is it to take the company out of the current state? The objective of this is for you to fathom the deeper purpose of why we are adopting quality practices.
Ascertain	Ascertain the audience persona.	In this step, you make an effort to understand the persona of the audience, their current context, and what will move them.
Comprehend	Comprehend the impact of the message on the audience.	Ascertain the impact of what people will gain or lose if they don't do what you are asking them to do. The gain or loss will be financial, social, emotional, or physical.
Determine	Decide which frame to take (gain or loss).	Decide the frame that you believe will deliver the messaging objective that you have in mind.
Codify	Codify the message.	Write down the proposed message. Don't take chances. Writing will bring clarity and will also standardise the message shared by all.

the current state, the messaging should be done using a gain frame. When the audience thinks that they have a chance of going down from the current state and losing what they have now, you should pick a loss frame.

So, what are the steps to follow while designing a message for quality. It comprises the steps mentioned in Fig 4.1 and Table 4.1.

One thing that you have to keep in mind while using the loss frame is that it should be designed in such a way that it makes people act, but it should not be so strong that it creates panic. If you are messaging for quality to a large audience, I always suggest that you test it out with a few people before officially rolling it out. Your goal should be to create a message with an action bias. And don't forget that you should also keep an eye on the sort of imagery that it evokes. If the message conveys a visceral connection, it will do the trick.

The way the message is communicated

The person who communicates the message and how he communicates make a difference to how a message is perceived. There are a couple of things that need to be kept in mind.

1   The person delivering the message must be credible. What this means is that if the CEO communicating about quality is perceived as someone who would do anything for sales, even if it's at the cost of sending out a bad-quality product, his message will never be taken seriously. Clearly, if the CEO is not trusted, his message will never get its due importance.

2   It's not technical competence but persuasive communication that makes a difference to the message. What I mean here is confidence. What this means is that the effective communicator makes the audience feel good about themselves and tries to make a positive association with quality. They elaborate on how it will make people's lives easy. They try to put the audience in a good mood, which will make it more likely for them to accept the message.

3   Humans are more easily persuaded by people who are like us and share our values. This increases their likeability. Hence, it always helps if the communicator is able to resonate with something which is common with the audience. So, if the audience is in their 20s and 30s, it would make sense for the leader to demonstrate energy, while if the audience has old people, the communication will be more subdued. We have all heard of Tupperware parties, wherein friends get together to buy products. More often, the reason people buy the products is because they like the person selling the product and not necessarily because the product is good.

For example, when a global manufacturing company launched a quality journey, the CEO did not give the job to communicate the launch message to all his direct reports. But he hand-picked those leaders who had high credibility and were popular among the employees to take the message firmwide. Many of these did not have the knowledge of quality but could flawlessly share why the company was embarking on it and the objectives it would accomplish.

Don't use data that highlights bad behaviour

We saw in Lesson: 1 information about social proof. During ambiguous situations, we copy others' behaviours and actions. This especially happens when we are uncertain of what needs to be done. So, you have to keep this principle in mind while communicating about adoption of quality practices by employees. Let me give you some examples:

- "The job abandonment rate in our company is at 11%".
- "Despite spending time and money of training, 8 out of 10 employees do not use quality-improvement tools".
- "Fifty-two percent of employees between the ages of 22 and 36 have not taken up the quality-improvement projects that they were supposed to."

Many times, this is done to sensationalise the issue and get people's attention. The goal is to share the enormity of the problem and shock the audience. This is done so that they can act. Unfortunately, the impact is just the opposite. Let's look at the message and see and see how it can be interpreted:

"The job abandonment rate in our company is at 11%".	"There are many people who abandon the job and walk out. I thought it was rare".
"Eight out of 10 employees don't use quality-improvement tools despite investing time and money on training".	"Why should I bother about using quality-improvement tools? After all, the bulk of the people don't use them".
"Fifty-two percent of employees between the ages of 22 and 36 have not taken up the quality-improvement projects that they were supposed to".	"Many of the employees are like me".

Note

1   I learned some of the insights on framing from a 2013 article by John Moses (2013) in *Benefits Quarterly*. The details can be found in the bibliography. Since then, I have used this idea successfully in many quality deployments.

Lesson: 5

Not always about people

People are the heart of quality. In the 14 principles enunciated by Deming, the importance of people is mentioned in many places. He talks about things such as driving out fear, involving people in the transformation, removing barriers that rob people of pride of workmanship, and eliminating the annual rating or merit system. Even if you look at Lean, which has emanated from Toyota, it has "respect for people" as one of its key pillars (Cardon and Bribiescas 2015). After all, when employees are respected and they are allowed to display their full capability, they do their best in a journey of quality and continuous improvement.

Charles has been coming late for early-morning quality-improvement training programmes. He was told about it a couple of times, yet he seemed to continue to be late. When this continued to happen, despite reminding him a couple of times, the training quality leader made a statement that Charles had been sloppy and had major issues with discipline and commitment. He went on to comment that such dysfunctional people derail and kill a quality movement. Later on, the employees got to know that Charles used to get in late because he used to take his ailing mother for dialysis, and every day, he got delayed as the process did not start and end on time.

This is a great example of a fundamental attribution error. When looking at the behaviour of other people, we have this tendency to attribute them to something personal about the person. We don't seem to look at situations that could have made the behaviour happen.

Fundamental attribution error is a cognitive bias wherein our tendency to overestimate the role of personal attributes and overlook the impact of situations is referred to as fundamental attribution in social psychology. We overlook context and make comments about someone based on competence and character.

This bias manifests in two ways:

1   Our inference about others is based on the behaviour that we see others engaging in.
2   We tend to make more personal attributions about others than we do about ourselves. While talking about ourselves, we tend to blame the situation.

DOI: 10.4324/9781003250517-6

Let me share two situations:

Situation: 1	Situation: 2
What happened?	**What happened?**
A person makes repeated errors during processing an invoice.	A business leader does not adopt a continuous-improvement practice which you are trying to advocate in your company.
How do you see it?	**How do you see it?**
The person is sloppy and incompetent.	He is not a supporter of continuous improvement and quality practices.
What might be going on?	**What might be going on?**
He may be untrained on the job.	He is currently undergoing a financial audit and would not like anything else to disturb it.
He is wrong choice for the role.	
He is going through a divorce.	He is not convinced of the impact that you are claiming the continuous-improvement initiatives can deliver.
He is worried about his financial debt.	
He has a problem with his eyes because of which he does data-entry errors.	He believes in quality but has a different approach in mind.
	He first wants to get team buy-in before he launches in his business.
	There is a technology implementation that is currently going on hence he has kept all other change initiatives in abeyance.

A fundamental attribution error happens when we have a limited view of others' worlds. Our inference about them is based on the limited information that we have or how they behave in front of us. We tend to base our judgement on what we see most of the other person, or because we lack sufficient information on what causes their behaviour. However, as far as we are concerned, we have a much better view of our world and situations; hence, we talk about situations and not much about competence and character.

As a manager, you could attribute poor work performance to people's personal attributes such as apathy, lethargy, and other traits without looking at other explanations and other contextual issues, which can be deadly. This could lead to your key people leaving the company. It could also put a question mark on your ability to lead people.

As you embed a culture of continuous improvement, you have to make sure employees shun the habit of attributing people's action to their character and competence. Like it or not, this is very pervasive in organisations. Making people aware of this bias can go a long way in creating a culture where people are treated with respect. Not arresting this bias could create a blame culture that can not only be toxic but also impede the creation of a continuous-improvement culture.

Always keep this principle in mind while doing a root-cause analysis wherein behaviours are involved. Don't just confine your analysis to personal attributes; look for factors from the person's context and other issues which could have caused the behaviour which may not be visible.

Hence, while making an inference about anyone's behaviour, keep the following in mind:

- Ascertain if there are any situational factors that have led to the behaviour.
- Try and put yourself in the other person's shoes and understand why he is doing what he is doing.
- List three positive qualities about the person (especially if you are resentful of him) to help balance your perspective.
- Have an empathetic conversation with the person to fathom what is beyond the obvious.
- Always assume that people have good intentions.
- Reach out to someone else for an external perspective.
- If you are managing a team, make the effort to know them more.
- The fundamental attribution error can create a blame culture; hence, it should be arrested. It will never allow you to build a culture that supports continuous improvement.

Lesson: 6

What quality experts need to know

We have all met employees in our careers who have very little understanding of the fundamentals of quality management, yet they would go out and advise others on what it takes to build a company that's known for product quality.

Or you might have met a quality–improvement practitioner who would brag in large meetings about his knowledge of tools and his ability to deliver business benefits through projects, yet if you ask his colleagues and bosses, they would tell you that he has very poor knowledge of tools and struggles to complete projects, so benefits are nonexistent.

These people are victims of the Dunning–Kruger effect, which was first brought to light by J. Kruger and D. Dunning in a 1999 paper published in the *Journal of Personality & Psychology*. This is a cognitive bias wherein people who are incompetent at something are not able to detect their own incompetence. Even when they are not doing a good job, they tend to believe they are doing a great job. As Dunning and Kruger describe it, ignorance carries with it the inability to accurately assess one's ignorance.

The work of David Dunning and Justin Kruger was influenced by a robbery that happened in April 1995 in two Pittsburgh–based banks. The robber, McArthur Wheeler, did this act in broad daylight. Thanks to the surveillance camera, he soon got arrested. When the police arrested him and showed him the surveillance tapes, he said, "I wore the juice" (Fehlhaber 2017).

He thought that lemon juice was used as an invisible ink. Hence, rubbing it on his face would make him invisible to cameras. He reasoned that lemon juice is used as invisible ink, so if he was able to be away from a heat source, he would be invisible. He even tested this theory before the heist by smearing juice on his face and taking a selfie with a Polaroid camera. For reasons that remain unexplained, the camera gave him a blank image. The test gave him sufficient confidence to go ahead with his plan. Most would consider this utterly foolish. But not McArthur Wheeler. As police found out, he was not under the influence of drugs or alcohol; he was mistaken. What was foolhardy for others was not for Wheeler. It was his perception of the properties of lemon juice that made people invisible. His faulty perceptions of the world impacted his actions. He had not questioned or given critical thought to his belief. Wheeler went to

DOI: 10.4324/9781003250517-7

jail and into the annals as one of the dumbest criminals. He was even featured in the 1996 World Almanac (Poundstone 2017).

This incident caught the attention of David Dunning, who was then a professor at Cornell University, and his graduate student, Justin Kruger, to see what was going on. They conducted an experiment on a group of university students. This was done in two phases. In the first phase, students were told to first complete a test to assess their capabilities in areas such as logic, grammar, and humour. Then they were asked to assess their own levels of competence in the tested areas. Simply speaking, they were asked to ascertain how capable they were of what they had been tested on. The results threw up some interesting findings: (a) people who were the least competent tended to overestimate their capabilities (Ludwig 2021), and (b) the more capable people had a tendency to underestimate their capabilities.

In the second phase of the experiment, they all got to see their individual results and those of others. Then they were again told to assess themselves. In this phase, the results threw up the following: (a) those competent individuals who had rated themselves low rated themselves better this time and (b) the assessment outcome of those who were less competent remained the same.

The change in rating of competent people happened because they realised their capabilities. The less competent people were still unable to ascertain that the capabilities of others were better even when provided with evidence (He 2020).

A person has this bias because of the following reasons:

- They tend to overestimate their own ability and skill level in a particular area.
- They misjudge other people's skills.
- They don't realise their shortcomings.

If not controlled, it can have a negative impact on what they believe, what they do, the actions they take, and decisions they make.

So how does this bias happen?

As David Dunning mentioned in 2014:

> An ignorant mind is precisely not a spotless, empty vessel, but one that's filled with the clutter of irrelevant or misleading life experiences, theories, facts, intuitions, strategies, algorithms, heuristics, metaphors, and hunches that regrettably have the look and feel of useful and accurate knowledge.

People who have this bias have an inability to evaluate themselves and fathom their own mistakes and errors. This makes them biased, exceptionally confident self-evaluators. As Dunning and Kruger say, it's a double curse. A person makes mistakes in a subject, as she is not competent, but the same incompetence blinds her from seeing errors in her work. Very simply, she does not have the requisite skill to assess that she is not good at it. This also makes her misjudge other people's ability and assumes she knows much more than them. Such people often feel more confident about a skill or a subject than they really should be. They are not aware of their overconfidence (Resnick 2019).

The other reason this happens is that these people tend to go on auto-pilot and never seem to stop and think about what they are doing and what the consequences could be. Also, it is caused by our ego and having this overestimation of oneself.

The Dunning Kruger effect was visible during the latest pandemic when political leaders made statements without realising the cracks and holes in their expertise. For example, they suggested citizens take the malarial drug hydroxychloroquine when there was little evidence of the drug acting against coronavirus (Beauchamp 2020). Or citizens were advised to wear scarves instead of masks for protection, when in fact, scarves provided no protection (Devega 2020). We have also seen similar problems with young start-up founders who tend to overrate themselves. Their arrogance, bluster, and little knowledge make them shun experienced talent. They don't listen to experts and push their decisions, only to repent later. Many times, such individuals are resistant to being taught, and since they believe they know the subject, they generously share their half-baked information, or should I say misinformation.

Have we not seen someone with little knowledge of subjects pertaining to quality suddenly declaring himself an expert? We have seen people acquiring a green belt certification and then behaving as if they have all the arsenal to solve quality problems. The problem with behaving as an expert is that we then stop learning, as we believe we know everything.

Confucius rightly said, "Real knowledge is to know the extent of one's ignorance" (Dunning 2003).

Contrary to that, real quality experts would always underrate themselves. Their depth and knowledge in the subject tells them how much they don't know. They need to have the virtue of intellectual humility and recognise that the things we believe in or think we have expertise in may be wrong or incomplete.

I have had the opportunity to interact with and teach many quality professionals in the last three decades of my career. One question that I have often asked students is how many of them rate themselves as above-average quality professionals. You will be surprised with the number: 80% of these quality professionals rate themselves as above average – a statistical impossibility. In reality, I have also known many of them to be quite incompetent, yet they rated themselves high.

Having this bias can impact you as a quality leader and also the culture that you are trying to build. It can make you closed to others' ideas. You will come across as an arrogant person who does not listen to or have respect for people. Most importantly, people around you will know that you are a hollow talker whose actions and subsequent results don't match your claims. What this bias also does is force a leader to push solutions to problems which he deems right.

When a problem is being solved through methods such as Six Sigma, Lean, or any of the structured problem-solving methods, a person having this bias will try and push his ideas even if they are not correct or half-baked. His confidence and arrogance may get his way but impact the final resolution.

Always keep in mind that those who are the most confident may not be the most competent. The corollary to this effect is that the most competent people often underestimate their competence.

A quality professional should never think of himself as an expert. He should have the humility to learn and unlearn from various contexts. It's always good to have doubts about what you know. Bring your humility to the workplace. Learn to say when you don't know or when you make a mistake. Remember, even an operator of a machine has a lot to teach you. Keep in mind that every employee has something to teach. Listen to them and learn whenever possible. You don't become a good quality leader by boasting about your knowledge of quality management and various improvement practices. You become a good leader by listening and catalysing an environment where others can contribute to the journey. If a quality leader believes that only he knows how to make his enterprise known for quality, he is wrong. Everyone has a role to play.

Quality and continuous-improvement professionals should also keep in mind that they have to beware of becoming overconfident. They need to be wary of how this bias can impact their decision-making. Here are a few examples:

Overconfidence can be a silent killer.

- A continuous-improvement professional worked on a TOC (theory of constraints) project in a manufacturing company. He was so confident of his solutions that emerged from the project that he did not feel it necessary to communicate and sell it to others in the company. He believed that people would be attracted by the power of the project recommendations and would implement them in the company. He loudly proclaimed, "Diamonds don't need to go to people; people come to them". Little did he realise that even the best solutions need to be sold to the employees so that they adopt them for organisational benefit. He had actually done a great job, but since he did not do a good job of selling it, the adoption was poor. The solutions, though brilliant, did not get adopted by those who needed to use them. The project had been successful, but there was no impact.
- Even experts need to sell their solutions and ideas and can't sit pretty on them. After Charles Darwin's book *On the Origin of Species by Means of Natural Selection* was published in 1859, he did not sit quiet, thinking his ideas would be accepted by all. He took the help of four stalwarts in diverse fields to defend and spread his revolutionary theory (Sutton and Rao 2014). The four musketeers who helped with this were the famous geologist Charles Lyell, the renowned British botanist and

explorer Joseph Dalton Hooker, the American botanist and author of the classic text *Gray's Manual of Botany* Asa Gray, and English biologist and anthropologist Thomas Huxley.

Too much data does not mean better results.

- Today, with the help of technology, getting customer data is not difficult. Rather, there is an inundation of data, which companies need to know how to manage. While data is good and is required for quality-improvement efforts, it makes people overconfident and makes overconfidence worse. I have seen quality professionals who believe that just because information exists, we should use it. I have even heard quality gurus advocating that the more information, the better the quality-improvement efforts. This is not true.

- An experiment done by Paul Slovic (Slovic and Corrigan 1973), a psychology professor at the University of Oregon, found something interesting in his horse racing study. He chose eight expert horserace gamblers ("handicappers") and asked them to predict the results of 45 races. They were given a list of 88 variables that were useful in predicting horses' performance in the past. They were told to predict the performance of horses and their confidence in their prediction. They did the exercise by picking different levels of data starting with 5 variables, then going on to select 10, then 20, and then 40 variables. The researchers found that the handicappers had the same level of prediction accuracy regardless of the number of variables they used. However, their confidence level progressively increased with more data points. Clearly, beyond a small amount of relevant information, we use additional information to feed our biases. More information can increase our confidence levels but does not have any incremental benefit.

  This experiment reinforces that just because data is available in plenty, we should not use it in quality-improvement projects. I have seen quality professionals use information just because it is available. It's a waste of valuable time and effort. Instead, a quality professional should know what data to pick and what data to reject.

Be careful of past successes.

- Past success can exacerbate overconfidence. One of my clients hired a person as a quality leader for one their businesses. This person was confident and had been very successful in three of his earlier roles as a quality leader. So he believed he had a recipe for success. Not only did this push him to become overconfident, he seemed to have become quite arrogant. He became a poor listener and easily snubbed people. He was hired by this company because the CEO was very impressed by his confidence, his aggression, and most important, his past success.

When he joined this company, he put together a blueprint that replicated the approaches of the past. He was confident it would work, and as a result, he did not take anyone's input. He tried to steamroll his approach, thinking he would get success. However, after a couple of months passed, he realised that his ambitious approach about which he was so confident did not seem to be working here. He seemed to have alienated many people. Very soon, there were a host of people in the company who were all against him. A year passed, and there was no result. Given the antagonism around him and there being no result, the CEO called him one day and asked him to resign.

This was a clear case of how past successes had made him overconfident. As Bill Gates (1995) has said, "Success can be a lousy teacher. It teaches smart people into thinking they can't lose". Past success does make you believe that your skills and capabilities are the primary reason for success. It also makes you believe that you have a standard approach to be successful, forgetting the fact that every context is different. What worked somewhere else may not work here. As a result, they tend to value their beliefs more than the contribution of those of those around them.

What is the remedy for this bias?

- Raise awareness of the bias.
- Use stringent performance standards and goals to expose those who only talk.
- Provide tools, training, and resources to help the individual understand their shortcomings.
- Provide frequent feedback.
- Demonstrate confidence in employees who perform well but lack confidence.
- Sometimes it's best to just let someone fail if it does not impact anyone else. A small serving of humble pie can do the trick. Failing will teach them their limitations.
- If you make quick decisions and make quick calls, just slow down. It helps to deliberate and then decide.
- Recognise when the bias can affect you, such as when you are learning a new skill or subject.
- Continue to learn and practise. Keep digging deeper.

One cannot climb the curve of competence without seeking knowledge and feedback.

It always helps to remember that irrespective of your level of expertise, your knowledge is like an island. It is surrounded by a vast sea of things that you don't know.

When facts are overlooked

Adolph Mazon was an aggressive and successful finance operations leader. He managed the performance-management team in a finance shared service centre of a global manufacturing company. His view was that quality improvements had little application in finance. This view was shaped by his experiences in his earlier company. Apparently, a continuous–improvement programme had been launched in his previous company. The efforts saw a Lean Sigma effort being rolled out across all functions in the company. While manufacturing, supply chain, and human resources functions did reap a lot of benefits, there was no explicit benefit in finance. The failure in finance was largely because of little leadership support. However, what got ingrained in Adolph's mind was that Lean Sigma does not work in finance. So when his current company launched a similar effort, he knew in his mind that it would not work in finance operations. For him, Lean Sigma was for manufacturing process improvement and was not applicable to finance processes. He even went out to prove to everyone that was a wastage of time, money, and resources. Hence, he would like his team to not waste their effort in it. When others in the company pointed out the benefits achieved by other teams, he said that "finance was different". He would typically proclaim, "Improvement in finance operations happens through people who understand numbers and accounting. What would an approach like Lean Sigma do? Process improvement in finance processes can happen through accounting skills, not through engineering shop-floor concepts called "Lean Sigma". He would go to great lengths to cite one example from his previous company, where one Lean Sigma project had failed.

However, there were other leaders in the finance division who were willing to try it out. These leaders used the principles of Lean Sigma to improve their operations and saw major efficiency improvement. Seeing the benefits, various teams in finance operations adopted Lean Sigma. Adolph's team was the only one not to be touched by Lean Sigma improvement. This initiative was sponsored by the CFO, but Adolph did not do anything due to his belief that this was not for finance. To confirm his belief, he went about looking for evidence where the Lean Sigma efforts were a bit slow and failed. He scoured the

DOI: 10.4324/9781003250517-8

internet and picked a few examples where Lean Sigma in finance had not been successful. He even tried to get one of his colleagues from his past company to have an informal meeting with the finance team to share why Lean Sigma does not work for finance.

In any continuous-improvement effort, managing change is a critical element. There are teams which resist change and impede deployment. This is very normal and has to be managed. There are always a few projects which have problems. Adolph went about looking for these instances and challenges. This was to reinforce his incorrect belief that Lean Sigma does not work in finance processes. He became a major voice highlighting these challenges and discouraging others who had embarked on the journey.

However, there were other teams which had gone ahead and adopted Lean Sigma and started seeing benefits. They knew that this was important and was sponsored by the CFO. A couple of months passed, and there were teams which saw how Lean Sigma helped them to reduce errors and improve lead times. When the CFO visited the finance shared service centre for the half-yearly review, he was very happy to see the benefits gained through Lean Sigma. But when he got to know that Adolph Mazon's team had made little progress, he was very disappointed. He also got to learn how Adolph was dissuading others. This made him very furious. He called Adolph and gave him a piece of mind. He told him that his behaviour was unacceptable. He further told him that if his team did not adopt Lean Sigma, he would be forced to think of changing the leader of the performance management team that was currently being led by him.

This is a great example of an individual cherry-picking information that supports his belief. Adolph Mazon's actions were a great demonstration of conformation bias.

Confirmation bias is about paying attention and upholding the information that supports our beliefs and worldview (Gilovich 1991). Hence, we look for information that supports what we believe in. We tend to interpret the world through our worldview (Fernam Street Blog 2021). We stop gathering information the moment we realise it has confirmed what we believe in. We also tend to reject information that does not confirm what we believe in.

This is actually a type of cognitive bias where the focus is to actively seek out and assign more weight to evidence that confirms a person's preconception and hypothesis about a situation or option and to ignore or under value evidence that could disconfirm their hypothesis.

The bias impacts how we look at information and how we interpret it. It prevents us from looking at things objectively. The outcome is that we become prisoners of what we believe in.

Confirmation bias makes a person prone to being too accepting of information they want to hear and too critical of information they do not want to hear.

Why does this happen?

Once a belief pattern has been established, our neurons want to fire in line with that pattern, which makes it difficult to change a belief system. It is also because of challenge avoidance, which happens because we want to avoid cognitive dissonance that contradicts what we believe in. It is always because of reinforcement seeking that helps us to cope with dissonance that may happen when we encounter information that contradicts what we believe in.

Let's now talk about quality and how this bias impacts it.

A critical facet of quality improvements is data and evidence. However, when there is bias, there could be instances when we shun the right answer even when there is evidence for it, yet our predispositions and pre-conceived notions get in the way of us getting this right answer.

Also, sometimes, despite having data and evidence, our decisions get negatively impacted as we care about the outcome that we believe in.

What also happens is that just because we have a preference for someone, we tend to believe the person, who could be wrong. This makes our view narrow and does not allow us to explore all possibilities.

The following are other examples of conformation bias in quality-improvement efforts:

- A quality professional makes an initial diagnosis of a problem. He believes this to be the cause of the problem, He then goes all out to prove it right, even when there is evidence that his recommendation will not deliver the required results.
- While solving a problem, data should be looked at from all angles. However, confirmation bias affects the way a problem is being solved. A person can only look for data which confirms his hypothesis.
- There are many approaches to solving a quality problem. It could be through Lean, Six Sigma, 8D, Theory of Constraints, seven steps, PDCA, intelligent automation, etc. However, a Master Black Belt (who is trained in Six Sigma) believes that Six Sigma can solve all types of problems and is closed to any other approach to problem-solving.
- A quality-improvement professional force fits solutions that he believes are correct. He achieves this by pushing his ideas when the solutions to the problem are discussed.
- Because you believe that a supplier is good, you go lax on vendor audits.
- An engineer has a preconceived notion that only those with an engineering degree make good continuous-improvement professionals. Hence, he does not hire people from other disciplines.
- After catalysing a couple of successful quality projects, a quality leader believes he has all the solutions and tunes out information that contradicts past experience in transformation.

- Despite putting in place countermeasures, customer issues erupt again. This is because the root causes were not addressed. During the process of root-cause analysis, a member pushed his ideas as he believed they were the causes of the problem.
- While embarking on a customer-experience transformation, a team prepares customer personas based on what the transformation leader believes. The data and other research which had been done were all overlooked as the overbearing leader got his way.
- Managers insist on executing things as they have done in the past. They shun the new ideas that have emerged from a quality-improvement effort.
- A continuous-improvement manager believes that quality practices can help to solve all types of problems and closes himself off to approaches such as design thinking, human-centred design, etc.
- A quality professional reads the writings/books that confirm what he knows.

Let's see how confirmation bias impacts problem-solving.

Pinser Wong was a customer experience consultant. He was approached by the owner, Simon Liu, of a popular fast food restaurant named Symphony Burger (names have been changed for confidentiality). Simon told Pinser about his business challenges. Business had completely gone down. Sales had been falling. According to Simon, the reason for this was the many customer service issues the store has been saddled with in the last few months. He went on to say that he was so passionate about customers and was sad to see the negative reviews on the internet.

When Pinser Wong heard this, he got influenced by the passion of Simon Liu. He thought the problem that he needed to solve was "poor customer service". So, what did he do? He googled "poor service + Symphony Burger" and "customer complaints at Symphony Burger". His search threw up a host of customer complaints. He analysed the complaints, distilled the root causes, and shared them with Simon Liu. Based on his recommendation, Symphony Burger adopted the recommendations. But a couple of months passed, and there was marginal improvement in sales numbers.

This was an example where confirmation bias had impacted the entire problem-solving approach. The recommendations made were not right. What had happened was Pinser Wong got hugely influenced by Simon Liu's suggestion that the cause of sales falling was poor customer service and took the entire problem-solving in this direction. The following are the ways confirmation bias impacts problem-solving.

The objective of his problem-solving should have been "improving sales of Symphony Burger". Instead, Pinser picked the problem as "improving customer service of Symphony Burger". Hence, his solutions were very narrow and just focussed on issues pertaining to customer service.

The second evidence of confirmation bias was when he looked for evidence that confirmed his belief that customer service was a problem. While searching for customer voices in Google, his query should have been "customer feedback on Symphony Burger". Instead, he searched for "customer complaints of Symphony Burger". This completely narrowed the problem.

The third evidence of confirmation bias was Pinser Wong's recommendations. Pinser Wong had, from two of his personal experiences in two other restaurants, found the servers to be rude. Incidentally, both of them turned out to be college students who were part-time staff. From these two incidents, he believed that all college students were rude in a restaurant. This was one of the recommendations that he made at Symphony Burger. This restaurant had many college students as part-time workers. Pinser recommended Simon Liu replace them with permanent staff. In psychology, this is called illusory correlation. Here, people find a correlation between events when none exists. Perceptions are formed about relationships between events, actions, and behaviours when, in fact, there is no relationship.

This happens because these events are rare and catch our attention. They act as mental shortcuts. So when people look for reasons, they go with what immediately comes to their mind. Though there was no data to prove that college students provided bad customer service, Pinser Wong believed so and recommended the same.

So, what are some of the things we should do to arrest this bias?

- Make people aware of this bias – everyone can be impacted by this bias.
- Urge people to process new information.
- Don't jump to conclusions. Gather a complete set of information before making a conclusion.
- Ask a lot of questions. A good question is: "Why do you believe in this?" or "What are your views?"
- Make you and your team's motto: Focus on truth and not correctness. By this, I mean it's okay if you are wrong. The focus should be to get the truth.
- Practise humility – Remember no matter how much you think you know about a topic, there is always more to learn.
- Let people know their strengths and weaknesses. Use tools like the Clifton Strengths 34[1] assessment from Gallup.
- Fill your team with those who have opposing views. The 16th president of the United States, Abraham Lincoln, filled his cabinet with politicians who had been his opponents. Three of his colleagues in the cabinet ran against him in the 1860 elections, which included Edward Bates, Salmon Chase, and William Seward. Even President Barack Obama had Hillary Clinton as Secretary of State, though she was his opponent in the U.S. presidential elections (Coutu 2009).

- Encourage people to disagree. I have seen teams having a devil's advocate who would also push participants to see a new perspective.
- Look for and be comfortable with data that conflicts with your hypothesis.
- When you talk to a customer or a stakeholder, listen more and talk less.
- When some data is presented, don't give too much weight to the information that has been presented early.
- While evaluating technology solutions to a problem, don't look at any solution with rose-tinted glasses. For example, don't just go for a software solution for your processes because the company is very visible and spent a lot on marketing.
- When talking to customers for their views, don't just engage with those who are happy. Also, talk to unhappy customers, sales teams, customer service teams, etc.

This is just a partial list of how we can work on this bias. What's critical is to keep it in mind and be conscious about it every time.

Note

1 The Clifton Strength assessment from Gallup is a tool used to understand the strength of an individual.

The intricacies of change

Quality improvement and change management go hand in hand. Rather, change is the other side of any quality-improvement effort. Managing change is one of the key elements of a quality journey. Thanks to the work of thought leaders and consulting firms, today, we have well-defined approaches to manage change. This includes the work of Lewin and Kotter; models such as McKinsey's 7S, Bridge's Transition Model, Prosci's ADKAR Model, and so on. However, companies still get it wrong. It is not that any of those models are wrong, but because there are many unsaid things that are not kept in mind while driving any change transformation, and this includes quality-improvement programmes. Many of these are things that are related to the psychology of people and how they get impacted by change. So, what are some of these that should be on our radar?

Stir positive emotions

There is no better way to catalyse change than to evoke positive emotions. Traditionally, the focus of quality-improvement professionals has been to influence through data and logic. The reason is very simple. We humans respond to emotions much better than to cold logic. Positive emotions evoke feelings of pride, a sense of belonging, self-efficacy, gratitude, and joy (Green and Katie 2019). The problem with negative emotions is that they cause defensiveness. Negative emotions can be stirred by fear, guilt, and so on. This is where leaders use the burning platform strategy (also discussed in Lesson: 25). The metaphor "Burning Platform" was coined by Daryl Conner in his 1993 book. The phrase comes from an incident that occurred on 6 July 1988. On that date, the Piper Alpha oil rig in the North Sea exploded – the result of a failure to check some simple systems that had worked faultlessly for the previous decade. The explosion in turn caused a massive fire and 167 men died – the largest number killed in an offshore accident (Conner 1993).

An event like this signals a do-or-die sort of situation in which an organisation needs to undergo a radical change. This entails the construction of an urgent message that conveys the strength of the top management and clearly

DOI: 10.4324/9781003250517-9

explains the path forward to drive critical behavioural change (Medhat 2019). While it does give results, we need to keep in mind that negative emotions are exhausting (Hill 2021). They work in the short run, but are very difficult to sustain in the long run. Hence, positive emotions work best. A study done by Patrick, Chun, and MacInnis (2009) on emotions and self-control had individuals imagine feeling shame from eating chocolate cake or pride if they resisted eating it. Forty percent of members in the pride group resisted eating the cake versus only 10.5% of the shame group. Clearly, positive emotions are a big propellant in a change effort. When a manufacturing company embarked on a journey to becoming a zero-defect company, the CEO gave a clarion call that the employees were all going to be creating a world-class enterprise, which was going to be a matter of pride for the country. This evoked a lot of pride among employees, and most of them came on board to make it happen. Quality practitioners need to stir positive emotions by creating the right messaging, using merchandise such as T-shirts, cups, and badges, and might tie the change effort with a larger cause which touches the hearts of all employees.

Manage the mismatch between improvement goals and personal goals

We humans value what we have. We tend to resist anything that comes in the way of our achieving personal goals, pursuing our passions, and things that we value. Hence, if the outcome of a change effort impacts any of these, we shall resist the execution. What this means is that if the outcome of a quality-improvement effort is in conflict with what an individual or a team values, it will not get done easily. For example, a continuous-improvement project recommended automating the various processes that the employees did in the office. This included invoicing, accounting, payroll, hiring, etc. There were individuals who had mastered these processes and were known for what they did. So when they learnt that their processes would get automated, they set out to scuttle the rollout. A quality leader has to extrapolate the unsaid dimensions of the team. They need to understand what motivates them, what they value, what their passions are, and what their experience with change has been previously. Only after they have done this sense check should they embark on improvements. In case there is a mismatch, they have to take proactive steps to take them on board. The other approach is to tailor a message that makes the project relevant to those impacted by change.

Seek feedback but avoid the bandwagon effect

When quality improvements are underway and you wish to take feedback from the employees on any of the things that would undergo a change, never seek feedback in public. For example, the outcome of a Lean Breakthrough at a bank was rolling out a new process for credit operations. With an objective to seek buy-in, the business head reached out to the employees in a town hall to seek feedback on what they felt about it. It began with one voice who expressed why the new process would not work. Seeing one person dissenting, many other people jumped in. Very soon, there were many who were voicing concern. It was not that the new process had any issues; it was that the employees had to work extra to learn and get familiar with the new process. After the town hall, when the implementation team came for deployment, there were many others who resisted the adoption. As a result, the implementation got derailed, and the project did not get implemented. There is an important lesson here. When taking feedback about change, always do it one-on-one. Even if it takes a lot of time, you should try and do it one person at a time. This prevents a bandwagon effect. This is the psychological phenomenon wherein people do something because others are doing it, irrespective of what they believe in. This does not allow individuals to examine the merit of a change effort.

Nowadays, technology provides another way you can seek feedback from people in a large group without having the bandwagon effect. This requires software to make this happen. For example, in information technology companies, during meetings, engineers are often required to each provide their estimation of effort to create a piece of software. This almost leads to a bandwagon effect, as many people tend to go along with the first estimate provided. However, there is software available today through which work is discussed and then each engineer has to provide their effort into a Planning Poker software system, where it is recorded. Only after all the engineers have provided their inputs are the estimates all exposed to the group. This leads to more diverse estimates of effort (since the bandwagon effect is eliminated and everyone has to think on their own), and it therefore leads to more discussions (due to variability) and, ultimately to better, more accurate estimates. This is just another way in which companies have tried to break this effect: rather than having individual 1:1 meetings, letting the software provide a virtual 1:1 to make sure everyone really gives their best input.

Role modelling should be used more often

In any workplace, employees closely watch what people around them say as well as what they do. Human beings unconsciously mimic the emotions, behaviours, moods, expressions, etc. of those around them (Basford and Schainger 2016). They especially get influenced by the behaviours of those in positions of influence. A key facet of any quality improvement is changing behaviours that positively impact the change one is proposing to undertake. Hence, it's important that leaders in the company demonstrate the new "ways of working" they are planning to embed. Not only leaders who are at the top of the company but also influencers at all levels of the company should do so. This is a very important dimension of any quality-improvement effort but is often overlooked. For example, a company that embarked on a journey of customer centricity had a new way of working which spoke about keeping the customer at the centre of all decisions. The employees had this perception that the CEO and top management would do anything for sales, even if it was at the cost of the customer experience. This was something the leaders wanted to change. Hence, they wanted to demonstrate the new behaviour of keeping the customer at the centre of all decisions. Over the next six months, they took a series of decisions which convinced the employees that the top management was serious. They did things like not sending a large product batch to the customer even though it had a quality level of 99%. This was because what they had promised to the customer was product quality at Four Sigma levels, which was 99.977%. This had a major financial impact, but the CEO and his leadership team wanted to send the right signal to employees. The other decision was the top management spending one day at each customer's place, talking to them, observing how their product got used, etc. There were a series of such efforts. The results of all these actions by the top people had a positive impact on the employees, and they too started to demonstrate the same behaviour in their work areas.

Today's connected and digital world provides more opportunity to share with others how we act and behave, and we should use it in all quality improvements. Role modelling is a powerful tool that should be used more often.

Show . . . don't just tell

Sometimes, despite all the communication, employees don't seem to buy into change. In such instances, it makes sense to show and not tell. Let me explain. There was a food company which had embarked on a cost drive. One of the effects of this was that the company went for cheaper labels. This was pushed by the CFO and other members of the C-suite despite opposition from the packaging development team. The outcome was that the labels on the jam bottles started falling off, the edges got lifted up, and they looked filthy on the bottles. When complaints started pouring in, the head of quality put all the data on a PowerPoint slide and reported the same to the CFO and other members of top management. Their response was that it was an aberration and that anything new takes time to settle. The quality leader then decided to adopt a different approach. He collected defective packs from various markets in Asia, and these were not from 1 batch but from 30 batches. He then got them displayed in the conference room where the executive board meeting (chaired by the CEO) was to happen. Next to the defective samples, he placed the packs of competitors, which were impeccable and stood out. When the members walked in, they were shocked to see the packets. The quality leader stood in one corner. It was shocking for everyone to see the state of the packs. The CEO heard the quality leader out and ordered that the company shift back to the original label supplier even if it cost more.

Sometimes, to convince people, you have to show them, and just telling may not work. This also works well for demonstrating product defects to shop-floor associates, who may find the approach to be much more convincing.

The three needs

Change can be arduous, change can be painful, yet it can be addressed if companies are able to address the three critical psychological needs of employees: autonomy, growth, and meaning (Monahan, Murphy, and Johnson 2016). Let's understand what each one of them means:

- Autonomy: This is about employees having the freedom to take decisions in the workplace.
- Growth: This is about individuals having new challenges, acquiring new skills, learning new things, and having greater responsibility.
- Meaning: This is about having clarity on how their work will impact the larger objective of the enterprise.

If we are able to provide clarity to employees on all three needs, it will have a positive impact on the change due to the quality improvement. Hence, before you embark on any quality-improvement project, ask the following questions:

- How will the changes to quality improvement impact the autonomy of employees?
- What sort of growth opportunity will the employees get due to the change?
- How do we ensure that the employees see themselves impacting the strategic objective after the improvements?

Being able to answer these questions can make the quality-improvement process much easier and less likely to meet with resistance.

Remember ABCD

This is an approach that has been adopted from the behavioural insights' toolkit from the OECD (Organisation for Economic Co-operation and Development 2019). The framework can be in a quality professional's quiver while driving change of behaviour. It serves as a guide to things that need to be kept in mind while working on problems that require behaviour change.

A = Attention

We humans have limited attention to things and get easily distracted. The challenge before quality and continuous-improvement professionals is how to get people's attention in a digitally connected world and amidst an avalanche of information. When talking about attention, we need to keep in mind that it is influenced by our state of mind and salience. Our state of mind impacts what we do and how we do it. This directly has a bearing on our attentiveness. We tend to make errors or make wrong choices when we are hungry or tired. In a back office where finance processing happens, I have seen employees making more errors during the end of the day when they are tired. Salience also has a big impact. The focus should be to make the key information salient so that it seizes people's attention. Our attention is impacted by whether in our line of sight the tool for driving change is placed. Placing wash basins at the entrance of a production shop of a food factory made the workmen regularly wash their hands. Even communication boards on change need to be placed at the right locations so that they get people's attention.

It should also be in the language that the staff understand. All these have to be backed with regular reminders and refreshers. Quality professionals need to make their recommendations (for behaviour change) salient so that they catch people's attention. Without this, the desired change will not happen.

B = Beliefs

Our existing beliefs drive what we do. We tend to shun information that does not align with our worldview. When this happens, we tend to underestimate the benefits of change that is expected. Our beliefs constrict us from exploring newer possibilities. Hence, quality professionals need to do a sense check of pre-existing beliefs and design interventions so that people can act. The focus should be to make people not become victims of confirmation bias. They should ensure that people don't misinterpret things and form inaccurate notions. Hence, they need to explain the reasons for change and provide coaching support whenever people need help. What also works here is social proof in which employees are made to look at those who have already adopted the new behaviour. This really works when people don't know what needs to be done in change and are awaiting direction. You can also share information in a way that influences others to come on board. This can be done by framing information so that the positive story is brought out (insights on framing can also be found in Lesson: 4 and Lesson: 20). For example, a quality leader wanted the employees to use the new expense-reimbursement software. He regularly shared with the entire company a flyer that reported the percentage of the employees already using the new software. His first flyer said "65% of the employees are already using the expense software. Why are you missing the convenience?" These flyers went out every three days, and everyone could see how the adoption was going up. The outcome was that within two months, the usage levels touched 95%.

C = Choice

The way things are presented to us drives our choices. The context around us influences what we do. The way something is presented has an influence on people. What continuous-improvement practitioners need to know is that when an intervention or a recommendation is made attractive, people are willing to try it. There are a couple of tactics that can be used here. The first tactic is to try and see if the change can be associated with people's identity. For example, when a factory underwent a Lean manufacturing implementation, the Lean master anchored the rollout around sustainability. This was because the team in the factory was very passionate about the environment and climate change. His pitch to people was that Lean manufacturing was about continuous improvement, waste reduction, and respect for people. And respect for people starts when they begin contributing positively to the environment and the community where they reside. Also, green is about waste reduction and elimination of all that is detrimental to the environment.

The second tactic is tweaking the context so that people don't need to think much while making decisions. These are called defaults, and they are pre-set options that take effect if we don't make an active choice (Samson 2014). For example, buildings may be designed in such a way that taking the staircase is easier and more attractive than opting for the lift. The other example is when new employees join a company, joining the pension scheme is a default option. If they don't want to be a part of it, they will have to opt out. The third tactic is messaging. It should be done in such a way that it can stir emotions and drive change in behaviour. People internalise messages when they make them feel a certain way, which forces them to act. For example, the Indian government launched a quality-improvement programme in 2014, a nationwide cleanliness drive. It was called the *Swachh Bharat Mission*. The programme was launched to address the sanitation concerns of citizens. It focussed on toilet access and stopping open defecation. The type of messaging used for this programme made a big impact. They created a message that provoked disgust. The change agents involved in this programme delivered the message that open defecation is tantamount to eating one's own excreta, as flies sit on excreta left in open spaces and then sit on food. This had a huge impact, and the programme was hugely successful, and more than 90% of Indian villages were open-defecation free by the end of 2019 (Indian Government's Economic Survey 2019). We discussed more about messaging in Lesson: 4.

D = Determination

Our willpower is limited, and it does get impacted by biases. People may find it difficult to stay motivated during a change programme. They need to be supported continuously so that they don't stop action and reach inertia. Quality professionals need to devise strategies to sustain the determination. The types of tactics that can be adopted here are as follows: Firstly, making it easy for employees to execute the process or carry out the task that you want them to do. The focus should be to reduce effort. For example, we find it easy to shop on ecommerce sites because of the one-click checkout, which allows repeat customers to purchase immediately without having to enter billing information every time. The second tactic is to make people commit in public. Having done so, they will find it hard to undo it, as it will impact their reputation. The third tactic is creating a social norm. This pushes people to comply because no one wants to appear not to be a part of the group. For example, as a part of its business excellence programme, Delta AutoSystems (not the real name), an automotive supplier, launched an initiative to shun a silo mindset. It was common, even in top management meetings, for the senior leaders to look at things from their departmental window and forget the interests of the customer and the company as a whole. It was decided that going forward, everyone would demonstrate a "one Delta" mindset. So if anyone did not comply with it, the behaviour would be called out. This made a big difference. Within a month, the leadership team had changed its behaviour, and over the next few months it was cascaded to the rest of the organisation.

Communicate the change that you are seeking

A continuous-improvement professional should ensure that the change that is being sought is generously shared with the organisation. This could be change of behaviour, adoption of a new process, or usage of a new technology solution. Make it a point to talk about the desirable change that you are seeking. We humans are influenced by what others do; hence, this becomes very critical. This can be done by sharing the adoption levels (such as: 72% of the people do ____). Talk about the increased prevalence of the desired change (more and more employees are riding cycles to the office). The other way is to make a social comparison (e.g. telling employees that they are not participating in CSR (corporate social responsibility) activities while those around them are doing so). The reason why this works is because we humans come under peer pressure to comply with those around us. We also tend to believe that if a large number of people are doing something, it must be the right thing to do. And we just like mimicking those around us. Studies done by Plumer (2015) and Meyer (2017) found that one of the key factors for a household purchasing solar panels is whether other households in the neighbourhood have them, more so than their age, race, income, or political affiliation. To communicate the desired change, the quality professional should take the help of senior leaders and other influencers in the company. The mode of communication can be oral, video messages, emails, town halls, etc.

Keep an eye on key biases

What are biases? They are one-sided views of things that are dominated by prejudice and one's perspective. What are cognitive biases? They refer to flawed thinking that happens due to issues around attention, perception, and mental shortcuts. They result in faulty judgement that is far from the rational objective. Cognitive biases are an integral part of human life. Throughout the book, we have discussed various types of cognitive biases. However, when we are talking about change adoption, a few biases always need to be on the radar of quality professionals. The first one is our tendency to value things that are closer to the present and not appreciate the benefits in the long term. This is called the present bias. We have discussed this in Lesson: 1 and in Lesson: 25. The reason this is important is that, because of this bias, people are not able to see the long-term benefits of change. This means that we need to share benefits in the immediate future.

The second cognitive bias to be kept in mind is the human tendency to focus on information that is consistent with our existing beliefs and confirmation. This is called confirmation bias (also discussed in Lesson: 7 and Lesson: 12). If the outcomes of change don't align with what they believe in, people will reject it. Quality professionals need to be cognisant of this behaviour and adopt tactics to manage this behaviour. The third cognitive bias is loss aversion, where the pain of losing is psychologically about twice as powerful as the pleasure of gaining (also discussed in Lesson: 1 and Lesson: 13). Because of this, you will see people resisting change even if the benefits are explicit and visible.

The fourth cognitive bias is availability bias, which has been discussed in detail in Lesson: 12. Here, individuals are driven by what they have seen, what they have heard, and what they know. They reject data and statistics. Hence, don't be surprised if you talk about change and provide data for the same, yet people reject it because they have heard and seen something contrary.

The fifth bias to be kept on radar is groupthink. As a part of the change effort, people may not share their concerns, as they may fear putting forth contradictory views could make them look like someone who is not a team player. We have discussed this bias in detail in Lesson: 12.

While there are many other biases, these five are the critical ones to be kept to mind while managing change.

Behavioural science mantras for change

When we look at change management through the window of social psychology and behavioural economics, keep these 15 mantras in mind.

1 Align the improvements with one's personal identity and values.
2 Stir emotions – positive emotions are long lasting.
3 Gather insights on what drives and motivates those impacted by change.
4 Create opportunities for people to make public pledges.
5 Those who are catalysing change must be highly credible.
6 Make change simple and effortless to implement.
7 Provide coaching and assistance in closing the intention–action gap.
8 Communicate through messages that are simple and easy to understand.
9 Share personal stories about those who have been successful with change.
10 Learn the art of managing key biases.

11 Recognise the behaviours that facilitate the change agenda.
12 Build a culture of accountability to call out undesirable behaviours.
13 Share how the quality improvements are linked to the strategic priorities.
14 Seek input from employees in every phase of the implementation.
15 Tweak the context to make the change attractive.

Remember, the success of any quality improvement depends on how effectively we are able to drive behaviour change. These insights can be very useful in the adoption and sustainability of the final change outcomes.

Lesson: 9

The power of familiarity

We have experienced this in our lives wherein when you first listen to a song on FM radio, you may find it weird and may not like it. However, if you listen to it a couple of times, you tend to like it. Or for that matter, when you first meet a person, you may not like him. He would have been a stranger to you. But as you start interacting with him on a regular basis, he becomes likeable. Or you are looking for a school providing courses in business psychology. You have two options before you. You finally pick a school that is very visible, advertises regularly on TV, and has a very impressive brochure. You don't go for the other school, which is much better but never advertises what it does.

I give the example of Mumbai, the financial capital of India, where I live. When people first come to Mumbai, from smaller cities, they don't like it. The fast living, the completion of tasks, and the concrete structures put off people who come from smaller towns where things happen at a much more leisurely pace. However, after some time, people don't want to leave the city. If you ask them, they would tell you that the city grows on you eventually.

These are examples of the exposure effect. The more you see something, the more you like it. The more time you spend with someone, the more likely you are to have a positive opinion of him. This is based on the research done by Robert Zajonc (1968), who published a paper in 1968 titled "Attitudinal Effect of Mere Exposure". The paper discovered that familiarity brings about attitudinal change, breeding affection or some sort of preference. The more exposure you have to something, the more affection you will feel towards it.

The reason people like something is not for any logical reason, but because of their familiarity with it. The preference for familiar things is purely based on exposure. This is irrespective of personal beliefs and attitudes. The familiarity can be with anything, such as songs, paintings, people, symbols, shapes, etc.

So it can be used for quality improvements, too. The following are a few examples of where the exposure effect can be used in quality improvement.

DOI: 10.4324/9781003250517-10

Repetition makes people believe in the power of quality

Leaders at all levels need to continually communicate the power of quality improvement and how it can take the business to the next level of performance. When we repeat the same message, it starts to appear real to the employees. Slowly, it gets stuck in employees' heads. A CEO committed to quality will keep repeating its importance. When employees get repeatedly bombarded with the message, they assess two things: the credibility of the information and the familiarity of the information (Dreyfuss 2017). The former is rational in nature, while the latter pertains to feelings. But as we saw in the mere exposure effect, familiarity trumps rationality. Slowly, employees start liking the idea. They start embracing it and start believing that it can help businesses wherein they have a role to play. Hence, relentlessly communicate the overarching power of quality improvements. It may take time, but it does stick with people.

Interact and just be around

A quality leader should be present and regularly network with senior business leaders in the company. He should meet them both officially and unofficially to interact on a regular basis. This actually helps to build the general reputation of the person who is going to catalyse quality improvements in the firm. We often don't realise it, but just being known has benefits which we often don't appreciate. Being known breeds familiarity, which develops a preference for the person. How does this help a quality leader? Well, when he (quality leader) reaches out to others for the various quality-improvement efforts, it can help to get support from senior leaders. Getting them on board can be a big challenge for quality leaders, but this approach does help.

Get chosen over other competing initiatives

Marketing of quality is very important. Create a brand around it. Let there be a logo or some sort of design which represents the quality movement in your company. It is important to make the quality movement visible to the entire company. Do it through banners, posters, knowledge sessions, ideation workshops, videos, rewards and recognition, quality-circle activities, etc. What is critical is to make sure that initiatives keep on happening year-round across the company, touching all geographies. When there is constant buzz around quality improvement, it will help to keep quality initiatives on top of employees' minds. This is especially true if there are a number of change initiatives underway in the company, and all of them are vying for employees' attention. So, when employees have to choose a change initiative amidst their limited time, they will go for the quality initiative that is more familiar to them. This is quite like being in a retail store when we have to choose between two brands. We will generally go for the brand that is more familiar, assuming they are similarly priced.

Let people get comfortable

Let's say you are a Lean consultant and want your prospects to hire you or buy your wares, which could be consulting assignments, training programmes, and so on. Don't go in with all guns blazing. Make it a gradual process. This is especially true if the customer does not know you and also does not understand what Lean can do to a business. Let them get familiar with you over a period of time. Look at various opportunities wherein you can keep meeting the decision-makers. This could be in their office, at industry events, on the golf course, at networking events, at conferences, etc. Give them the time to be comfortable with you. This can aid in generating goodwill and acceptance over a period of time. The positive relationship that you build helps when you talk about what you bring to the table and how you can help make their company better.

Write blogs and articles

Make it a habit to write blogs, articles, and papers about various aspects of quality. Every blog or an article that you write is an opportunity for your customers (internal or external) to know about you.

This is an excellent opportunity for them to learn not only what you bring to the table, but also how you think. You can start by sharing your ideas on social networking sites like LinkedIn, which have a diverse set of people, many of whom could be your customers.

Banner in intranet

In your company intranet, keep a banner for quality efforts in one corner. Even if employees don't click on the advertisement, "quality" is always on the top of employees' minds. What it does is increase the likelihood of them getting involved in quality-improvement activities.

Clearly, familiarity has a lot to offer on a quality journey. A quality leader should know how to judiciously generate exposure for the agenda that he is driving. Unlike what we have been told, that familiarity breeds contempt, repeated exposure to something creates a liking for it.

Lesson: 10

The role of emotions

We often don't realise that emotions have a role to play in quality-improvement projects. Have we not seen quality projects that are full of positivity where participants don't mind going above and beyond to make things happen? On the other side, there are projects wherein people struggle to feel included and wonder when it will be over. Clearly, the type of emotion that is brought to the project is a big factor in its success or failure. After all, projects are composed of humans, and humans are emotional creatures. One has to manage the emotions that run through the entire life cycle of the project.

But what exactly are emotions? How are they different from feelings and moods?

Thanks to the pioneering work of psychologists such as Nico Frijda (2006, author of the book *The Law of Emotions*), Paul Ekman (2007, author of the book *Emotions Revealed*), and Robert Plutchik (2001), we have great clarity on this subject today.

Emotions:

They are motivating forces that prepare us for action. Emotions are beyond our control and spontaneously arise, and alert us to their presence through physical sensations such as the heartbeat going up when there is fear. They typically accompany a biological arousal that makes us notice them. They are automatic, fast, and temporary.

As proposed by Paul Ekman, there are six basic emotions, and they comprise anger, disgust, fear, happiness, sadness, and surprise. Each emotion has its own unique facial expression.

Psychologist Robert Plutchik has suggested that there are eight basic emotions, and they comprise anger, fear, sadness, disgust, surprise, anticipation, trust, and joy. He also created a wheel of emotions to describe how they are related. Quality professionals should have a look at it, as it gives you a range of emotions that are possible.

DOI: 10.4324/9781003250517-11

Feelings:

They are how we interpret the emotions that we have experienced and have a more conscious element. For feelings to happen, one has to be aware of the emotion, and there has to be a thought process connected to it. Feelings are emotions processed by thinking. When we feel something, we are able to have thoughts and make decisions about it. Feelings tend to last longer.

Moods:

They are related to a specific incident. It's difficult to identify their trigger; they could be caused by weather, lighting, people around us, what we have been doing, etc. They tend to last much longer. They could last for a few hours to a few days.

In any quality-improvement projects, these are four critical things that need to be kept in mind to manage emotions.

1. Being aware of the kaleidoscope of emotions

During the entire life cycle of projects, various emotions come and go (Eze 2017). A quality professional should be aware of them. In each phase of the project, there could be both positive and negative emotions. The project leader should have a good sense of the type of emotions that can erupt in each stage. For example, when the project is in its initial stages, when the problem is being defined, and the overall time frame is being put in place, the type of emotions that you can expect are joy, excitement, anticipation, etc. The negative emotions that can be there include uncertainty, fear of failure, pressure of timeline and responsibility, doubts, concern about whether other members would collaborate, etc.

The second phase of the project is about cause analysis. In this phase, the type of positive emotions that can be seen are joy, happiness, and optimism at having found the right causes of the problem and getting the project moving in the right direction. The negative emotions that team members have emanate from not having deciphered the root causes and include fear, lack of clarity on how long it will take, etc.

The third phase is about deployment of countermeasures. The types of positive emotions that you can see here are happiness, joy, admiration, trust, etc., all due to the successful implementation of the countermeasures. The negative emotions could be frustration, disgust, annoyance, or apprehension, all because the countermeasure implementation is not going as planned.

The fourth and last phase is about installing measures to sustain the benefits and closing the project. The type of positive emotions that one can see here are happiness, joy, or ecstasy for having successfully closed the project as planned. The negative emotions here could be disgust, anger, annoyance, grief, etc., for not having closed the project as desired.

Whenever I facilitate a Kaizen Blitz or Lean Breakthrough event, I consciously plan for the moments when the energy plummets. For those unfamiliar with Lean Breakthroughs, they are short-duration projects with the objective of delivering spectacular improvement in a short period of time. These are typically five-day exercises wherein a team comes together to solve a business problem. From my experience, I have seen the third and first half of the fourth day as being filled with negative emotions. Team members struggle with root causes, and the deployment challenges begin to appear. The types of emotions that have been seen here are annoyance, anger, disgust, boredom, grief, sadness, etc. This is when I plan a series of physical exercises and games that are done not only to break the monotony but also to get back the energy.

A quality-improvement leader needs to be aware of the emotional seesaws, anticipate them, and then take proactive steps.

2. Having the ability to manage emotions

We know that behaviours are contagious. So, if any team member on the quality project team has a grumpy face, it affects the other team members. This is especially true of the mood carried by the project leader. If he demonstrates high energy, others catch on to it. Similarly, if he puts on a gloomy face, it impacts all of the team members. Rather, it heavily depends on the project leader to manage the emotional temperature of the team. Hence, a project leader needs to be high in emotional intelligence. Rather, a high EQ should be a criterion for selecting any person to lead a project.

What is emotional intelligence (EQ)?

Emotional intelligence is the ability to manage one's own emotions and the emotions of others.

In an ideal setting, the project team members should have the emotional intelligence to manage the ups and downs of emotions. Expecting everybody to have a high EI is expecting too much. However, the person leading the project should have the emotional intelligence to manage the emotions that run through the life of a project.

So how does one develop their emotional quotient (EQ)?

As proposed by Goleman, Boyatzis, and Mckee in their 2002 book *Primal Leadership: Learning to Lead with Emotional Intelligence*, one can develop one's EQ by focussing on competency in the domains of personal competence and social competence. Personal competence is how we manage ourselves, while social competence is how we manage relationships.

Basically, emotional intelligence has four components:

a   **Self–Awareness:** This is the ability to understand one's strengths, weaknesses, and emotions and how they impact others (Laundry 2019).
b   **Self–Management:** This is the ability to manage one's emotions, particularly in situations that are stressful. It also includes being able to put up a positive demeanour.
c   **Social Awareness:** This is the ability to discover others' emotions and how they play out in the organisation.
d   **Relationship Management:** This is the ability to manage relationships, influence others, and even resolve conflict (Goleman 1995).

The first two are personal competence, while the last two are social competence.

To be adept in each of the four components, Goleman recommends specific competencies, which have been summarised as follows:

Self-awareness

The competencies to be developed in this area are as follows:

Emotional Self-Awareness: This is the ability to understand our own emotions and how they impact others, performance, and so on.
Accurate Self-Assessment: This is the ability to understand one's strengths and weaknesses.
Self-Confidence: This is about having a strong sense of self-worth.

Self-management

To be adept in this area, one has to develop these competencies:

Emotional Self-Control: This is the ability to keep disruptive emotions under control.
Transparency: This is about demonstrating honesty, integrity, and trustworthiness.
Adaptability: This is the ability to adapt to changing situations.
Achievement: This is the ability to perform to meet standards of excellence.
Optimism: This is about seeing the bright side of every event.
Initiative: This is the ability to seize opportunities.

Social awareness

There are three competencies that need to be developed in this area:

Empathy: This is about looking at things from others' view point and understanding how they feel about it.

Organisational Awareness: This is about knowing the power centres, politics, and various networks in the firm.

Service: This is about knowing others' needs and meeting them. These can be internal or external customers.

Relationship management

The following competencies are the ones required for being successful in this area:

Inspirational Leadership: This is the ability to craft a compelling vision for others to follow.

Influence: This is the ability to persuade others to come on board.

Developing Others: This is about developing others through coaching and mentoring.

Change Catalyst: This is about the ability to drive change and show new direction.

Building Bonds: This is about building relationships.

Teamwork and Collaboration: This is the ability to work in teams and collaborate with others.

Emanating from Daniel Goleman are the following actions, which every quality professional should know:

1   You need to know your emotions.
2   You need to learn to manage your emotions.
3   You need to motivate yourself.
4   You need to recognise and understand other people's emotions.
5   You need to know how to manage relationships and others' emotions.

Goleman et al. say that leaders who are highly effective usually show "strength in a half dozen or so EI competencies". Quality professionals planning to lead projects should sharpen these competencies. Just knowing tools and problem-solving methods is not sufficient; you have to have these EI competencies to take things forward and navigate through the emotionally charged moments.

3. Lack of communication can be demotivating

Communication plays a very important role in quality improvements. Projects may have various participants who could be involved in various things. If the members of the project team don't get to know what others are doing or where the overall project is moving, it can lead to distrust. As Turner and Müller (2004) found in their research, there are four emotions tied to the project, and they are: 1. trust, 2. interest in the project, 3. the perception of progress, and 4. comfort and the need to control. It's imperative to share with all team members the health of the overall project and how each person has been progressing in their area. The onus lies with the project leader to make sure he holds meetings at least twice a week so that all members are on board. Encourage everyone to share the successes and the challenges and collectively decide a way forward.

When people feel positive about things, we not only feel good but also relate to others well.

4. Have an activity roster in place

Managing myriad emotions during a project is not easy. However, there is no way around it. The quality-improvement team leader should know how to manage various emotions before, during, and after the project. It is recommended we adopt a series of strategies to keep the emotional temperature of the team under control. Here are a few suggestions that can be adopted during the life cycle of the project:

- Before the start of the project, go out with the entire team. This will not only help with familiarisation of the team members but will also break down barriers among them.
- Do a team-building workshop with the entire project team.
- Nudge teammates to share one of their secrets. This would help to explicitly state the expectations and who does what.
- Specify the ways of working and the behaviours that need to be demonstrated during the entire project.
- Once in a while, go out for a drink together as a team.
- Celebrate milestone achievements.
- Have many one-on-one conversations. Listen to people without judging.
- Regularly, go out jogging or cycling together during the life of the project.
- Don't nit-pick but provide regular feedback when someone's behaviour has been unacceptable.
- After every phase of the project, do a reflection session with the team to ascertain what went well and what failed.
- If there are two people who don't get along together, don't try to make them become best friends, but ask them to be civil and keep their focus on how to leverage the relationship for the success of the project.
- There will be setbacks during the project. Learn to accept it. Everything will not be as planned. Learn to accept failure.
- Have a 15-minute catch-up stand-up meeting every day to take stock of how things are going, learn if there are any challenges, and gauge the emotions.
- Give a crash course on the biases that could creep in during a project.

- Teach team members the fundamentals of mindfulness and encourage them to practise it.
- Make teams play games and exercises which break the monotony and get back the zing.

This is just a practical list of what you could do. You can choose strategies based on your context and requirements. From my experience, I have seen that many quality-improvement projects are over-managed and under-led. If the project leader and the team members had demonstrated emotional intelligence, things would have been better.

Lesson: 11

Engaging hearts and minds

Building a company known for consistently producing quality products and ensuring flawless service does not happen by chance. It's a multi-year effort which is accomplished with the help of employees. Leaders at the helm of this journey need to know that catalysing improvement projects does deliver financial benefits, helps to arrest chronic customer issues, and addresses deep-seated business problems. But the real value is derived when quality is embedded as an integral part of the organisational culture. The CEO and other members of the C-suite own the agenda of quality, but the employees make it happen. The execution is not complete without the active participation of the employees.

Many companies have failed in their quality journeys not because they lacked intent. They were unsuccessful because they were not able to take their employees on board. The employee participation was superficial, as a result of which the deployment did not take root. The top management has to do much more than setting up a vision, crafting a blueprint, and investing in time, money, and other resources. They have to create an environment that encourages the involvement of employees. It's this involvement that, over a period of time, turns into commitment. As a matter of fact, the employees are the real custodians of quality. A promising quality deployment is one in which all employees contribute to the journey.

Here is where a very important idea from psychology can come in handy.

I have a CEO friend who is also a pianist. When he is playing the piano, he seems to be in a completely different world. Not only is he absorbed in it, he seems to completely enjoy it. No amount of distraction can take his attention away. He seems to be in a state of ecstasy. This is what psychologists call flow (TED Talk 2004).

Flow is a psychological state when an individual is completely immersed in an activity. He forgets all concerns and is completely absorbed and fully focussed on it while enjoying every bit of it. His mind, body, and soul are being utilised to the fullest.

This concept of flow was proposed by Mihaly Csikszentmihalyi and beautifully explained in his 1990 book *Flow: The Psychology of Optimal Experience*.

DOI: 10.4324/9781003250517-12

He described flow in his book as follows: "a state in which people are so involved in an activity that nothing else seems to matter; the experience is so enjoyable that people will continue to do it even at great cost, for the sheer sake of doing it".

He further mentioned that flow starts with "a narrowing of attention on a clearly defined goal. We feel involved, concentrated, absorbed. We know what must be done, and we get immediate feedback as to how well we are doing". A musician knows instantly if the music he plays sounds as it should.

A major part of the enjoyment of flow is the sense of being outside everyday reality, totally separated from the worries of everyday life.

Mihaly Csikszentmihalyi had made specific recommendations on what should be done. But how does one use this concept in a journey of quality to create an engaged workforce?

Here's what you should do:

Balance skills with challenge

Csikszentmihalyi (1997) suggested that the individual should not only have the required capability but also be stretched to work on a challenging problem.

Hence, just training people on quality-improvement tools and methods is not sufficient. What is also critical is to give them challenging assignments so that their skills can be used. This is one of the key elements that you have to keep in mind to achieve engagement in quality efforts. Let's understand using Figure 11.1.

- When employees are taught all the tools and techniques and acquire high-end quality capabilities such as Certified Master Black Belt, Certified Customer Experience Catalyst (CXC), Certified Lean Service Catalyst (CLSC), or Certified Quality Manager (CQM) but never get an opportunity to work on challenging projects, they are in a state of relaxation and even get bored. Have we not seen companies where employees trained on quality methods, when they're not utilised, don't take much interest in the movement? Some of them who are in a full-time quality role decide to even leave the company or look to move to other departments. For example, I know of two leading financial services organisations where Master Black Belts are used for mapping-process flow charts.
- When the employees are expected to work on chronic business problems but don't have knowledge of quality methods and tools, they are in a state of anxiety and worry. The other example is expecting shop-floor associates who have never been trained on quality tools to work on customer issues and problems. When employees have not been trained on quality methods and tools, they find it difficult to get involved even if they show interest. This too causes anxiety.

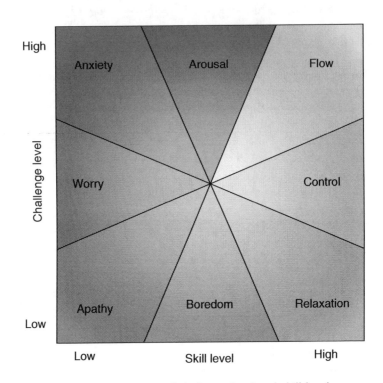

Figure 11.1 Mental state in terms of challenge level and skill level

Source: Wikipedia.com

- When employees are not trained on quality tools and they are not given challenging assignments to work on, they are in a state of apathy. They don't care about quality movement and are bystanders watching from the sidelines. For example, a manufacturing company embarks on a quality journey with a big bang. However, they do not invest in training the shop-floor staff. They also don't expect the employees to work on shop-floor problems. The result: the journey is a false start. As the shop-floor employees have not been involved in it, they don't seem to care about it.
- When employees are trained on one aspect of quality yet they are expected to do something about which they have little knowledge, that too leads to anxiety and worry. For example, expecting a Six Sigma Black Belt to lead a business excellence journey. A Six Sigma Black Belt knows how to solve problems using the various tools, while a business excellence journey requires knowledge of models such as Malcolm Baldrige or EFQM (European Foundation for Quality Management).

- When employees are trained on relevant tools and also get an opportunity to work on challenging assignments, they are in a state of flow. They get addicted to problem-solving and enjoy the quality journey.

One thing that we need to keep in mind is that the assignment that I am talking about does not just have to be about solving business problems. It can also be getting involved in activities and tasks that are enablers in the journey, such as getting organisation buy-in, changing the company culture, designing new processes, understanding what the customer's needs and wants are, quality planning, etc.

To provide sufficient stretch to the assignments, it is recommended that we give opportunities to employees to work on various types of problems, tasks, and initiatives. The problem they work on should have sufficient stretch so that they feel intellectually challenged. Of course, one needs to make sure they have the requisite skills, knowledge, or experience so that they don't feel skill deficient. A person will experience flow when he is prepared for it. Without adequate preparation and knowledge, he will struggle. A cyclist experiences flow when he is prepared for it. This is achieved through discipline and regular practice. Hence, it's the responsibility of the leaders of the organisation to make sure that the tasks that employees do have sufficient stretch, and this has to be ascertained on a regular basis. They also need to make sure that employees are skilled in new areas and upskilled in exiting areas.

Clear objectives around quality

Csikszentmihalyi suggested that having a clear set of goals is a must in achieving flow.

This means making sure employees have clear performance objectives. They have key performance indicators that push them to use various methods of quality for taking the company to a new level of performance. Right from the CEO to the shop-floor person, everyone should have one objective during the year that impacts issues around quality, process, customer satisfaction, etc. Or they have goals around business problems that require the use of quality tools and techniques. Table 11.1 encapsulates objectives that were taken up by executives of a company on a journey towards becoming an institution that is known for world-class quality.

Such performance objectives should be taken up by employees at all levels year after year. What is critical is for the employees to see how their work is impacting the strategic objectives of the firm. This is key for them to feel their work is contributing to the larger journey of the company.

Remove distractions and keep aside time

Csikszentmihalyi suggested that when a person is in flow, he has a high level of concentration.

Table 11.1 Performance objectives taken up by various levels in a manufacturing company

Role	Performance Objectives take up	KPIs
CEO	Build the most customer-centric company in the industry that we operate	• Revenue • Net Promoter Score • Cost to serve
Chief Sales Officer	Six Sigma project to improve effectiveness of sales force	• Revenue per salesperson per month • Accounts per person per month
Chief Manufacturing Officer	Lean project to improve supply chain performance of key products	• Cash-to-cash time • Supply chain cycle time • Inventory turnover
Chief Human Resource Officer	Reduce attrition of sales team	• Attrition %
Quality Manager	Reduce quality complaints about Product 234	• Complaints%
Production Operator	Reduce rejection of Machine 123	• Rejection %

This means when involved in things that are important, which includes quality improvements, we should remove all distractions. This becomes increasingly relevant as we all are a part of a digital world and notifications keep popping up. This can be addressed with individual effort and also the organisation making it possible by providing an enabling environment. The following is a list of things that can be done to remove distraction from the workplace:

- Educate employees on the concept of work prioritisation by using the urgent-and-important framework. The Eisenhower matrix and Stephen R Covey's principles of aligning our work to life's larger mission can be used here. This has been discussed in Lesson: 13.
- Institute meeting blackout periods to prevent employees from being pushed into them in the middle of important tasks.
- Encourage people to follow a clean-desk policy. This can be supported by teaching employees the principles of 5S, a Japanese technique for workplace organisation.
- Ensure that meetings are tightly run. They begin on time, they end on time, and pre-read materials are sent in advance so that participants come prepared.

- Turn off distractions like instant messaging, social media, and email before beginning an important task.
- Raise enterprise-wide awareness of the cost of distraction to self, their work, and the larger company.
- If someone interrupts you while you are working on an important task, tell them you are in flow.
- Use apps like Dewo, Freedom, FocusMe, and others to protect you from constant notifications, email, and social media alerts, and to help you focus on what matters.
- Leaders should make it clear to their teams what is expected of them.
- Employees should have clear goals for what they want to achieve.
- Do not multitask. Do one task at a time.
- Before you start working, make sure you have all of the tools you'll need.
- Ensure that feedback is provided on a regular basis. For a person to be in flow, they need to know what they are doing and whether they are achieving what they set out to achieve.

To be in a state of fluidity where mind and body are aligned and you are completely absorbed in your task, unaware of how time is passing by, you need to shun distractions.

Regular feedback

Feedback is critical for flow. Provide regular feedback on the quality improvement that has been taken up. Don't wait for the assignment to get over. Share both things that are not going well and those that are happening well. Your feedback should be on the task being done and related behaviours; it should never be on the person. Focus on one piece of feedback at a time. Keep it short and sharp. I would recommend that you prepare well for the feedback. Once in a while, go deep. The feedback process should be such that the recipient should see value in it.

Sense of control

Without control, a person cannot be expected to be in a state of flow. Give complete control of the quality-improvement assignment to the person. Control means having the freedom to decide and do what is right for the quality project without anyone's interference. This will not only give him complete ownership, but also the freedom to execute it freely. Never micromanage the assignment, as that can take away the sense of control and the person can feel claustrophobic. The assignment can be reviewed at a pre-defined interval at the various toll gates.

Making it effortless

What's also required for flow is that the person has all the relevant wherewithal to complete the quality assignment. He has the required capabilities in quality tools and practices. He also has access to all relevant resources, which includes money, assistance, infrastructure support, technology solutions, etc. which are required to complete the assignment at hand. He does not need to squander time to convince decision-makers who don't believe in quality. It's on the top management, the quality leader, and the team catalysing the quality transformation to make this happen. It is also suggested that there be a help desk for the employees to reach out to for any help as they navigate the quality task at hand.

Cleary, these strategies do help in improving employee engagement on quality. I have experienced it myself in my deployments. As Csikszentmihalyi mentioned in his 1990 book *Flow: The Psychology of Optimal Experience,*

> The best moments in our lives are not the passive, receptive, relaxing times . . . the best moments usually occur if a person's body or mind is stretched to its limits in a voluntary effort to accomplish something difficult and worthwhile.

The biases in problem-solving

Problem-solving is an integral part of all quality-improvement efforts. As a result, problem-solving and a quality journey go hand in hand. One cannot exist in the absence of the other. In this journey, teams take up myriad problems. These could be around customers, employees, processes, operational risk, revenues, organisational simplification, productivity improvement, cost reduction, etc. Typically, a problem-solving effort follows a structure, a set of tools is used, and we get the desired income.

For the success of a problem-solving effort, we need to keep in mind a few biases which, if not managed, can derail the effort. Biases are unconscious drivers that influence how we see the world. They can impact every person and all teams. You cannot get into problem-solving without these biases being there. Hence, we need to be extra careful so that they don't lessen the desired impact.

We demystified what a bias is and how different it is from cognitive bias in Lesson: 8. Table 12.1 gives a brief difference between a cognitive bias and a heuristic. We shall explore heuristics in detail in Lesson: 16.

Understanding the difference is critical to understanding the various biases that impact problem-solving. Biases limit how well teams solve problems. They cause leaders across levels to make decisions in a sub-optimal way. Not only do quality leaders need to have an understanding of cognitive biases, but all decision-makers need to know them and must consciously work towards minimising their impact.

The biases that need to be kept in mind while solving a problem are as follows:

Belief perseverance

This is a bias in which a person's evaluation of the logical strength of an argument is distorted by the conclusions that he believes in. He is more likely to accept a cause/causes of a problem that aligns with his already-held beliefs, prior knowledge, etc. He decides whether a cause is strong or weak on the basis of whether he agrees with the conclusion.

DOI: 10.4324/9781003250517-13

Table 12.1 Difference between cognitive bias and heuristics

What are cognitive biases?	What are heuristics?
They are patterns of thought that produce illogical results.	These are mental shortcuts that allow people to solve problems and make judgements quickly. They are rule-of-thumb strategies that shorten decision-making time without extensive deliberation.

For example, while catalysing a quality project on employee attrition, if you believe that the reason for attrition is company policies, while brainstorming for root causes, you will only support those that are related to policies and reject or even ridicule all other causes which may not pertain to policies at all. So, what happens here is that just because a person believes that he knows the results, he uses that belief to distort the results.

Here are ways to avoid belief biases in problem-solving:

- Pause and check when you have a strong belief about something but no data to back it up.
- Get an outsider's perspective on what you are proposing.
- Be willing to consider all points of view and potential causal candidates.
- Follow the structure of problem-solving; don't skip steps.
- All decisions on causal candidates for problems and next steps should be based solely on data.

Confirmation bias[1]

This is a bias wherein you seek evidence to support what you already believe in. We have seen this in detail in Lesson: 7.

For example, if you are working on a quality improvement focussed on reducing bacterial count in ice cream, if your belief is that the cause of high bacterial count is due to poor-quality milk, you go all out to get evidence to support your claim. During project discussions, you steer the conversation around milk quality and try and support it with all sorts of available information such as data, past research, etc.

Availability bias

This is a bias wherein a decision is based on what comes to the mind or what is easily available. This results from cognitive shortcuts (known as availability heuristics) or things that help in quick decision-making. This happens when we overestimate the likelihood of occurrence of an event by the ease with which examples and instances come to mind easily.

For example, after an *E. coli* (a pathogenic bacteria) outbreak in a competitor's chocolate products which grabbed national headlines, the quality leader at a frozen-meat factory, while working on a project on food safety, focussed his entire attention on how to prevent *E. coli* in the product. This was despite the fact that it was not a cause of concern in the product. But still, the improvement effort focussed on how to prevent *E. coli* in their frozen meats.

The other example that comes to my mind is when Six Sigma was at the height of its popularity in the early 2000s, companies adopted it for things where it was not the solution. For example, a company CEO tasked his team to use Six Sigma for installing processes. What the CEO missed was that Six Sigma was not what the organisation needed at this juncture. He just recommended it as it was then the talk of the business world.

Here are ways to avoid availability bias:

- Ensure that the members in the quality-improvement project have diverse points of view.
- Any idea that is proposed should be subjected to the rigour of data and effectiveness tests.
- Get an outside perspective.
- Brainstorm ideas and ensure that everyone has given their opinion and that you have carefully considered them.
- Determine whether the proposed idea is similar to what is currently in the works.

As per Crawford Hollingworth and Liz Barker (2020), a related concept is **WYSIATI** or "What You See Is All There Is" where there is a tendency to make decisions based only on the information that is accessible and we fail to envisage the information that is not with us.

Anchoring bias

This is a type of cognitive bias in which an individual makes a decision based on the initial piece of information. Here, we tend to rely too heavily on the first piece of information that we come across and use this to make subsequent judgements. This is another of those heuristics our brain uses for quick decision-making. This is an automatic process in which we baseline our judgement based on what we see first.

For example, when a team was trying to solve a problem on how to improve sales force effectiveness, the conversation began with one member talking about a specific technology solution which had helped a competitor who was also a market leader. Due to anchoring bias, the bulk of the discussion during the rest of the day moved to technology solutions, and the team did not look at other dimensions such as training, process design, career planning, selling approach, how they spent the day, product knowledge, etc.

How do we avoid anchoring bias in problem-solving?

- Consider all possible causes when evaluating causal candidates for a problem.
- Use data for evaluation, analysis, and assessment.
- Make sure that everyone on the team is aware of the list of biases (including anchoring) and call it out if anyone demonstrates it.
- Determine whether you are under pressure to make a quick decision and whether you have rushed to make a decision on what should be done.

Planning fallacy

Proposed by Daniel Kahneman and Amos Tversky, this is a phenomenon in which people underestimate the time it will take to complete a future task despite knowledge that previous tasks have generally taken longer than planned (Robson 2019). This happens when one is too optimistic about one's estimate.

As Daniel Kahneman (2011) mentioned in his book *Thinking, Fast and Slow*, there are two reasons this happens:

- The fallacious plan assumes best-case conditions (any sort of disruption is not taken into account).
- It does not take into consideration the data presented by similar cases.

Beyond the two suggested by Kahneman, I also believe this delay happens because of the following reasons:

- **Unpredictable Unplanned Events:** There can be shifted priorities. This is the case when you make an estimate of a certain number of days to perform a task, but due to unforeseen business priorities (e.g. production issues, customer issues, etc.), you end up being temporarily assigned to address the urgency and missing your estimated date. This is especially true when a person's expertise is temporarily needed elsewhere and that is not factored in the estimate, since they are unpredictable, unplanned events.
- **Motivated Reasoning:** We tend to look for evidence that suits the goal that we have set out for ourselves. We dismiss clues that tell us that it might take more time. We tend to rationalise past delays by saying things such as, "the software implementation delay was just a one-off" or "all our suppliers will be more reliable this time". This emanates from our desire to feel more confident about the project. The focus here is to look for evidence that suits our goals.
- **Rewards:** Sometimes the planning is done to meet specific reward criteria set out by the company, which makes people overlook potential delays. The behaviour is driven by the prize on the horizon for quick completion of the project.

This is typically a planner's problem. This happens because it's easier to imagine success than failure. The best way to evaluate time is not what you think, but the time that others have taken on the project in the past. Even if we look at past projects, we only look at what has been successful. We also tend to think that the project is unique when many of the elements could be compared with similar tasks done in the past. Sometimes incentives or rewards increase our assessment of the likelihood of success. I have seen so many quality-improvement projects get delayed because of planning fallacies.

What are some of the things you can do to avoid planning fallacy?

1 To decide on the timeline, ascertain the time taken by similar projects in the past.
2 Get an outsider who is not associated with the project to look at the timeline.
3 Remember Murphy's Law: What can go wrong will go wrong. Make sure you factor various things that can go wrong into the project. I would suggest you do a what-if analysis and list what can go wrong.
4 Focus on individual tasks and steps and just don't get lost in the time taken to complete the overall project.

One rule of thumb that I follow and recommend my clients is that for a quality-improvement project which is estimated to be over in 90 days, I tell them to add another 45 days. And for projects that are expected to be over in 180 days, I tell them to add another 60 days. And typically, for multiple-year transformations, my recommendation is always to keep a 30% to 49% stretch on the timelines. There is no science to these recommendations, but I have found them to work.

Sunk cost fallacy

Sunk costs are payments and investments which cannot be recovered. This bias is based on this idea. It says that there is always a hard time giving up something after having invested resources, even though the investment can't be recovered. The items that one does not want to give up could be strategy, time, talent, money, energy, skills, processes, an employee, a tech investment, etc. The resources that have been invested include time, money, effort, training, etc. (Arkes and Blumer 1985).

This fallacy happens as we stick with a decision because we've already put the money and resources down for it and want to make sure it isn't lost. It's about holding on to a losing proposition because it has cost you.

The reasons this happens are:

• We don't want to undergo the pain of the loss of our investment.
• We don't want to admit we were wrong and don't want to look foolish.
• We become attached to our commitments, and it becomes difficult to let go.

- We tend to forget the bigger purpose and get pre-occupied with the time and effort we have put into something.

Any loss is painful, and it grows over a period of time. When a decision is made to avert such losses, there is a chance that it could lead to a sunk cost fallacy.

Probably the example to cite is Concorde, the supersonic jet which flew between the UK and France between 1976 and 2003. It had a speed of over twice the speed of sound. It was used mainly for wealthy passengers who could pay a high price for high speed and great luxury. Despite its economic rationale being dead, the British and French governments continued to run it. It was a clear example of the sunk cost fallacy, where good money was being thrown after bad money.

The following are examples of the sunk cost fallacy in problem-solving:

- A company invested substantial money in value-stream software. This required licences to be bought for each user. Despite being established that it was an ineffective aid for value-stream mapping, the company continued to add more licences, as it wanted its employees to use it. This was because money had been spent on buying it, and the CFO wanted it to be utilised.
- While brainstorming for solutions for a quality project on sales conversion, the team recommended to use the existing lead-management system despite having proven that it was not delivering the promised results. The sales manager who was a part of the project said that we couldn't throw away the lead-management system because a lot of money had been spent on it. We had to find a way to use it.
- Having brought on board a training partner for Lean training, a company continues with it despite having sub-par feedback.

What are some of the ways to avoid sunk-cost bias in problem-solving?

- Always focus on the larger objective of the problem-solving exercise. If you decide to stick with your current approach, do it for the right reasons.
- Look at the potential future value of the current option that you are recommending, instead of past cost (Sweis et al. 2018).
- Remember that past effort and investment do not obligate you to continue investing in the future.
- Be open to jettisoning an idea even if you have invested time, effort, or money in it.

Groupthink

Problem-solving happens in groups. Hence, how individuals perform in a group plays a big role in the quality of outcome. Problem-solving gets the best results when individuals are able to give their best towards arriving at the desired solution. This is where the psychological phenomenon of group-think needs to be kept in mind. This happens when people focus on consensus within the group, and individuals put aside contradictory views. The term "groupthink" was coined by William H Whyte Jr (1952) and popularised by Irvin Janis through his 1972 book *Victims of Groupthink: A Psychological Study of Foreign Policy Decisions and Fiascos.*

The focus of individuals in groupthink is conformity and maintaining bonhomie. They don't report negative issues, despite their being very valuable for quality improvement. They just shut up and share with others what they need to know while solving a problem. There are many reasons for this to happen. Firstly, the members in the group don't want to go against the view of the leader or the expert who has already shared his views. They want to be respectful towards them. Secondly, they don't want to appear as if they are not a team player or someone who is not a part of the group. They don't want to contest the prevailing thinking in the group. Thirdly, they want to just maintain a cordial relationship and believe that going against anyone may impact this. Fourthly, this happens when the team members think they are less knowledgeable and their insights may not count. They forget that not knowing the domain can often be very beneficial for the group, as they bring in fresh insights.

Fifthly, this can also be cultural. In certain countries, being a part of the team means going along with the majority view (Guszcza 2015). Sixthly, it can happen because of time pressure when team members are forced to decide and move on. Seventhly, it could be because of a strong persuasive leader who encourages a high level of group cohesion, and sticking together as a group is valued more than freedom to speak. Eighthly, when we don't have a clear view, we simply adopt the majority view. Lastly, just because some people are silent, it's assumed that they are on board.

The problem with groupthink is that it can impact even the best and the brightest who are in the group. Even knowledgeable people make flawed decisions. Hence, a lot of care needs to be taken to make sure it does not show up during group deliberation.

Quality professionals need to be on the lookout for the following symptoms that could indicate groupthink:

- The group is a homogenous set of people. Members mimic others' views. They adjust their views based on what others say.
- The group is insulated from outside inputs and there is limited opportunity for outside insights.
- There is no debate and conflict in meetings.
- The leader has a strong view on the outcome that the discussions should deliver.
- Members have low self-esteem, and they agree with others' opinions to avoid appearing wrong.

- There is a lot of "happy talk" in meetings, and there is an effort to maintain harmony in the group (Sunstein and Hastie 2015). Conflicts are avoided at all cost.
- Members are afraid of being criticised.
- Rivals or those with contrarian thoughts are given names, and negative stereotypes are constructed around them.
- Silence from members is treated as consent.
- Team members quickly agree with the leader.
- Anyone with a dissenting view is attacked, insulted, or called disloyal.
- Members are optimistic about the solutions and are willing to take extreme risks.
- There are individuals who come down heavily on anyone who does not agree with the majority view.
- The group has a sense of infallibility and that they can never go wrong.

While working on a problem, quality practitioners need to keep the following in mind to avoid groupthink:

1. Appoint a "devil's advocate" whose job is to be a contrarian. He questions and challenges the group's consensus.
2. Encourage everyone to participate. Make sure no one is left out and everyone's ideas are sought, even if they are not in sync with what others prefer to hear.
3. The person leading the problem-solving project should have an open leadership style and encourage others to share their views.
4. The leader should encourage dissent and make it clear that he is expecting every idea to be discussed and debated.
5. Put together a diverse team to seek diversity of thought and fresh perspectives.
6. Create an atmosphere of trust so that people find it comfortable to speak up. One way to achieve this is by taking time to get to know each other, both at a personal and professional level.
7. Reach out to experts outside the group to gather their insights on how to solve the problem.
8. The leader should not speak until everyone else has shared their ideas.
9. Practise "red teaming" wherein an internal team in the organisation acts as an adversary (competitor, critic, hacker) and finds short-comings in the solutions to the problems that are being solved.
10. Break the large group into smaller groups and let them work on the same issue/problem and deliberate ideas under different leaders.
11. Seek opinions anonymously; have team members submit their ideas privately. It removes the pressure to conform to the majority view.

Let me share one example of groupthink from quality improvement. When Damzo Organic (not the real name) embarked on a journey of customer centricity, one of their focus areas was providing a differentiated experience to the customers. Towards this, they had to define the customer's persona. The customers in every segment are different; hence, their personas are different. The CEO who had set up this business had fixed notions about the needs and wants of the customer. He had started the company in the 1980s, and we were now in the year 2021. The preferences of customers had changed. Though they were in a B2B business, selling a commodity item, customer experience was as important as the product. After all, B2B clients have people who have needs and wants, and their expectations have morphed with the changes around us. They expect convenience and want many things to happen digitally, more so because the pandemic is getting over and they experience contactless processes. Somehow, the CEO had pre-conceived notions about what the customer expected. These were archaic, yet he believed he was right. When the quality leader held a workshop to define the persona of the customers of a certain segment, the CEO was the first to speak and strongly shared his views. His proclamations set the tone. This was a company where the CEO, who was also the founder, called the shots. Once he took a position, no one ever took a position against it. The CEO was in his 70s. In this culture, there was this unwritten rule that younger people didn't speak against an elder's views, even if they were wrong. This was done as a sign of respect.

As result, the other leaders who reported to the CEO could not give their views on the persona. They all shook their heads and said that the CEO was right. The quality leader tried to push back, but he was snubbed. The outcome was that the final persona was just based on what the CEO thought. The others did not share their insights, though they did not agree with the CEO. The customer experience was designed using this persona. It was launched and had very little positive impact on the customers. Rather, there were complaints from the customers that the processes were becoming cumbersome. The CEO waited for 6 months. When there was no sign of positive feedback, he went back to the earlier way to service the customer. This is a great example of how groupthink can mar quality-improvement efforts.

Clearly, cognitive biases need to be averted, or else they can hurt an organisation's problem-solving efforts.

Note

1   Please note that belief perseverance and confirmation bias are not the same. In confirmation bias, a person seeks information that supports his preconceived notion, while in belief perseverance, the focus is to reject information that doesn't confirm the belief. Here, there is no effort to seek or use information for the process.

Minimising cognitive overload

Declaring a war on cognitive overload is not new. If you look at Lean manufacturing, we talk about the reduction of *muda* (Japanese for waste), *mura* (Japanese for unevenness), and *muri* (Japanese for unreasonableness). *Muri* is about doing something that goes beyond one's power. While there are many causes for *muri*, one of them is clearly cognitive overload. However, given the connected world that we are in and with so much continuous inundation by information, it's important to talk about it separately.

It may not be right to generalise, but the focus of most quality problem-solving efforts is process improvement. However, what we should also see is if there is an opportunity to cut the cognitive load for those impacted by the solution. These could be for internal or external customers. As companies grow, we tend to add newer processes, newer metrics, newer roles, newer products, newer geographical regions, more plants, more IT systems, more organisational layers, etc. When these things are done, they make the company more complex. Little do we realise the impact of all these on employees, one of the outcomes being cognitive overload. This has increased more today, as we live in a digitally connected world and there is information overflow from all over.

So, what is cognitive overload?

Cognitive overload is having too much information to process at once. This happens when unnecessary demands are made on a person, making the task of information processing difficult. Our brain can only do so much; hence, we should be careful about what we want it to do. The result is that it overwhelms our "working memory" and impacts our memory and decision-making (Yablonski 2018).

The fact that "working memory" has limited capacity was first proposed by psychologist George Armitage Miller. He went on to say that they can store seven (plus or minus two) elements. The working memory also organises information "chunks" to overcome informational bottlenecks. For example, remembering a 21-letter word is difficult. Hence, if we break it into chunks of 3-letters, it will be easier to remember.

When a person is exposed to numerous bits of information when doing a task, the information is stored in the prefrontal cortex for 10 to 15 seconds.

DOI: 10.4324/9781003250517-14

The prefrontal cortex participates in functions such as reasoning, planning, decision-making, and thinking. The Working memory is also a function of the prefrontal cortex. Working memory is the process of maintaining a limited amount of information in an active representation for a brief period of time so that it is available for use (Courtney et al., 1998)

The impact of cognitive overload on willpower and decision-making was brilliantly established in an experiment done by Baba Shiv of Stanford University (Shiv and Fedorikhin 2002). There were two groups of students in this experiment. One group was given a two-digit number to remember, while the second group was given a seven-digit number. After this, they were told to walk down the hall, where they were presented with two different snack options: a slice of chocolate cake or a bowl of fruit salad. And here, something very interesting happened. The group which had to remember with seven digits were nearly twice as likely to choose the cake as students given two digits.

And why did this happen? As Professor Shiv says, it was that the extra numbers took up valuable space in the brain, resulting in a "cognitive load" on the students. This made it much harder for them to resist an unhealthy dessert. What happens here is that the prefrontal cortex of the brain is so overtaxed with this extra bit of information as to make a person give into temptation. It actually impacts the person's willpower.

As companies grow, we often don't realise that lots of activities get added which increase the cognitive load on employees. We have seen finance shared service centres wherein employees have to exert themselves a lot during month-end closing and period-end reporting. The pressure is so high during this period that even processors who never make errors start making errors, and their productivity also drops.

The other reason for cognitive overload is when the person is provided with too many choices that impact speed of decision-making.

The British and American psychologists William Edmund Hick (1952) and Ray Hyman (1953) proposed, in what is now called Hick–Hyman Law or Hick's Law, that *the time it takes to make a decision increases with the number and complexity of choices available*. The more options available to a person, the greater the amount of time he takes to choose the best option.

A great example of a product causing cognitive overload is traditional remote controls, which have so many buttons that it requires a lot of mental processing to know how to use them. This causes a lot of frustration for customers, and they hate using them.

Our workplaces, too, are filled with examples of cognitive overload. Let me share a few:

- A contact centre agent has to navigate through multiple software programmes and screens while answering a call.
- Employees are being asked to take up multiple tasks at a time.
- Shop-floor employees are being held accountable for more than 10 metrics.

- A customer has to go through a bureaucratic process to get a mortgage approved.
- People are part of too many unnecessary meetings.
- A customer is having a tough time selecting from a menu in a restaurant that has a long list of options.

How does one address cognitive overall as a part of quality-improvement efforts?

Stop multitasking

Many employees take pride in being great multitaskers. But if you probe deep enough, you will see that under the veneer of productivity, there is quite a bit of inefficiency. Multitasking happens when we try to do two tasks at a time. It also happens when you try to do a couple of tasks in quick succession. It also involves switching from one thing to another.

The human brain is incapable of paying attention to multiple tasks at the same time. Multitasking not only impacts productivity, it reduces accuracy of work and makes you less attentive.

This majorly impacts productivity because of the cumulative time that people waste due to switching between tasks (Petter 2018).

Research done by Joshua Rubinstein, Jeffrey Evans, and David Meyer found that participants lost significant amounts of time as they switched between multiple tasks and lost even more time as the tasks became increasingly complex.

According to Rubinstein, Meyer, and Evans (2001), there are two stages in executive control:

- Goal shifting: This is about deciding to do one thing instead of the other.
- Role activation: This is about changing the rules for the previous task to rules of the new task.

Switching between these may look small, but when you add them up, it becomes big.

Another study done by Eyal Ophir, Clifford Nass, and Anthony Wagner at Stanford University in 2009 found that people who multitask have poor attention spans. According to him, even when the chronic multitaskers were doing just a single task, their brains were less effective and efficient.

What is the solution? The best thing to do is to complete one task and get into another. However, if you still need to do two tasks together, follow the rule of "chunking". As Clifford Nass proposes, follow the 20-minute rule. Spend your attention on one task for a 20-minute period before switching to the next task (Cherry 2021).

The simple rule to be kept in mind is that when doing something that requires thinking, don't focus on anything else.

So, when you work on quality improvement, do one activity at a time. Try to avoid task switching. Complete one task and then get into the other. While you work on the problem, deep dive to see what the person is doing and whether they are being inefficient due to multitasking.

However, if you are doing things unconsciously, multitasking is fine. For example, you are in the gym and listening to music or making doodles in a boring class. The doodles that a student makes keep him alert. What needs to be remembered is that multitasking is not okay if two tasks are done simultaneously and they require action, for example, trying to respond to an email and participating in a conference call.

There has also been some evidence which says that trained musicians are able to switch between tasks. They seem to have the ability to alternate smoothly and easily between two sets of mental tasks. This was reported in the journal *Cognitive Science* in 2014. York University psychologists Linda Moradzadeh, Galit Blumenthal, and Melody Wiseheart report that musicians appear to have a "superior ability to maintain and manipulate competing information in memory, allowing for efficient global processing". To put it another way, their minds can efficiently process information from a holistic perspective. What they further said: "Musicians' extensive training requires maintenance and manipulation of complex stimuli in memory, such as notes, melody, pitch, rhythm, dynamics, and the emotional tone of a musical piece". This, they add, "may help them to develop superior control to respond efficiently to stimuli in an environment where both switching and non-switching components exist". I think there is a need for more research in this space.

As far as quality efforts are concerned, there is no evidence otherwise. If you switch tasks, you will do so at the cost of productivity and even effectiveness.

Re-design work

Sometimes, cognitive load may be due to the way work is designed in the workplace. This would require revisiting the job description but also the way the work gets executed by the employees. Let me give you an example of a quality-improvement project that we did for a packaging company. The assignment was focussed on improving the productivity of the sales team. As a part of solutioning, we performed "a day in the life of" with many of the sales associates to understand how they spent their working hours. What this exercise brought to light was that the sales team did many things which were not a part of their job description. Their activities included sales calls, sales closure, order delivery follow-up, collection of payment, after-sales service, follow-up with finance on billing, ensuring closure of quality problems, helping the R&D team on commercialisation, personal expense reports, etc. What became very obvious was that, with so much on their plate, the sales force was not able to focus on what was important, which is sales. One of the solutions that we recommended was that the sales team should only focus on sales and collections. Every other activity was taken off of their plate. The impact was that they saw a 45% increase in sales. Of course, we also recommended other solutions around process improvement, process automation, decisioning, and career planning.

Shut yourself of from distraction

In today's digitally connected world, distractions from apps, emails, and mobile phones can be a big irritant. When you are working on something important, I would suggest that you just shut off your mobile phone so any notification does not distract you. A single ping of an email can completely take away the focus of a team.

Educate employees on prioritisation

One of the things I recommend to my clients is to teach people how to prioritise work. When people know the difference between urgent and important work, and are able to link it with the larger plan of their workplace and their lives, it can help to reduce cognitive load and improve productivity. I strongly advocate the principles suggested by Stephen Covey in his book *First Thing First* (Covey, Merrill, and Merrill 1994). Prioritise work by focussing on important activities that are required for leading a meaningful life and the various roles that we play. It's imperative to craft a larger mission for life and then break it down into goals for the year, month, and week. This includes goals around the various roles that an individual plays, such as an employee, parent, partner, and community leader, and aspects like physical fitness, spirituality, and so on. Figure 13.1 is the Eisenhower matrix, which should be followed regularly. Proposed by President Dwight Eisenhower, it's a tool that helps to prioritise tasks according to their urgency and importance. List all the activities that you do and categorise them into one of the four boxes. Our focus should be to enlarge

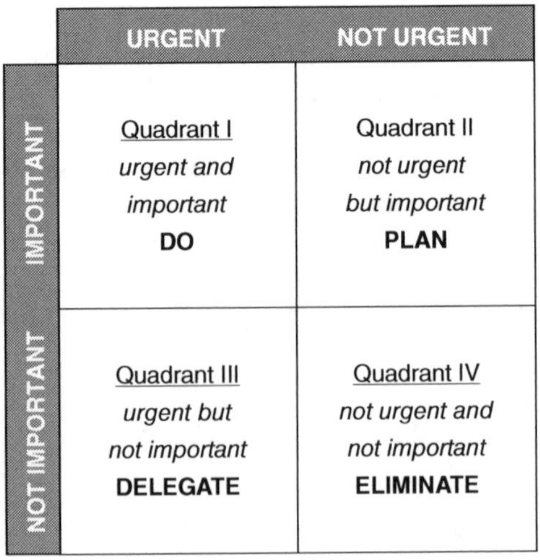

	URGENT	NOT URGENT
IMPORTANT	Quadrant I urgent and important **DO**	Quadrant II not urgent but important **PLAN**
NOT IMPORTANT	Quadrant III urgent but not important **DELEGATE**	Quadrant IV not urgent and not important **ELIMINATE**

Figure 13.1 Eisenhower matrix

the QII (Quadrant 2) activities in our schedule. They should be planned well, as they are important and impact your larger mission. QI (Quadrant 1) activities are urgent and important; hence, they should be taken up right away. QIII activities are not important and just urgent. They don't require your time and hence should be delegated. QIV activities are neither urgent nor important. They should be removed from your list.

Metrics refresh

Refresh the set of metrics for your workplace. What often happens is that new metrics keep on getting added to processes and no one looks at them. Instead, once a year, check the existing metrics on current performance, their relevance, and whether you still need to measure them. Also check if existing metrics need to be replaced with new metrics. At any given time, don't let your employees focus beyond three to five metrics.

Remember, when you tell a person to focus on too many metrics, he will not be able to do them all justice.

Remove unnecessary tasks

Another exercise that should be done is to look at everything from the window of "value". Here, the principles of Lean thinking can be of help (Sarkar 2007). Dissect all processes and practices in minute detail. Ascertain how many of them create value for the customer or user (value add), how many are business enablers (business value add), and how many can be eliminated (non–value add). Remove all those unnecessary activities that don't create value yet exist in the process.

Use anticipatory design

In traditional designs, a product is created, and the customer or user is expected to use it by touching, swiping, holding, etc. These are things done to accomplish the goals of the customer.

In anticipatory design, the product is designed in such a manner that it's easy and effortless for the customer. The customer needs to navigate a minimum number of steps to accomplish his end objective. No instructions are needed, and things are very intuitive. The user is provided with relevant information, he takes a decision, and things get done.

As Aaron Shapiro (2015, CEO, Host), the person who coined the term "anticipatory design", mentioned in an article in *Fast Company*:

> Anticipatory design is fundamentally different: decisions are made and executed on behalf of the user. The goal is not to help the user make a decision, but to create an ecosystem where a decision is never made – it

happens automatically and without user input. The design goal becomes one where we eliminate as many steps as possible and find ways to use data, prior behaviours and business logic to have things happen automatically, or as close to automatic as we can get.

Take booking a flight as an example. Rather than being given options – airline, time, seat location – an anticipatory approach would be to automatically monitor the user's calendar, and book a ticket when a meeting is scheduled in a location that requires air travel. Seat preference, preferred airlines, the decision between price and a specific flight time are all based on prior travel behaviour and payment information can be electronically transmitted.

Since anticipation is based on prior knowledge, the user may initially be asked for feedback on the choice before or after booking, but once the system is reasonably accurate the job will be done without question. The result is a fully designed system that performs a powerful set of functionalities without the need for step-by-step interaction.

A few examples of anticipatory design are as follows:

- Google Now anticipates your needs and wants based on your search history.
- Amazon's recommendation engine.
- Netflix shows movies based on users' past preferences.
- Uber app, when opened after a trip, shows the return journey.
- Nest thermostats from Google learn the heating/cooling habits of consumers' homes and automatically adjust the temperature according to their preferences.

Anticipatory design focusses on creating great experiences for the customer by reducing cognitive load and minimising choices. It will liberate customers from decision fatigue.

Doing a *Brahma, Vishnu, and Shiva*

In the Hindu pantheon, the gods Brahma, Vishnu, and Shiva (2021) are responsible for the creation, upkeep, and destruction of the world. Brahma is the creator, Vishnu is the preserver, and Shiva is the destroyer in order to recreate. It is the destruction created by Lord Shiva that allows for positive re-creation. Preservation and destruction will be needed if something is created. If nothing is created, there is nothing to preserve or destroy. So, when the creation occurs, there should be a Vishnu or Shiva to either preserve or destroy the things which are created/creating. Shiva is the god who destroys the world when it is in a state of chaos and ungodliness.

Taking the analogy to the business world and quality, there need to be Vishnus who ensure the current business is efficiently effective. They not only operate at best efficiency but also ensure desired profits. They also need Shivas who kill businesses, processes, practices, policies, etc. when they don't make sense or cause pain to the organisation. Then there should also be Brahmas, who would innovate and create new products and businesses (Dave 2016). They would create a potent new future that will replenish what time and circumstance have destroyed.

When we get used to something, it becomes very difficult to get rid of it. This is more so when we have been its creator. It could be a process, practice, technology solution, business strategy, procedure, way of working, idea, etc. There are a couple of psychological reasons for it.

We tend to over-value something that we own irrespective of the current market value. This is called the endowment effect. This because we are loss averse, and we give more significance to losses than we put on gains. We have discussed loss aversion in Lesson: 1 too.

Hence, as a part of a quality journey, a leader should know when to kill a process, approach, or practice that is currently underway. When their relevance has decreased or they are not delivering what they were supposed to, they should be killed or improved without hesitation. Employees should know that they have to play the role of Brahma, Vishnu and Shiva. They may have been involved in creation of a process or put effort into maintaining it, but they should also play a role in destroying it when its relevance ends.

This is very relevant in the context of cognitive load, as many times, employees don't want to let go because they are used to a process, practice, or way of working, or have been part of its design. However, they should know that if something makes them inefficient and unproductive, they should just kill it or work towards its improvement. This has to be done even if it makes people squirm in pain.

Lesson: 14

Five rules for customer solution design

Everything in quality happens for the customer. The customers could be external customers, internal customers, or other stakeholders. External customers are those who buy and use the product. Internal customers are employees. Other stakeholders include shareholders, partners, vendors, the community, the environment, regulators, etc.

As you design products and services for them, it's important to keep a few principles in mind. This will help you to design solutions that meet customer requirements.

Rule 1: Think in terms of experience

If you want to create a lasting bond with your customer, don't think about providing a product to your customer. Instead, see how you can convert it into an experience. This is not because a company can create more value for itself by charging a premium; it's also because it makes the customer happier.

Two decades of research done by Cornell University's Professor Thomas Gilovich also establishes the fact that happiness is derived from experiences and not things (Cassano 2015). His research focussed on ascertaining how people felt after buying goods and services. He found that people were happier after spending on experience. This is despite the fact that people think of experience as something that will come and go and hence don't think it's wise to spend on it. Yet when they buy experiences, they are happier (Gilovich 2014). This aligns with the research done by Richard Ainley Easterlin, which was published in 1974. He argued that money buys happiness, but up to a certain point. This phenomenon is now called the "Easterlin Paradox" and states that at a point in time, happiness varies directly with income both among and within nations, but over time, happiness does not trend upward as income continues to grow. As Gilovich's study has found out, people's satisfaction with physical objects went down with time, but satisfaction with experiences went up. Why does this happen? Let us look at the reasons:

- We get used to our possessions. We don't feel like talking about them after some time. We tend to remember experiences long after we have purchased them.

DOI: 10.4324/9781003250517-15

- Happiness with physical objects fades as they become part of the new normal.
- We tend to enjoy the anticipation of having an experience more than owning a possession.
- When we buy physical things, they make us happy in the beginning, but after some time, they lose their novelty in our perception and don't excite us anymore (Gilovich and Ross 2015).
- When we buy experience, it enhances social relations more readily and effectively than material goods.
- Experiences become ingrained as a part of our identity. Though you may be fond of physical objects, they always remain separate from your physical self. Experiences are important to us because we are a sum total of our experiences.
- When we share our experiences with others, they like it. But they don't like hearing much about our possessions.
- It's very difficult to compare the experiences of two people. But physical objects can be compared, which can be a cause of heartburn.

For those who say that our products cannot be converted to experiences, I always tell them to look at Starbucks. It's a great example of how a simple cup of coffee can be transformed into an experience.

We are already seeing change in this direction. We live in an experience economy in which companies are making efforts to convert their products to services. Today, many companies are realising this and are working towards converting their offerings into experiences, though a lot has still to be done.

The journey of converting your business into an experience starts with understanding the customer's persona and context, deciding on the experience, designing the relevant journeys, and seeing how they can be differentiated across touchpoints. What's key here is to focus on customers' emotions, how they act, and what they do. Always decide on the experience first and then work on the technology and other things to make it happen.

Remember, while thinking about your employees, vendors, or other stakeholders, also think in terms of experience. This is because when your employees and suppliers are happy, they will go out of their way to provide a differentiated experience to customers. Not surprisingly, companies are embarking on initiatives around employee experience and vendor experience.

Rule 2: Give a sense of control

This is another very important element of what you provide to customers. We humans want control in everything we do. Being in control is one of the deepest needs of humans. When we don't have a sense of control, it creates a lot of discomfort and uncertainty. Psychologically, it delivers the following to us:

- It brings certainty.
- We learn how things are done.

- We can predict the outcome (at least, we think so).
- It brings harmony. We humans dislike anything that causes chaos.
- When we have a sense of control, we feel less vulnerable and thus feel less pain.
- We are confident that nothing will go wrong.

Humans don't always need to be in control, but what they seek is a "sense of control", which essentially means a perception of control even if there is no real control.

When a company puts control in the hands of the customer, you not only make him feel comfortable but also create a boundary within which he can play. The reins of his play are still in the company's hands.

The more control the customer feels on his journey with the company, the greater is his engagement.

To give control to customers, do the following:

- Keep customers up to date on the status of their product deliveries.
- Allow them to do things on their own.
- Clearly state what the product will and will not offer.
- Make it easy for customers to find out about a product's details and how it can be operated.
- Provide them with all pertinent information and allow them to make informed decisions.

Let me give you examples of how companies are translating this into action:

- **Instead of filling out a paper form, bank customers now use a tablet to complete an application form.**
  Nowadays, banks do customer enrolment with tablets instead of physical application forms, and the data is filled in by customers. The customers love this, as they can ensure there will be no errors. Earlier, the data was filled in by customers on a paper application form and had to be re-entered into a computer system by someone else. This created opportunities for error.
- **Customers of e-commerce and couriers are kept informed of their package's location.**
  Courier companies keep customers aware of where their package is on its journey to the customer's door.
- **Progress bar**
  While downloading software in a computer, we see a progress bar which keeps us informed of the time it will take to complete the process.
- **Kiosk check-in**
  Kiosk check-in at the airport is an example of where the customer does not need to stand in a queue but can do the check-in easily all by himself. He can also choose the seat he wants.

Rule 3: Make it easy for customers

We know from the work of Daniel Kahneman (2003) that our brain has two operating systems. One is called System 1 and the other one is called System 2. System 1 is the intuitive thinking system, while System 2 is the rational thinking system. The defining characteristic of System 1 thinking is that it is quick, unconscious, automatic, and happens with little effort, energy, and attention. System 2 thinking is a slow, deliberate, rational, effortful, and controlled mental process that is done with logic. It requires energy and attention.

The outcome of System 1 thinking is prone to errors, while that of System 2 thinking is not.

More than 95% of our thinking happens through System 1.

We humans are cognitive misers. We conserve our cognitive efforts for vital tasks. Most often, we use System 1 thinking for our day-to-day tasks. System 2 thinking is used only for vital tasks which need thinking and deliberation. What helps us with System 1 thinking is heuristics or mental shortcuts and rules of thumb. We have discussed this briefly in Lesson: 12.

As we work on customer solutions, our focus should be to create a product or service that the customer can use effortlessly without much thinking.

As a company Amazon.com is guided by sixteen leadership principles (2021), and one of them is "customer obsession". The company strives to be Earth's most customer-centric company. Not surprisingly, it is one of the best in customer experience. In July 2021, it included two new leadership principles which are "strive to be earth's best employer" and "success and scale bring broad responsibility" (Day 2021). The former is focussed on employees, while the latter is focussed on the planet and communities. Both have an impact on Amazon customers and stakeholders. The company tries to make things easy and effortless for customers. Here are some examples:

- Amazon has a no-questions-asked return policy.
- If you want to get in touch with customer service, you click on a link, and you get a call on your registered phone within a few seconds.
- One-click buying allows customers to make purchase decisions with the payment details which have been entered earlier.
- Amazon Go, the brick and mortar store from Amazon.com, allows customers to grab a product and walk out. They don't need to stand in line and checkout.
- Amazon helps you to decide by providing ratings and feedback.
- They personalise and send you offers based on your past searches.

Rule: 4 Understand the customer's context

While designing customer products and solutions, it's imperative to understand the customer's context. This is to understand why they do what they do.

We humans may think we are logical, but very often, our buying decisions are based on emotions. Before you begin working on customer solutions, it's important to spend time with the customer to understand their daily experiences, frustrations, and challenges. Don't look just at the people and the products they use. Observe their entire surroundings. Look for anomalies in what people say and what they do.

Hence, perform ethnographic studies, "a day in the life"; shop along with customers to see how they decide, talk to them, experience simulation, etc. Look at physical, cognitive, social, cultural, and emotional elements in the situation in which the customer operates. Also, look at customers who are not using the product and why they are missing it. The final solution that you decide should bring a new value to the customer.

Rule: 5 When customers labour . . . they value something more

There is this story that in 1950, General Mills wanted to find ways to sell its Betty Crocker brand of instant cake mixes (Mortimer, Mathmann, and Grimmer 2019). To achieve this, they appointed psychologist Ernest Dichter. After meeting customers and running focus groups, his recommendation was that the instant cake mixes made things too easy for the customer. His recommendation was that the recipe be changed to replace the powdered eggs in the cake mix with fresh eggs. This made the customers experience the baking process and also feel greater ownership of the results. This solution produced an increase in sales.

This was a great example of making the customer labour to value something more. This came to be known as the Ikea Effect, as proposed by Michael Norton, Daniel Mochon, and Dan Ariely in 2012 in the *Journal of Consumer Psychology*. (For those unfamiliar with Ikea, it's a Swedish retailer that requires customers to assemble products in their homes.) They found "that labour alone can be sufficient to induce greater liking for the fruits of one's labour". When customers do part of the work, they feel good about it and have a greater perception of the value of the product. But why do people demonstrate this behaviour?

We humans want to have a feeling of being successful. Hence, the more effort that gets into doing a task, the more people have a greater sense of accomplishment when it's completed.

Humans want to feel competent and use this ability complete and achieve goals by using what they possess. Also, when you put effort into a product, you tend to focus on the positive attributes of the product and tend to like it more. As Marsh, Kanngiesser, and Hood shared in 2018, the Ikea Effect leads us to believe that our creations are more valuable than items that are identical but constructed by others. This is attributed to the feelings of ownership that emerge from it (Sarstedt, Neubert, and Barth 2017).

So, what are some examples of applications of this idea?

- Build-a-Bear allows customers to assemble their stuffed animals.
- Vacations spent on agriculture farms.
- Spending time during a vacation restoring age-old research, looking after endangered animals, helping in scientific research, etc.
- When you are designing a new process for employees, involve them in its creation.

As you design a customer solution, it is recommended to incorporate the Ikea Effect strategies. Ideally, you make customers do a "high-value" but "low-effort" step like adding the egg to the instant cake mix. Letting them be involved in product creation in some small way will go a long way in enhancing perceived value.

Making quality issues known

When a company is faced with a quality problem, the normal approach taken by the management is pretty defensive. A team is put together to work on it while management tries to talk about it in hushed tones. All efforts are taken to make sure that the news does not go out of the organisation. The thinking is that if external stakeholders get to know about it, the perception of the company will be impacted. Moreover, if customers get to know about it, they will stop their purchases, and this would impact company revenues. If investors get to know about it, they could lose trust in the top management and their ability to manage the enterprise. If regulators get to know, the company could struggle with court cases. My belief is that we need to question these assumptions.

What is recommended is that a company that is serious about building an enterprise known for quality should tell the world about the chronic problems that it is facing and then put the might of the enterprise into solving them.

When you call out a problem and share it with the external world, it is almost like putting one's neck on the line. It brings the entire company's focus on it, and the employees know that top management is serious about it.

In 2010, when Patrick Doyle became the CEO of Domino's Pizza, the company was in trouble. The stock price was down, and the company was not growing as expected. Among the many actions that he took was to go out and tell the world that their pizza was bad. His team laughed at a campaign in which he appeared. The TV advertisements repeated comments from focus groups about what they thought about the product. The advertisement shared comments from these people, such as "the sauce tastes like ketchup" and "the crust tastes like cardboard". Doyle appeared in this campaign and took responsibility for the same and promised to "work days, nights, and weekends" to get better (Taylor 2016). Patrick Doyle led a transformation at Domino's that paid off. When he was the CEO of the company, it generated one of the highest shareholder returns in the market; he increased its share price by more than 2,100% while returning $3.4 billion to shareholders (*Globenweswire* 2019). He moved on from Domino's in 2018.

I am not saying that going out and talking about quality issues was the only reason the company transformed during his tenure. Adoption of information

DOI: 10.4324/9781003250517-16

technology, mobile and online orders, leadership, better store design, and effective franchise management also played big roles. But clearly, when a CEO goes out and puts his neck on the line on customer and quality issues, it can do wonders. As Doyle mentioned in a video released by the company that was also carried by the magazine *Restaurant Business* in June 2018, "You can either use negative comments to get you down, or you can use them to excite you and energise your process to make a better pizza", Doyle said in the video. "We did the latter" (Maze 2018).

So, committing publicly is the right thing to do. But, why? Here's my take:

Brings focus

When the management commits to a few quality problems in this manner, it brings focus. It ensures that instead of squandering their bandwidth on a large number of quality problems, they put their might behind a few big-ticket problems. These are the problems that directly impact the company's performance. The CEO and other members of top management jointly oversee these problems and take ownership of their resolution within the committed time frames. By the way, by top management, I mean the CEO and his direct reports.

This does not mean that no other quality problems are taken up by anyone else. Of course, other quality problems would be underway, but they may not deserve top management's attention. They could be sponsored and overseen by other leaders.

Articulates intention

When the top management goes out and talks about the key quality problems that the company is working on, it's not just about solving a few problems, but articulating the intention of management to build a customer-centric organisation. It demonstrates that the top management does not just talk about quality but has embraced it as a method for business improvement. They take up problems and report progress through measurable outcomes.

Gives a psychological push

A public commitment not only puts social pressure on the organisation, but it also creates a psychological push within the organisation to get things done as committed. There is a psychological reason for this. We, as humans, want our actions to be consistent with our beliefs. So, when we have made a declaration in front of others, we want to stick to what we have declared. When quality is the agenda, it can have a great positive impact on the company. If the CEO has made the commitment, no members of the C-suite can deny being a part of it. Even if someone is partially committed to it, he has to go ahead and make sure the commitments are met. As a matter of fact, commitments made in public are probably one of the most powerful ways to get things done.

Embeds transparency

When you declare your problems in pubic, you are actually putting the organisation up for scrutiny. This is an important signal to the outside world that the company believes in transparency, and this is one step in that direction. This would also foster greater cooperation between customers and the company, and they would get to know what's happening regarding quality issues that directly or indirectly impact them. So, if the customers believe a key issue being faced by them is not being taken up, they should flag it and convey it back to the organisation.

It also provides visibility to investors into what the company is doing on issues that have a direct bearing on company performance, and this, in turn, impacts the share price. Actually, when citizens believe that a company is transparent, it creates trust, which is quite priceless. When a company hides problems from its customers, the top management appears to have an accountability problem.

No one likes humiliation

When CEOs declare quality problems in public, they are putting themselves in harm's way. This is not easy and not for the faint hearted. When they do that, if the problems are not resolved in the promised time, it could make their position precarious and lead to public humiliation. This brings immediacy to the problems and the agenda of quality.

Brings a sense of urgency

Humans have this nature that we do not take up anything that does not have an immediate benefit. We always want to focus on things that have benefits here and now. Anything that does not have immediate gain, even if it has a long-term benefit, does not attract our attention. We humans have the tendency to seek instant gratification. When a CEO and members of top management announce the key problems that will be taken up for the next few months, it is almost like a clarion call which unites all employees to come together and support the project.

What happens if there are no customer issues to be worked on? Top management should then talk about other business problems. For example, there could be problems with sales productivity, customer conversion, or employee attrition. There will always be some other problems to work on. Yes, this is not going to be easy, as you are putting yourself up for scrutiny. However, when quality problems get this focus, they help to reduce the noise that is generated by customer complaints, negative press, and social media backlash.

My recommendations for the CEO and other members of the C-suite are the following:

- Create a pipeline of high-impact quality-improvement projects. These could have an impact on customers, quality, cost, revenue, risk, etc.
- Pick the top three that have the maximum impact on the company's performance.
- Every quarter, go out and share with the external world the problems that you are addressing.
- Report progress to the same audience when the next round of quality problems is announced.

Going out and speaking about quality issues faced by the company can be tricky. If it is not done well, the company can end up with court cases, investor ire, or even impacted stock-market performance. Hence, the CEO and the top management need to keep in mind the following:

Purpose: Be clear on the purpose. What is the objective that you hope to achieve by going public about your customer or quality issues? Is it to show commitment to quality, or is it to show the beginning of a transformation, or is it to unite the company, or is it something else?

Clarity on the impact of the complaint: Be clear on the type of quality problem that you are going to speak up about. Does it have an impact on customer health? Does it impact company reputation? Does it impact customer safety? Does it impact the environment? Does it impact customer confidence? Does it cause economic loss to customers?

Ascertain clearly the impact of your going out and talking about it. Could it lead to court litigation? Would it make customers leave the company? Would it make the board and shareholders unhappy? Will it impact the company's reputation? Will it impact the share price? It is important to keep in mind that whichever quality issues you are going out with, they should not result in any of those issues.

Who is the audience? You need to be clear as to who the audience is for whom you are going out and sharing the problem. This is closely linked with the purpose. Is it meant for the customers or employees or regulators or competitors or someone else? Your tactics should depend on the customers whom you are targeting.

Authenticity: Make sure the process appears authentic and does not seem like a charade in front of customers and other stakeholders. It is important to demonstrate that the CEO is serious about customer concerns and sincerely wants to eliminate the quality problems.

Get a handle on social media and customer service: Before you go out and talk about the problem, make sure you're prepared to manage social media (Buss 2018). Because after the CEO goes out and speaks about it, one can expect many complaints from customers. There is a bit of a bandwagon effect here. Even those customers who are unsure of the quality issue would go out and speak. This is quite normal. This is when the company should respond to all issues that come on social media or through any other channels at high speed. The company should also keep its customer service team ready to address and respond to customer problems. In this phase, the company may need extra resources in both social media and customer service teams because of the surge in customer complaints, social feedback, etc.

Be ready to manage the press: The company should be solidly ready to respond to queries that come in from various newspapers, TV channels, etc.

Get ready for total scrutiny: When you go public about issues, be prepared for all operations of the company to come under the scrutiny of the outside world to find out what else could be wrong at the company.

Enterprise might: Make sure that the CEO and top management is able to galvanise the entire company to work on this issue. It's critical to establish a visceral connection with employees so that they understand the sense of urgency and importance. Ensure they are ready to put all their effort towards resolving the issue. If the bulk of the company is aligned on this matter, the resolution will be easy.

Don't let morale sag: As the company embarks on resolving the issues, make sure the employees don't lose steam. They need to be kept charged up. It's the priority not just of the CEO and top management but of leaders across all levels to get this right.

Lesson: 16

The halo effect

Let me start with a real-life incident. John Martin (not his real name), the COO of a global organisation, was hiring a leader to manage its product development centre. For the interview, a gentleman by the name Andy Moze turned up. This gentleman looked more like a Bollywood star than a corporate executive. He was tall, handsome, and well attired and had the gift of gab. The COO was so impressed upon seeing him that he decided to hire him within two minutes of the conversation. He did spend the rest of the meeting time talking to him. But the physical appearance and his gift of gab made John believe that Andy was the right person for the role. The human resource team did have some views about his people management skills, but they could not strongly put it across, because the COO had approved his candidature. A few months later, it was discovered that he was not the right choice, and he had major issues with the way he managed the teams. He was a toxic boss who believed that goals could be accomplished by terrorising people. He was finally asked to go.

This is a great example of the "halo effect".

So, what is the halo effect?

This was first identified by US psychologist Edward Thorndike. It is about making specific inferences based on general observations. It is a cognitive bias wherein one trait good or bad clouds one's judgement, and as a result, he does not see the other traits. These traits could be personal characteristics, behaviours, beliefs, or actions.

When the trait that overshadows other traits is positive, we call it the halo effect. When it is negative, we call it the horn effect. What happens is that great weight is given to the first impression, and subsequent information is overlooked.

A very simple example of this is that if a chef is known for making brilliant pizzas, we tend to believe he can make other Italian dishes also with equal proficiency.

It means if someone is found to be good in one dimension, they are assumed to be good in other dimensions, too.

DOI: 10.4324/9781003250517-17

Let me give you examples of how the halo and horn effects impact a business organisation:

1   A company is being assessed as a part of a vendor audit. The company has been doing well on revenues and profits and keeping costs down. The stock markets have also rewarded it with a gradual increase in its share price. Just because these critical parameters have a positive trend, the assessors tend to believe the company has engaged employees and a great quality system.

2   A strategic business unit (SBU) of a fast-moving consumer goods company has a low level of cost of poor-quality numbers. Seeing the encouraging numbers, the SBU head decides that continuous-improvement activities should be suspended. This he does without realising that continuous improvement is an ongoing effort that has no end.

3   When I worked for a bank in the early 2000s, there was this young man who came for an interview to join the quality team. His name was Mukesh Kumar. He had worked for an automotive company. He had a simple-looking demeanour and lacked all the gloss that one would expect from someone working in a high-profile bank. He had graduated from one of the Indian Institute of Technology schools (IITs). IITs are the top engineering schools in India. They have produced some of the finest engineers and business leaders. During the interview, we learned that he was a farmer's son who had succeeded in getting through the IITs due to his brilliant cerebral power. His external demeanour lacked the polish that is expected of a high-profile banking job. He did communicate in English, but it wasn't as fluent as one would have expected of a high ranking banker. The panel which was interviewing him had three people, including me. Seeing him and hearing him speak, both the other panel members seemed to have lost interest in him. They had been influenced by his external demeanour. However, on probing him, I realised that we were talking to an excellent mind who might not have the required gloss but had great quantitative and analytical ability. He had solved some of the toughest problems in his previous company. It also unfolded during the discussions that he had great influencing ability. He had persuaded not only senior leaders but also people on the shop floor of a large automotive company. It was also obvious that he was indeed a great learner who was hungry to continuously learn and sharpen himself. I vetoed the decision of the other two colleagues and hired him. My judgement was correct. He went on to become one of the finest quality professionals that I have ever worked with. He brought heft to the team and played a key role in the bank's transformation, which I had catalysed. He later moved on and joined a telecom company, where he continued to do well. Today, he is part of a top team in that organisation.

4 Great ideas can come from any source. However, if a person whom the boss does not like suggests an idea for improvement, it does not mean that the idea is useless. Or if an innovative idea emanates from a non-performer, does it mean it should not be considered? Remember, a good idea is a good idea irrespective of its source.

5 If a quality team has incompetent employees who are not able to successfully deliver Lean Six Sigma projects for the customers, the perception of the entire quality team gets tainted. Leaders in the company start questioning the relevance of the quality team and also the power of Lean and Six Sigma to solve problems.

6 The halo effect is also seen in performance appraisal. Based on an employee's enthusiasm and high energy, the boss rates him in overall performance. He does not go through his goals and accomplishments or talk about whether he has lived the organisational values.

7 A Six Sigma Black Belt working in a global food company has great statistical skills and solid analytical ability. The COO is so impressed with this that he makes him lead a transformational project that cuts across geographies and touches leaders across levels. The success of the assignment is based on the Black Belt's ability to influence, manage stakeholders, carry a diverse team, and manage change. The COO gets so carried away by the halo of analytical ability that he does not assess his other abilities. The project starts with a bang but can't move much, as the Black Belt does not have the required leadership skills to ensure the success of the project.

8 A CEO of a leading healthcare company was impressed with the writings of a quality expert. He had not only read his books and read his articles in newspapers, but he had also heard him speak at a conference. This individual was more of a thought leader who had very little experience in leading a quality function. When the company decided to hire a new chief quality officer, he invited this expert to join the company. He was so impressed with his writing and ideas that he overlooked the deployment angle. This expert came on board, but with a year's time, it was clear he was not fit for the role that he was hired for.

9 The halo effect is also found in survey questionnaires administered to customers. What happens here is the overall responses of customers are generalised by one element that they like. For example, input about a new product launch can be biased by customers' favourable experience with past products.

10 A high-performing improvement professional gets away with showing up late, leaving the office early, and even missing deadlines.

11 When a company does well in the marketplace, its culture is celebrated by management writers. The observations are made without any scientific basis. When a company's performance shows a downward trend, the observations are just the opposite.

What is the psychology behind this?

Let's understand the psychology behind this. When things are ambiguous, the situation is emotionally charged, and the person is not an expert on the things that they are evaluating, they look for easy ways to accomplish the task. The first impression acts as a heuristic and helps to form a judgement. Human beings are "cognitive misers" and avoid using cognitive resources, about which we read earlier. They tend to look for shortcuts called heuristics. I have discussed heuristics in Lesson: 12, but you can learn more about them in Table 16.1.

Customers and the halo effect

The halo effect and horn effect also play a role in how customers perceive an organisation. So, if a company is not careful about these issues, it can impact customer experience. Let me give you an example:

1   While filling out a customer satisfaction survey, the customer recalls their overall satisfaction with the brand and assigns scores to each question to make them consistent with what they have overall felt about the brand. When this happens, the questions which are essentially the driver of the overall satisfaction don't tell the whole story.
2   If the look and feel of a website are not attractive, it can disappoint customers despite having good usability. Research done by Lindgaard and Dudek (2002) found that visual appeal played a big role in how customers perceived a website. They asked users to rate a group of websites for look and feel. The websites which received a high rating on look and feel were tested for usability. The average failure rate on these websites was above 50%, which means there was a less than 50% success rate[1]. However, despite this high failure rate, the user satisfaction rating was high. Clearly, the look and feel had a halo effect.
3   Products from companies which have good reputations are more likely to be chosen by customers. They are also less price sensitive and even more willing to be more forgiving if there are minor quality issues.
4   When one product becomes successful from a company, the halo effect extends to products which are released in the future.
5   Just because a celebrity endorses a product, we tend to believe that the product is of good quality.
6   When evaluating a product, customers tend to view it more favourably if the sales person is attractive and has good product knowledge.

Table 16.1 All about heuristics

What are heuristics?

They are a rule of thumb that people use to achieve a goal. They may not be perfect, but they do help in discovery, problem-solving, and learning something new. They also act as shortcuts to help in decision-making. Heuristics reduce the cognitive load in decision-making. They focus on one aspect of the matter under discussion or problem being solved and overlook others which could be relevant. They may be imperfect, yet they help achieve the immediate objectives. As a result, they work in some contexts, yet in others they don't, leading to deviations. The resulting errors are called cognitive biases.
Heuristics can be of many types but the ones that are most popular are:
—
1. **Availability heuristics:** This pertains to relying on information that comes to mind quickly. They operate under the principle that "if you can think of it, it must be important". When you are deciding something, there may be an event or instance that may come to your mind. Because this is the first thing that comes to mind, you tend to believe it is the most common and frequently occurring, and you base your decision on it. Here, the decision-making is based on how available examples are in our mind.

For example: you read in newspapers for a couple of weeks about growing attrition of employees in service companies. So, when you are doing a root-cause analysis on errors in onboarding a customer, you may attribute it to attrition of people.
—
2. **Representative heuristics:** While making decisions, we tend to compare something with the existing prototype or how similar an example is to something else.

For example, Debbie loves mathematics and spends a lot of time working on solving problems at home. During her free time, she enjoys reading and attending a Toastmasters group to sharpen her communication skills. Based on the description, is Debbie more likely to be a quality manager or an artist? Many people would tell you that she is a quality manager because she fits the profile of a quality manager, who is supposed to have problem-solving ability, communication skills, and good quantitative aptitude.
—
While availability has more to do with memory of specific instances, representativeness has more to do with memory of a prototype, stereotype, or average.
—
3. **Affect heuristics:** Here, the decision-making is influenced by how an individual is feeling at the moment, which could be fearful, pleased, sad, frustrated, surprised, etc. (Slovic et al. 2002) If they are in a good mood, they see the potential upside of a decision, while when they are in a bad mood, they see the downside of their decisions. It is typically used for judging the risks and benefits of a choice depending on the positive or negative feelings that people associate with the outcome. For example, if you like an activity, you may see fewer risks and more benefits.

When you love scuba diving you will see it having less risk and great benefits.
Another example is that if you have a negative attitude towards something (let's say a nuclear plant). When being told to decide under time pressure, instead of looking at the positives and negatives separately, you may look at more risk and fewer benefits in nuclear energy.

Ways to avoid this bias

What are things that a company needs to keep in mind to avoid the halo effect? It is not easy, as each situation is unique. However, let me list a few things that can help to avoid halo and horn effects:

1   Before you make a decision that could impact the strategic business objective of the company, make sure all angles are looked into. Don't jump into decision-making. Sleep on it after looking at the critical factors. Give an opportunity for the unconscious mind to mull it over. Take a walk, play, or listen to music while your unconscious mind works on it without the usual biases.

2   While hiring a person, make sure the stipulated interview process is followed. Make sure a candidate is interviewed by at least three people. Even if it appears arduous, make sure all comments about the candidates are written in the evaluation form and that this is done independently, without consulting each other.

3   Before making any conclusion about an event or a person, dig deep to understand the assumptions that you have made. Ask yourself if what you believe about the person is accurate. See if you have looked at the complete picture or if your inference is based on one or two data points or traits.

4   Don't get swayed by a first impression. Try to evaluate the person/company/situation critically, and don't get carried away by your feelings. Look for data. Reach out to others for their opinions.

5   Don't get carried away by what you hear or what people say.

6   Avoid confirmation bias. Just because you believe in something, don't look for data to confirm it.

7   Don't confuse correlation and causation. Just because the attrition levels have gone down and the head of human resources is an upbeat person does not mean this is the reason for low attrition. Delve deep before making a conclusion.

8   Beware the delusion of a single explanation. When someone gives a tidy explanation for an event, you can be sure it's nonsense. For example, if someone says the reason for a great omni-channel experience for a retailer is strong leadership, think again. A single variable can never deliver a desired business outcome. It is always an outcome of many variables working together.

9   We should not have the delusion of lasting success. Everything regresses over a period of time. A great product, an improved process, a superior experience, a great company performance, etc., all decline in performance over a period of time. So please pre-empt this bias and do something about it.

10   Businesses don't follow the laws of nature, and the outcomes can't be predicted with the accuracy of science. Even if you do everything right, things can go wrong. While designing a new product, you may have followed all

the right steps, yet it may have issues in the marketplace. A product may have been processed with utmost care, but there can be quality issues in the customer's hand. What we tend to do is to reduce the uncertainties. It's a game of probability, and by doing the right things, you increase the probability of success.

11 Absolute performance does not mean anything. Everything is relative. A company may have great product performance yet fail in the market. What really matters is how you are doing relative to your competitors. A process may be at Six Sigma levels, but if a competitor has a process that provides a better experience, you lose the game. Psychologically, humans need to compare with something to perceive value. They cannot judge absolute performance.

Before we end this lesson, remember that the halo effect can be for people, leadership, a company, a product, a process, etc. It can be applied to anything.

Note

1 A website's "success rate" is the percentage of users who have successfully completed a task. It is calculated as follows:

Task success rate = Number of corrected complete tasks / Total number of attempts

So, if the success rate is 60%, it means 60% of the users are ability to complete the task on that site. This, of course, means that 40% of the users fail in executing the task, which is the failure rate.

Lesson: 17

Building psychological safety

Creating an engine of continual improvement is an integral part of quality improvement. When we talk about building a culture of continual improvement, we do many things, such as training, leadership, employee involvement, employee engagement, revisiting our assumptions, working on our values, etc.

However, one thing we seem to forget is the need for a psychologically safe working environment.

So, what does it mean to work in a psychologically safe work environment?

It means having a workplace where employees are fearless about acknowledging their mistakes. The company looks at these as a part of the learning process and doesn't penalise employees for them. In a psychologically safe environment, employees openly share their ideas, talk about issues, report problems, and even hold colleagues accountable. When they take risks, they do it without worrying about their image, status, career, and retribution (Edmondson 1999).

As a matter of fact, Google launched a study called Project Aristotle to find out why some teams did well and why some did not (Duhigg 2016). In this, they found a workplace that provides psychological safety to be a key element for team success (Delizonna 2017).

In a psychologically safe environment, employees are more innovative and take more chances to improve their workplace. What a psychologically safe work environment does is to provide a context where people fearlessly question what's not working or needs to change, and this helps in a journey of quality.

A study done by Amy Edmondson at Harvard University in the mid–1990s found some very interesting results. The question of her research was as follows: Do nurses with better relationships perform fewer errors? (Edmondson, Kramer, and Cook 2004).

She thought that a collaborative and friendly environment would make people focus better on their jobs and they would make fewer mistakes. However, she found something very different. The better the relationship the nurses had with their managers and co-workers, the more errors they made. On probing deep, her study revealed the following:

- In a closely knit group, nurses don't actually commit more errors, they just report more of them.

DOI: 10.4324/9781003250517-18

- In a psychologically safe environment, nurses feel safe to report the problems, and mistakes are viewed as safe (Edmondson 2003).
- When employees report errors, they learn from each other.
- Encourage employees to report problems as a part of establishing a culture of continuous improvement.
- When fear of failure is strong, employees don't experiment sufficiently and get into the root cause.

Amy Edmondson is probably one of the topmost experts in this field. She has written a book called *The Fearless Organisation: Creating Psychological Safety in the Workplace for Learning, Innovation and Growth* (Edmondson 2018).

As she describes in her book, psychological safety is "a climate where people feel safe enough to take risks by speaking up and sharing concerns, questions or ideas" (p. 22). In other words, employees will be able to speak freely without fear of humiliation or retribution.

However, let's understand the psychology behind this. Our ancestors lived in jungles, and they had to be very vigilant for any form of threat, be it wild animals or anyone attacking them. This trait continues in us. If anything threatens us, either physically or even our identity or what we stand for, we want to protect ourselves. Hence, we don't want to get into a situation where when we share an idea or make an observation, we get scolded, humiliated, or laughed at. We also don't like it when someone ignores our thoughts and ideas. So typically, in a meeting, we watch, test the waters, and then give our views. To avoid all these situations, humans prefer to be quiet. And this culture of silence is deadly. Or to maintain the harmony of the group, we just go ahead with the decision of the group even if we feel strongly otherwise.

As Edmondson found in her research, fearless organisations promote continuous learning and innovation. These are essential components in fostering a culture of continuous-improvement.

Before we go ahead, it's important to understand the subtle difference between "psychological safety" and "trust". They have some differences which we should understand. I have tried to summarise the differences between the two from the works of Edmondson and others in Table 17.1.

So, what are some of the things that companies need to do to create a psychologically safe environment that facilitates continual improvement? Here's is a list:

1. Create a shared purpose

A critical element of building a psychologically safe work environment is to communicate with the employees on the purpose of the organisation, its long-term vision, the purpose of the team, and what objectives they need to achieve.

So, if you work in a pharma company, you must regularly share with your employees who the company's customer is, how their efforts make a difference,

Table 17.1 Difference between psychological safety and trust

Psychological Safety	Trust
1. This is a condition where team members believe that no one will be rejected or humiliated for sharing ideas, questions, concerns, or mistakes.	1. Trust means being able to predict what the other person will do. The other person is aware of your vulnerability, but he will not misuse it.
2. The point of focus is oneself.	2. The point of focus is others.
3. This is experienced at a group level, and people working together tend to have similar perceptions of whether or not the climate is psychologically safe.	3. This is between two people.
4. This is a temporally immediate experience.	4. This describes an expectation about whether another person or organisation can be counted on to do what it promises to do in some future moment.
5. This encourages learning behaviours.	5. This reduces the need to monitor behaviours (Duica 2019).

the complexities of the manufacturing processes, the associated regulatory guidelines that must be followed, how a quality issue can impact a life, and how there can be opportunities for things to go wrong. After you have shared your perspective, reach out to employees to seek their perspectives. In the beginning, people may be closed off, but once you do it a couple of times, they should open up. Ask what should be done differently, what needs to be taken care of, and whether we are missing anything. After they have given their views, thank them for their input. Then ask them what support they need from you.

This is not a one-time exercise but something that has to be done repeatedly by leaders. This idea has been adapted with modification from Amy Edmondson's book, and I have found it to be a powerful tool for establishing a psychologically secure working atmosphere.

2. Encourage employees to speak up

If creating a psychologically safe workplace is your goal, encourage employees to be themselves and speak out on issues that bother them. This could be things that are not working in the workplace; there could be orphans or issues that no one wants to own or customer pains which the organisation should be aware of. There could also be ideas for product or process improvement or recommendations on practices that need to be upgraded and made employee friendly. They may also talk about the mistakes that they have made and know that they will not have an impact on their career. They can also speak out on issues that impact the reputation of the organisation and things that could impede performance.

3. Educate employees to hold fellow employees accountable

Employees are urged to hold people accountable if fellow workers and even bosses don't do what they have committed to do. This has to be done by communicating clear expectations to all members and seeking the commitment of all team members. Train employees on how to give feedback without being caustic and how to do so to senior colleagues. Having done so, ascertain progress and provide feedback whenever required. All employees may not have the internal motivation, and hence, there may be a need to link the outcome with consequences.

For example, if a worker on the shop floor finds that a certain task has not been completed by his supervisor which is impacting the outcome, he does not hesitate to call it out. He knows that by pointing this out, his performance would in no way be impacted. Let me give you another example from a food business, where everyone entering the processing floor is required to wash and sanitise their hands, rinse their shoes, and wear hats and masks. So, if the CEO enters the manufacturing floor and misses washing his hands, a shop-floor worker points it out and takes him to the wash basin.

4. Urge teams to embrace vulnerability

Traditionally, team members put on a façade that they are perfect. They don't want to share their shortcomings with other team members. The reason they don't do it is because they don't want to be caught on the wrong foot or appear to be ignorant and incapable. However, great teams do just the opposite. They embrace vulnerability. The team members openly share their strengths and weaknesses and talk about areas where they are not good and need help. These vulnerabilities could be in areas of capability deficits, interpersonal shortcomings, mistakes, past failures, and so on.

The core of vulnerability-based teams is that individuals are willing to abandon their ego, fear, and pride for the good of the team and its larger purpose. When team members share their shortcomings and remain transparent with each other, it builds trust. They aren't shy to say that they need help or they screwed up.

Knowing each other's shortcomings, the team members support each other and work towards achieving the larger team objectives. The brilliant thing about such a team is that members don't focus on saving their own backsides but work towards maintaining the credibility of the team. In short, it's holding each other's hand for larger goals.

There are tools to find these vulnerabilities, and they include personal history exercise, 360-degree feedback, experiential games, personality profiling (using the Myers Briggs Type Indicator), etc.

5. Ask questions

A company serious about creating a psychologically safe environment should nudge its employees to ask questions. This has to begin with employees being trained to ask productive questions. And this should be rooted in critical thinking that enables employees to ask questions that benefit the company.

The reason employees don't ask questions is that they don't want to look stupid or demonstrate their ignorance.

A culture in which employees ask questions has to begin from the top. The CEO and top management should ask a lot of questions. These questions should not be the ones that interrogate employees (such as Why have you not done this? or What would be the cost?) but should be to explore newer possibilities (such as What are your thoughts about our latest business strategy? or How do you think we should solve this problem?). These have to be open questions that allow the employee to contribute to the organisational agenda. The top management should also open itself for scrutiny and answer tough questions.

For those uncomfortable asking questions, there could be online channels so that they don't need to confront the person whom they are asking the questions. Companies should also ensure that employees are not punished for asking questions or the problem is pushed back to them to work on. Consider this: an employee asks a leader a question about a company process that isn't working and his boss becomes irritated and tells him to take care of it on his own. If this happens, employees will stop asking questions.

One thing that needs to be kept in mind is that when you make people ask questions, they could come up with answers that are irrelevant or even negative. They may complain about things that are not working. Don't get rattled by the negativity of people. You need to know that your focus has to be on what is important for them and the organisation.

Most importantly, employees should be rewarded for asking questions. For example, the most voted-on question could be given an award.

6. Nudge people to fathom what needs improvement

Create opportunities for employees to look at things in the organisation and decipher what's not working. Allow them a few hours each month to investigate what's wrong with the organisation, what behaviours need to be changed, and who on the team is blocking progress. For example, one business leader told his team to spend half a day a month to walk around the company and find what needed fixing. At another company, the quality manager asked his team to come up with absurd ideas that normally would be poo-pooed. When they do this, the pressure goes off for the team members, and they feel comfortable sharing any ideas that come to mind.

7. Create shadow boards

Many companies create shadow boards or groups that work with top management. These boards are not only focussed on strategic imperatives, but also serve as a vehicle for gathering input on crucial issues that affect a company (Jordan and Sorell 2019). Typically, the composition of these boards includes younger people who normally may not be exposed to senior management. While the normal bias of companies would be to put high-potential employees into this group, it is recommended that we also look at other employees. When the application process for this is open, the company can not only find other hidden diamonds but also signal that people are free to share their opinions. The biggest advantage of shadow boards is that they connect the younger generations with top management. For example, Mahindra and Mahindra (an Indian multinational that is into various businesses) initiated shadow boards in many of its companies, in which the younger generations come together and work on business challenges and present them to the topmost leadership of the Mahindra Group (Philip and Vijayraghavan 2015).

The shadow boards not only signal an open culture but also provide an engine for business improvement. French Accor Hotels took the help of a shadow board to come up with a value proposition for millennials which could compete with Airbnb. As a result, the Jo&Joe brand was born in 2018. This was positioned as "an urban shelter for Millennials". The Finnish paper and packaging company Stora Enso used its shadow board (which it calls Pathfinders and Pathbuilders) to revise how the executive committee assigned work (Jordan and Sorell 2019).

Keep reviewing the function of shadow boards and even change their membership every 12 to 18 months.

8. Meet beyond the workplace

One effective way to break down barriers between members is by creating forums and providing opportunities for employees to meet, often beyond their workplace. This could be for a game of tennis or soccer or doing Pilates together. Nudge people from across the hierarchy to join these forums. This will help the employees to break their fears and barriers that they may have about other colleagues, especially those higher up in the organisational pyramid. It can also help to break cultural barriers. At the New Development Bank (the multilateral development bank set up by BRICS countries) based in Shanghai, there are employees from various countries such as Brazil, Russia, India, China, and South Africa. To break barriers among these divergent cultures, teams go out regularly for games of badminton and ping-pong.

9. Embrace positivity

Research done by Anthony Hood et al. (2016) found that team disposition has an impact on psychological safety. According to the report, the extent to which a team's environment is perceived to be psychologically safe is influenced by its members' general disposition towards positivity (e.g. optimism, joy, gratitude, cheerful, energetic, etc.) or negativity (e.g. fear, annoyance, guilt, discouragement, apathy, anxiety, anger, etc.).

This puts the onus on leaders to make sure teams are positive and happy.

Making people happy and energised in a workplace is not easy, because positive emotions wear off after some time. For example, when you finally get to visit a well-known restaurant to have caviar, the first one or two bites are most special. After a couple of bites, the enjoyment slowly peters out. When you go back to the same restaurant again to get the caviar, it may not be as exciting as the last visit. This tells us that positive events don't remain special after some time. Hence, when we are talking about the workplace, we have to make sure that instead of having one event in a year to embed positivity, there should be regular events that pump in positivity. So, instead of holding one annual celebration in which all employees participate, hold a series of events during the year. These need not be mega-expensive events, but small, frequent events that pump in positivity. To address this issue, companies can offer free cappuccinos and free snacks, giving workers movie tickets, etc., or organise activities throughout the year such as master chef (where employees get together to show their culinary skills), dumb charades, treasure hunts, music events, group cycling, etc. All these help to elevate the mood of employees and send a signal that the company cares for them. Offering a fat bonus at the year's end may not create positivity. These small things can be great positivity boosters. One thing that you need to keep in mind is that there has to be variety in the positivity boosters. Our brain likes novelty. Our mind needs newer experiences to keep us emotionally engaged. Also, don't forget the power of surprise. When things are not expected and they happen, it just energises you. For example, you visit your office after a holiday and are welcomed with a flower bouquet. Or suddenly, you get a ticket to hear a famous orchestra.

It is recommended that a company should appoint an individual who takes care of all these activities. Some companies have a CFO, or chief fun officer, for this. For example, Cap Gemini in India has a chief fun officer (Murali Shankarnarayanan Profile 2019). His mandate entails bringing joy into the lives of over 100,000 employees and their families through creative strategies, thereby making the company a fun place to work.

10. Leaders need to be mindful of their behaviours

Leaders need to improve their listening skills. When they are with an employee or a team, they should be both physically and mentally present. It should not happen that while they are listening, their eyes pop over to the computer next to them or they pry into their mobile phone. Rather, they should make it explicit before beginning the conversation that they will keep the mobile phone off and keep the computer in a log-off mode. Senior leaders also need to create various forums when leaders get to talk to employees – not just their direct reports but also those below them. The other thing that needs to be kept in mind is to keep a check on how they react to employee feedback, observations, or ideas (Windsor 2019). They should not react in such a way that shuts off the employees permanently. And leaders should encourage teams to ask for help. Many of us feel uncomfortable reaching out to others, as we don't want to look stupid. But when you reach out for help, you are demonstrating vulnerability.

11. Ways of working

Come up with detailed ways of working for the team. This stipulates behaviours that are expected from each member. This could be things such as how we talk, how we collaborate, never to get personal, letting everyone speak, treating all members with respect, calling a spade a spade, etc. Make sure this is created with the involvement of all team members so that they own it. There could be differences of opinion, but we should know how to sort it. As movie producer Darry Zanuck said, "If two men on the same job agree all the time, then one is useless. If they disagree all the time, both are useless".

12. Roles and responsibilities

It's upon the leader to make sure the roles and responsibilities are clearly defined and made known to the team members. They should know what is expected of them and how their performance will be managed. Ambiguity here can show that the leader does not care for his team members and does not value them. The leader should also make sure that the team members know how their work impacts the larger objectives of the organisation and the department in which they function. Also, make sure that learning opportunities are provided to them. This learning can be in the classroom as well as on the job. The role of on-the-job coaching and mentoring is very key.

13. Stop blaming people

When things go wrong, our immediate reaction is to blame someone. When creating a psychologically safe workplace is the goal, this has to stop. No one likes to be blamed. Blaming people makes them defensive, and they become negative and disengaged. Instead, replace blame with curiosity. Your effort should be to focus on the issue and not the person. So, if there is a quality-improvement project that is behind its targeted deadline, don't blame the leader. Instead, adopt a learning approach in which you probe with a set of questions.

How does one do it in real life? This is how you can go about doing it.

Begin with stating the problem: "The quality-improvement project is behind schedule and will not be completed by the due date".

Then seek the team leader's permission to explore further: "Do you think we could explore this issue together?" When you ask for permission, you are disarming the person's possible defensiveness. Also, you are treating him with respect.

Then reach out for causes. People who are part of the project would have the reasons: "What is it that could have caused this delay?" "What are your thoughts around it?"

Then summarise the takeaways and learnings: "So we are believing that the causes are . . ." "What have been our key learnings from the project?" Then close the discussion: "What is it that we should do differently so that this problem does not happen again?"

The best teams for quality are not those that are trained in quality tools, but those wherein members feel fearless in expressing their ideas. Team members feel free to speak up without the worry of being pulled down by someone else. When a team feels psychologically safe, members feel they can use each member's uniqueness to enhance workplace performance. They know they can speak openly without the fear of getting embarrassed by the group.

Lesson: 18

The power of open-ended questions

We have spoken about how questions are an integral part of creating a safe working environment. When the goal is to establish a firm that is known for its quality, questions can be useful in a variety of ways. This is something that should be understood and consciously practised. As a matter of fact, I call it the silent tool of the workplace. This is because it's the most underutilised item in a manager's arsenal. Many of us are unaware of its power and what it can accomplish in terms of establishing a reputation for excellence.

Companies that recognise its importance ensure that their staff hone their question-asking skills (Berger 2014). All employees should be taught the art of questioning and how to get value out of it. The CEO and top management have to encourage employees to ask lots of questions. However, this has to be supported by a mechanism that ensures employees are responded to. Also, there may be a need to have communication channels beyond face to face. This is especially when employees do not have the opportunity to meet senior leaders. Hence, the questions can be asked through emails, online chats, webchats, dedicated voice mails, town halls, etc. Top management also has to be ready to answer some uncomfortable questions. At times, this may be tough, but it helps to create trust between management and employees.

The reason leaders don't ask questions is that they don't want to appear weak, indecisive, imperfect, and unsure. They don't want to appear not to be on top of issues, and hence don't encourage questioning. However, great leaders know the power it. As a matter of fact, the former CEO of Google, Eric Schimdt, once said, "We run this company on questions, not answers".

Actually, it's this constant questioning that makes a company better. The problem in many companies is not capability, but they don't seem to ask sufficient questions.

So what do questions do to an enterprise?

Questions help to involve

A simple question – "What do you think?" – can do wonders for a workplace. Open-ended questions like these are actually a great tool for involving

DOI: 10.4324/9781003250517-19

employees in various initiatives that are underway in the company. One of the reasons employees are disengaged in a workplace is because they feel their opinions are not taken for the various initiatives that have been launched. Often, the general feeling is in the air that top management treats them as robots, and they are just told what needs to be executed.

For example, a chief sales officer before, putting together a sales strategy, reaches out to all the sales force and asks, "What are the things that should be included in next year's sales strategy?" A simple question like this can trigger all the minds in the sales force to suggest what should be and should not be included in the strategy. What's most satisfying for a front-line salesperson is that his views have been taken for the strategy development.

We often don't realise the power of untapped ideas and thoughts that reside with our employees. Sometimes, the finest ideas emerge from the lowest levels in the organisation.

Examples of questions to involve employees:

What do you think? What's your feedback on our strategic choices? What do you think about our new product design? What should we do to arrest the manufacturing problem?

A company serious about quality should ask such open-ended questions more often, especially on issues that are important to the company.

Questions prevent us from becoming complacent

With so much change around us, the CEO and top management of a company can never afford to be in their comfort zone. When employees are allowed to question everything in the company, it prevents them from becoming complacent. There are so many eyes which are constantly on the lookout to find what's not working. It also provides a great opportunity to learn about newer practices and to get to know about things of which they are not aware. A curious mind may pop a harmless question, which could trigger new thinking. Leaders have to get used to a culture in which they continuously learn and unlearn about what they are doing.

Examples of questions to prevent us from becoming complacent:

Why isn't anyone owning this issue? Why are we not able to attract the right talent? Why is our employee engagement going down? Why are we not becoming digital? Why are we not as good as our competitors? Why don't we see our C-suite on the shop floor?

Questions help to influence

Open-ended questions help to influence people to do what you want them to accomplish. Instead of making directive statements, an open-ended question steers an individual in the direction that you want them to go. A directive question can be threatening, create fear, cause passive aggression, and lead to frustration. After all, no one likes to be ordered. So, if a leader wants a certain behaviour to be embedded in his subordinate, he could share a directive statement such as, "I want you to complete the training programme on leadership blind spots by December without fail." Instead, he could ask an open-ended question as follows: "What are your dates for developing the skills around leadership blind spots that are expected of all successful business leaders in this company?"

The latter question is more empowering and gives leeway to the individual to decide on the date, yet he knows it has to be done. The manger indirectly tells him to do what is required without appearing autocratic. A study done by David Brendel (2015) and reported in *Harvard Business Review* found that the ratio of open-ended and directive statements should be 10:1.

This strategy helps to build trust. The approach that a leader should adopt is firmness, and no-nonsense style can be communicated by body language, while he can be collegial and supportive verbally.

Questions help to solve problems

Powerful open-ended questions help critical thinking. When framed well, they trigger our minds to solve tough problems. Brilliant thinkers never stop asking questions. Some of the finest inventions ever emerged from a question. Isaac Newton asked, "Why does an apple fall from a tree?" This led to his pioneering work in the space of gravity. Charles Darwin asking, "Why do the Galapagos Islands have so many species not found elsewhere?" led to his work on evolution.

Similarly, some of the finest business breakthroughs have happened because of an inquisitive mind asking a simple, open-ended question. For example, the invention of the Polaroid instant camera in the mid-1940s was triggered by inventor Edwin H. Land's three-year-old daughter (Berger 2016). Her question to her father was, "Why do we have to wait for the picture?" She did not like waiting for the development of the film.

For example, one CEO asked his retail banking team, "How could our bank branches provide a unique service which no one else does in the market"? This led to the teams launching a service guarantee for some of the products delivered at the branch. This meant that if the customer did not get a demand draft within a stipulated time, they were compensated by paying $5.

Have we not seen Japanese *senseis* (or coaches) when they make the rounds of factories? They never provide answers but always ask questions. Their focus is to push people to use their minds to find solutions. This ensures that employees are involved in the process, and they also own the decision.

Don't forget that powerful questions enable and build critical thinking in an enterprise.

Questions improve communication

When people ask open-ended questions, it can help to improve communication between employees. It is a great tool to get rid of confusion and improve interpersonal relationships. Let's say the chief quality officer has interpersonal issues with the chief manufacturing officer. Open-ended questions can be a great tool for open communication and understanding what's not working. Probably the most powerful open-ended question that the chief quality officer can ask is: "What is it that I need to do differently that can improve our relationship?"

This simple yet direct question not only disarms the other person but suddenly opens up an opportunity to solidify the relationship.

Examples of questions to improve communication:

What are the issues that bother you? What are the things you want me to do differently going forward? What are you worried about? What can I do to support you better?

The invisible gorillas

Let's begin this lesson with a short exercise. I know you could be reading this book in your study, in a library, on an airplane, in your office, in a park, at a beach, or beside a swimming pool. It does not matter where. Start by closing your eyes. Now, open them and try looking for everything that's green in colour. I am sure your eyes are only seeing things (both living and non-living) green in colour. Make a list of all green objects. Close your eyes again. Now, when you open them, look for objects which are red. Make a list of all red things you see around you.

So, what happened? Amidst the many objects and colours, your eyes just see what you want them to see. They filter out what is important and focus on what they are looking for.

There is a famous Harvard experiment called Invisible Gorilla by Christopher Chabris and Daniel Simons (2010). In this experiment, people were asked to watch a short video where two groups passed around a ball. These groups had three people each. One group had people wearing black T-shirts while the other had white T-shirts. The question for those watching the video was that they needed to keep a count of the number of passes made by the people in white shirts. Somewhere during the video, a person walks by the court wearing a gorilla suit. When those who were watching the video were asked if they had seen anything out of the ordinary, a large percentage had not noticed the person in the gorilla suit.

This is called *inattentional blindness*. This is the event when we fail to see what is visible to others. Together with this, we also are not able to see large changes to scenes and objects, which is called *change blindness*. We tend to see and observe things that are in our minds. There could be plenty of other critical stuff, but we tend to overlook it even if it is in front of us.

The take for a business organisation is as follows:

- We miss things right in front of us.
- We watch very little of what's happening around us.
- We are aware of far fewer things than we think.

DOI: 10.4324/9781003250517-20

- We can't do two things at the same time; instead, we can switch from one task to another.
- We develop our experience and intuition based on what we notice.
- We have to make the visible perceptible.
- We may not even be aware of big-ticket changes around us.

Why does this happen?

Our brain has limited capacity when it comes to attentiveness. The human brain senses much more information than it can process. To manage this information overload, the brain peels off just a few pieces of information to process further. Natalie Angier shared in a 2008 *New York Times* piece that our brain scans about 30 to 40 pieces of information (e.g. sights, sounds, smells, tactile data) per second until something captures its attention. Our attention selects a small amount of information to process, and the rest never reaches our consciousness, causing inattentional blindness. As Marc Green (2004) mentioned in a piece in Visual Expert.com,

> The overload becomes even worse when we recall information from memory and engage in deep thought. To cope with the problem, we have evolved a mechanism called attention, which acts as a filter that quickly examines sensory input and selects a small percentage for full processing and for conscious perception. The remaining information is lost, unnoticed and unremembered – we are inattentionally blind to it since it never reached consciousness. This all happens without our awareness, so it is not a behaviour which people can bring under conscious control.

Why does this happen? Based on Marc Green's (2004) piece and a Matthew Grissinger paper published in *P&T* in 2012, the reasons have been summarised as follows:

1 **Contrast:** The way information is displayed has an impact on whether it catches our attention. What matters is a high degree of contrast with the background. Here, luminance (brightness) contrast is more important than colour contrast.
2 **Relevance:** Relevance plays a big role in the type of information we pick up. Have we not seen the phenomenon in a cocktail party where you are having a conversation, yet when someone utters your name, even in a different corner, it grabs your attention? This is also called the cocktail party effect.
3 **Expectation:** Expectations have a big impact on what we pay attention to. This is often influenced by past experience and the expertise we have gathered over the years. For example, if medicine X comes in a carton

with a certain blue label, we look for this presentation every time we look for this drug. If a new medicine (let's say medicine Y) comes in a similar carton and has a similar presentation, we may think it is medicine X. We may inadvertently administer medicine Y to a patient who needs medicine X. This happens due to confirmation bias, as we are looking for information we already believe in.

4   **Mental Workload:** Inattentional blindness happens when part of our attention is diverted to a second task, for example, writing a prescription while talking on a cell phone. Certain tasks need full attention, and you cannot get them right by focussing on two things.

5   **Boredom:** Working on tasks that require monitoring of processes or activities that are automated or happen on autopilot requires little mental load. People become bored when they have a low workload, and they cease paying attention. This is because the arousal level drops and our attention wanders. This can cause errors.

6   **Capacity:** The capacity to pay attention is influenced by drugs, alcohol, tiredness, and age. Under these circumstances, attention level is reduced.

How it connects with quality improvement

How do the previous points relate to a company that is focussed on quality? Let's understand:

Adherence to Processes

In workplaces, we often display work instructions and operating processes. This is done with the objective that people will look at them and follow them when required. Yet there are cases when employees don't follow them even when they are in front of them. Have we not seen these processes being displayed at the desks of operators in transaction processing or even on manufacturing workstations? Sometimes, the operators would tell you that they have never looked at the "process display", and it seems to be gathering dust. Well, the reason for this is the "invisible gorilla". Employees are so busy with their other priorities that their attention does not go to the process displays.

Uncommon Events

We examine what can go wrong in products, procedures, and business systems as part of our quality initiatives. We employ techniques to identify any potential failures. Then we put corrective measures in place. This could be for both failures that occur frequently and those that occur once in a while. However, countermeasures for events that happen rarely may not work if they are manual and require human intervention. For example, in a milk-processing factory, there could be procedures that need to be followed to manage deviations.

This happens as we tend to observe things and events that happen often and not those that happen rarely. The human mind is not good at discerning things that are not common. What's important to remember here is that the solutions that are decided should be foolproof. When you think about embedding quality, don't be surprised if people miss practices which are not common.

Hospitals

Hospitals these days are highly concerned about quality. Many of them are adopting practices to ensure reduced misdiagnosis, better treatment, faster discharge, and enhanced patient experience.

However, despite these measures, errors continue to happen. There are areas where doctors, nurses, and other staff may miss out on things that are important. For example, a patient complaining of toothache visited an endodontist—someone who specialises in root canal treatment. The endodontist performed a dental x-ray (or orthopantomogram) and concluded that the cause of the pain was a badly infected tooth. He performed a root canal procedure on the affected tooth and sent the patient home, assuring him that his pain would vanish. However, the pain did not subside. The patient came back to the dentist after a week. After looking at the OPG again, the endodontist realised that he had done a partial job and had missed the adjacent fractured tooth, which was also the cause of the pain. He then worked on it, and the patient was pain free. Since the majority of his patients had dental cavities, he focused on the same in this patient as well, despite the OPG showing both the cavity and the fractured teeth. He just saw what his mind wanted him to see.

Training and Practise

If you want people to follow a process, it will not happen by displaying work instructions. A standard process will consistently be followed when it becomes habitual. This can be achieved through training and repeated practise. If you decide to put a person on the job when he is still learning, it is suggested that he be under strict supervision. Only when he is adept in his area of work should he be allowed to do the job independently.

Problem-solving

When solving a problem, one should put together a cross-functional team. A specialist attempting to solve a problem always refers to his area of expertise. This closes the door to alternate views. Hence, a cross-functional team should be put together. For example, let's look at a healthcare setting. To ensure misdiagnosis does not happen in hospitals, it's suggested that a patient's ailment be looked at from multiple perspectives (Frimpong et al. 2017). When a patient is treated by a single doctor, he will likely treat only one issue and overlook areas beyond it. Just imagine if the line of treatment was decided by a multidisciplinary team comprising the physician, specialists, nurses, and doctors. Not only would it reduce the chances of misdiagnosis, it would also enhance communication among staff with the patient. Additionally it breaks the hierarchy and one-way sharing of information from the doctor and dispersed to the rest of the staff. All these lead to enhanced employee engagement and better outcomes.

Managing invisible gorillas – the eight cardinal rules for quality improvement

As quality professionals, we should remember the eight cardinal rules:

Rule: 1

The only way people follow processes is when they are trained and repeatedly practise. Expecting employees will follow a process by looking at displayed processes is a short-sighted view.

Rule: 2

Visual vigilance can prevent failure, but only to a certain extent. It can never make products and processes foolproof. Processes, practices, and products are made foolproof by adopting a failsafe design.

Rule: 3

Always solve problems through a cross-functional team. A truly multidisciplinary team can offer cognitive diversity and ensures various aspects of the problem are looked at through myriad lenses.

Rule: 4

Develop a workplace environment which allows diverse perspectives to survive. Create capacity among employees to embrace multidisciplinary views. This is both cultural and leadership-led. Managing a cognitively diverse team is not easy, but when done well, it can be a big strength for the enterprise.

Rule: 5

While displaying information, remember the degree of contrast with the background should be there so that it catches attention.

Rule: 6

Have well-established protocols on what people need to do when monitoring activities that are automated or are on autopilot.

Rule: 7

While on an important task, don't focus on another activity.

Rule: 8

Don't involve people in important activities if they are tired. It's important
to give them a break from working on important tasks before they get
fatigued.

The opportunity in invisible gorillas

While one needs to be aware of invisible gorillas when creating an organisation known for quality, it also provides an opportunity for the CEO and top
management. Based on the strategic aspiration, the CEO and top management
can steer the focus of the teams in the direction that they deem fit. For example, if "zero defects" is a focus of an enterprise, the CEO and top management
should take every opportunity to drill it down in the minds of the employees.
So, irrespective of what they do or which function they work for, they will
strive for zero defects.

This does make a difference. As this becomes the focus for an employee, he
will shut out all distractions. If the focus is not there, the employees wonder and
misinterpret what they should focus on. Or every team could have different
focus areas that take them in different directions. A strategic focus like the one
that we discussed unifies the team, and they know what to focus on.

I know of a CEO who joined a manufacturing company that had severe
quality issues. Customers repeatedly complained, and the direct impact was
that they were shunning repeat orders. Clearly, this was a red flag for the
company, and the CEO knew that if it was not addressed, it would lead to an
existential crisis. Hence, he set three priorities for the company, and quality
was one of them. The priorities comprised (a) revenue, (b) quality, and (c)
new products. This was done not only to increase revenue but also to reduce
the chronic quality issues being faced by the company. There was an enterprisewide effort to drill these priorities into his employees. Whether it was at
a town hall, a business review meeting, founders' day celebration, a training
programme, or an ideation workshop, these three priorities were repeatedly
mentioned at the beginning. Not only were these priorities displayed on the
wall, they were also discussed by top management and other leaders when
they met the employees. For example, when the members of the C-suite
(chief financial officer, chief sales officer, chief human resources officer, etc.)
met someone in the elevator, they would begin the conversation by checking

on the three priorities. There was also an enterprisewide effort to make sure everything that happened was linked to the three priorities. As a result, the employees started looking at these priorities in their workplace. What happens is that a human mind focusses on things that are at the top of the mind. By repeatedly communicating these priorities, they become the team's focus. The automatic nature of our brain prioritises tasks that are relevant and blocks out everything else. In this company, the employees' focus on quality started delivering the desired outcome. Soon, the chronic quality issues started dropping, and the sales volumes started recovering. Clearly, inattentional blindness has positives in that we pay attention to one thing while blocking the rest. It brings focus to what is important.

Goals, measurements, and targets

Stephen Covey (1994) had said, "Begin with the end in mind." This is also true for all quality-improvement efforts. Whatever you do, it's imperative that we have an end goal in mind. Goals form the backbone of a quality organisation. Without goals, the efforts can be directionless, and one would never see progress. In an enterprisewide quality deployment effort, the focus should be to instil goals in all individual and team pursuits. Having defined the goals, they should be written down with stipulated time frames and clear responsibilities.

When we talk about goals, it is also said that they should be SMART. The mnemonic SMART stands for specific, measurable, achievable, relevant, and time bound.

- *Specific* means having a sharp goal targeted to a specific area.
- *Measurable* means it should be amenable to measurement.
- *Achievable* means the goal should be doable, and there should be required skills and resources.
- *Relevant* means the goal should align with your values and long-term objectives.
- *Time Bound* means the goal has to be achieved within a stipulated time.

The effort in quality is about improvement. It's about making things better than they are today. Hence, every improvement effort needs to have a goal and should follow the SMART guidelines.

However, there is something more to goal setting that we often overlook. The way the goals are constructed can have an impact on employee motivation. Goals can be created in two ways:

Approach goal: These are goals that are focussed on positive outcome. They target reaching or maintaining a desired outcome. They are focussed on doing more of something good.

Avoidance goal: These are goals that are focussed on reducing or eliminating undesirable outcomes. They are focussed on doing less of something bad.

DOI: 10.4324/9781003250517-21

Having a large proportion of approach goals is found to be of greater well-being to humans. People perform poorly on avoidance goals versus when they are pursuing approach goals. Research done on types of goals and their impact on grades, by psychologists Andrew Elliot, K M Sheldon, and Marcy Church (1997) at the University of Rochester, found that avoidance goals depressed performance by about the same amount as approach goals.

Approach goals are enjoyable, while avoidance goals are stressful. There are reasons this happens. Focussing on avoidance goals may lead us to have a negative bias. We may tend to be oversensitive about the potential failure, and this may become a self-fulfilling prophesy; the thing you are trying to avoid translates into unwanted behaviours and actions. This happens because when you believe in something, it translates into behaviour.

The other reason is that in the case of an avoidance goal, the focus is on potential loss and not on potential gain. When we have this sort of psychological framing, our attention constricts, and thinking becomes rigid. We find it difficult to see the big picture. We also resist trying to find a solution. As a result, these insights become elusive. On the other hand, when the focus is on an approach goal, it energises us. This is because we are excited about the potential gain and the accomplishments. This mental state allows a better mental exploration, and we can see wide varieties of options for potential solutions. We are much more creative, which is a pre-requisite for superior problem-solving.

Also, when a person's focus is an avoidance goal, it appears a lot harder and quite stressful to accomplish. When the occurrence of avoidance goals is large, it results in burnout.

So in a quality-improvement effort, it's imperative to have an approach goal so that the focus is on potential gain. It's imperative to do the right psychological framing while framing the goals.

In Table: 20.1 there are examples of how goals can be reframed in a quality-improvement effort.

Actually, it's not just about the goals but also the type of conversation that you are having in the workplace that has an impact. Create a culture wherein employees get into a habit of positively framing issues. If this can't be achieved for all employees, make sure the top management, functional heads, and departmental heads do so.

When the conversation in an organisation has a positive bias and issues are positively framed, teams take it favorably. They are excited about what they are getting into and don't brood over the challenges. Even if there are impediments and things are arduous, they know it's for something meaningful. There are more happy faces as employees find work fulfilling.

However, if the general conversation in the workplace has a negative bias, teams are less happy, more anxious, and distressed (Elliot and Friedman 2007). What bothers them is that what they are avoiding or trying to reduce should not be a reality again. There is also a tendency to procrastinate, which delays the

Table 20.1 Reframing of quality goals

Quality-Related Pursuit	Avoidance Goal	Approach Goal
Goal for staff in the engineering department	We are focussing on removing dirt and filth from our workplace.	We are focussed on making our workplace clutter free, efficient, and productive.
Message to shop-floor workers	Focus on reducing errors.	Focus on getting our products right the first time.
Communication from CEO to employees in company	Reduce inefficiencies and process dissonance,	Create a lean and agile enterprise.
Call to reduce process non-compliance	Reduce incidences of shortcuts to process adherence.	Process adherence will be a way of life.
Improve quality of team participation in problem-solving meetings	I will not lose my cool in the problem-solving meeting.	I will look for opportunities to collaborate in the problem-solving team meeting.

final outcome. Teams feel less competent, and the whole experience impacts their self-esteem.

The three laws

Measurements are an integral part of any continuous-improvement effort. They help us to focus and get desired results. They also help to ascertain how we are performing. They reveal the health of the organisation and its components. Metrics tell us where we are going and how we are progressing vis-à-vis the target that we have set out for ourselves. Peter Drucker said, "If you can't measure it, you can't manage it". Metrics also are a tool for self-correction, and people can correct when things don't happen as desired. They also drive focus. They tell you what to deep dive into and what not to spend time doing. The metrics help to deliver the highest standards of product and service quality through transparency, accountability, and credibility.

However, quality professionals need to know the unintended consequences of metrics. And here, it would help to know the following laws:

Goodhart's Law

This law was proposed by British economist Charles Goodhart. He was a member of the Bank of England's monetary policy committee. In 1975, he proposed this law in a paper which was later used to criticise Margaret Thatcher's monetary policy.

The law states:

"When a measure becomes a target, it ceases to be a good measure" (Anzil 2021).

Though the law was originally used in economics, it is now used in other domains.

It means that when you set one goal as a measure of performance, people optimise everything to achieve it. It does not remain a good measure because people start to game it. They don't mind manipulating it to achieve the target. This implies that when the measurement of a goal itself becomes a goal, this may result in the goal not being aligned with the larger objective for which the goal was set up.

An example of Goodhart's Law is a contact centre specifying an average call hold time of 4 minutes, for the agents. This negatively impacts the quality of services, because the focus of agents will be reducing customer hold times and not solving their problems. Their focus would be to somehow close the call within 4 minutes even if the customer issues are not closed. This can even peeve the customers.

As reported by Jessica Morris in her blog in 2018, which talked about the British National Health System (NHS), when the NHS pushed for decreased wait times in emergency departments, hospitals forced patients to wait in ambulances instead of emergency department waiting rooms. They succeeded in decreasing the time in the waiting room, but to what benefit?

The other examples are: bankers inflating or deflating interest rates for London Inter-Bank Offered Rate to inflate their performance ratings and bonuses. And in schools, some teachers may erase and improve student answers to protect their own reputations, pay, and jobs (Rodamar 2018).

Let me also share an example from a credit card company. Here, the performance of the sales team members was measured against a single target of "number of customer application forms sourced per month". To meet this target, the sales team members went all out to get customer application forms without really ascertaining whether they met the eligibility requirements. The outcome of this was that around 40–45% of the forms were getting rejected as the customers were not eligible for a credit card. The focus on a singular target did more harm than good. The back-office staff squandered time in verifying application forms of ineligible customers. It not only reduced the sales team's overall effectiveness but also added to the acquisition cost of business. A focus on a single target had made the sales team focus on "quantity" while "quality" suffered.

Campbell's Law

This law is a cousin of Goodhart's Law. This was proposed by psychologist and social scientist Donald T. Campbell.

The law states:

"The more any quantitative social indicator is used for social decision-making, the more subject it will be to corruption pressures and the more apt it will be to distort and corrupt the social processes it is intended to monitor" (Campbell 1979).

This means when you measure performance or effectiveness solely through quantitative indicators, people tend to demonstrate less ethical behaviour and most likely less effective results as well.

There is this interesting story from British India (Bakshi 2017). Apparently, the officials of the British government were very worried about venomous cobra snakes in the city of Delhi. To address this issue, they rolled out a programme wherein people would be paid for dead cobras. The outcome was that the residents of Delhi started breeding cobras. When officials got to know about it, they stopped the programme. As a result, the citizens released the cobras, and the population of cobras went up. This is known as the Cobra Effect, and the name was coined by German economist Horst Seibert (2001).

As mentioned by Sam Adams in his 2020 book *War of Numbers: An Intelligence Memoir of the Vietnam War's Uncounted Enemy*, when the US military began relying on body counts and estimates of declining enemy strength to demonstrate that things were going well in Vietnam, body counts became inflated, and unfavourable strength estimates were squelched. We shall talk more about this later in this lesson.

These are all examples of people gaming the system to achieve the target while the larger objective is lost. The fundamental reason why Campbell's Law happens is because the measurement system that has been installed is incomplete. To ascertain progress, both quantitative and qualitative indicators should be looked into. When quantitative indicators are installed, precautions should be taken so that there is no manipulation and distortion.

When targets are not right, people tend to game the system, erode moral values, demonstrate wrong behaviours, and even harm the customers (Crockett 2019).

So, what are some of the things that quality leaders should keep in mind while installing metrics?

1   Before installing any indicator, please think through the consequences.
2   Avoid falling into the trap of putting in place a single indicator for the measure of success. Shun the concept of the North Star Metric (NSM) or the single metric[1] that best captures the core value that your product delivers to customers.
3   Install a good measurement system that captures multiple factors . . . hence, embed a range of key performance indicators (KPIs[2]).
4   Use the Balanced Scorecard created by Robert S Kaplan and David Norton (1996).

5 Keep reminding people of the larger objectives with which the indicator has been established.
6 See if it can be changed regularly, though this may not easy in a business setting. I would still recommend to refresh the metrics every 12 months.
7 Please include quantitative as well as qualitative goals.

McNamara Fallacy

This is named after Robert McNamara, who was the US Secretary of Defence from 1961 to 1968 during the presidencies of John F Kennedy and Lyndon Johnson (Mahony 2017). This idea emanates from the Vietnam War, wherein enemy body counts were taken as a measure of success. Also known as the Quantitative Fallacy, the focus here is to make decisions based solely on quantitative observations and shun all others.

For McNamara, war was more like a mathematical model. He thought that by increasing enemy deaths and minimising one's own, victory would be achieved. He did not realise that measuring the success of a war through body count was myopic. This is because he was ignoring the mood of the public, territory gained, chaos, destruction, etc. McNamara later conceded that over-emphasis on a single metric blinded and oversimplified the complexities of war. His name got inextricably linked to the USA's not being successful in Vietnam.

The term "McNamara Fallacy" was coined by sociologist Daniel Yankelovitch in his 1972 work. He outlined the four elements of the fallacy as follows:

1 Measure whatever can be easily measured.
2 Disregard that which cannot be easily measured.
3 Presume that which cannot be easily measured is not important.
4 Presume that which cannot be easily measured does not exist.

The takeaway quality professionals need to keep in mind is that decisions should not just be made on numbers while overlooking qualitative factors. If you are doing this, you are becoming blind to other important factors. Also, don't make inferences based on numbers that are easy to gather or you have gathered yourself.

The following are common examples of the McNamara Fallacy:

a After a training programme on quality, the trainer measures the effectiveness by measuring the reactions of participants. This he does by taking feedback from them immediately after the session ends. He does not ascertain their knowledge or whether the lesson has an impact on results and behaviour later.
b In a retail bank, the customer satisfaction scores show a positive trend, yet the customer complaints continue.

c   When leading a process–improvement project, a quality professional focusses only on achieving the quantitative objective of the project. He believes that if he is able to improve the process as desired and achieves the quantitative goal of the project, he will get the desired outcome.

d   Installing metrics in a company is good and required. However, if you want to be a company known for quality, look beyond numbers. Address issues concerning people, culture, engagement, communication, and so on. We often don't realise the power of these things in building a continuous-improvement culture.

e   Quality-improvement approaches such as Lean, Six Sigma, Theory of Constraints, 8D, etc. are great methods for solving problems. When successfully implemented, they can help you achieve the target that you are gunning for. However, when used in isolation, without understanding the context and addressing human dimensions such as culture, motivation, engagement, preferences, coaching, and motivation, they can be less effective. Not surprisingly, the Toyota Production System puts an important emphasis on people (Husar 1991).

Data is important. It helps businesses. But we should not overdo it. It should not govern us in a way that it delivers more harm than benefit. We should not be driven by data analysis when other things could be missing. Data has done a lot of good for Google, and it's a company that many of us are impressed by. But there something that I read about from Google's early years. It will give you an idea of what data fetishisation can do to employees. As Kenneth Cukier and Viktor Mayer-Schönberger mentioned in an article titled "The Dictatorship of Data", which appeared in *MIT Technology Review*, on May 31, 2013:

> Google's deference to data has been taken to extremes. To determine the best color of a toolbar on the website, Marissa Mayer, when she was one of Google's top executives before going to Yahoo, once ordered staff to test 41 gradations of blue to see which ones people used more. In 2009, Google's top designer, Douglas Bowman, quit in a huff because he couldn't stand the constant quantification of everything. "I had a recent debate over whether a border should be 3, 4 or 5 pixels wide, and was asked to prove my case. I can't operate in an environment like that", he wrote on a blog announcing his resignation. "When a company is filled with engineers, it turns to engineering to solve problems. Reduce each decision to a simple logic problem. That data eventually becomes a crutch for every decision, paralyzing the company".

To avoid the McNamara Fallacy, the following are the points a quality leader should remember:

1   Shun the idea that "if it cannot be measured, it's not important".

2   Running a business is full of complexity. Don't think you can make full sense of an issue through metrics only.

3   Don't set metrics that don't result in improvement.

4   Never shun qualitative dimensions which have an impact on organisational performance.

5   Don't embed a target culture. This is because we tend to measure what can be counted rather than what is important. How can you infer the quality of an activity when the outcomes are a result of the interaction and inter-dependencies of many processes?

6   One should not install metrics that dissuade employees from doing things that cost the customers or any other stakeholders.

7   Be judicious in how you drive performance through metrics. There are drawbacks to metricising the entire organisation and all activities. It can lead to naming and shaming, people being asked to go, etc., which can lead to wrong behaviours such as gaming the system, obsessive checking, bullying, etc. It actually creates a very negative culture, which you need to be careful of. Metrics work well when people are supported to achieve them. If you are using metrics as targets, use them very carefully so that the discussed issues don't happen, and use them sparingly, and don't just use them as dictates for enterprise adoption.

8   When you are ascertaining performance, don't just look at metrics; ascertain the overall context.

9   Don't be so fixated on numerical quantification that you fail to appreciate that outcomes are a result of multiple factors. The metrics give a certain perspective on the outcome. We should not forget that not everything that matters can be measured.

10   The focus on metrics to drive accountability signifies a culture marked by low social trust where leaders don't rely on their ability to influence the teams to get desired outcomes.

11   Measuring what's easy can lead to short-termism. Things that have a long-term impact are often difficult to measure.

Quality- and continuous-improvement professionals need to keep in mind the three phenomena that we discussed. I suggest you keep this set of actions in mind whenever you work on improvements.

Notes

1   Metrics are quantifiable measures to track performance.
2   KPIs are those that are most aligned with the company's strategic objectives and that make the real impact.

Lesson: 21

When employees are defensive

A CEO serious about quality should make it a point to make a conscious effort to create an environment in which employees are not defensive. This is something that should be advocated by the entire top management. We often don't realise how our actions and behaviour can make employees defensive. When an employee is defensive, he takes steps to avoid any form of attack, and this is detrimental to building a culture that facilitates quality and continuous improvement.

Let's understand what really happens when a person is defensive. The survival circuits lie deep within the automatic system of the brain. When they pick up signals of potential danger, they get activated and launch their response. These responses could be fight, flight, or freeze.

In a fight response, the person tries to strike back. He could do this by responding aggressively, becoming more competitive, snapping at people, or just arguing the point endlessly.

In a flight response, the person tries to run away from the situation. This he could do in many ways, such as avoiding the person, leaving the room with an excuse to go to the washroom, changing the topic of the conversation, or being absent from work.

In a freeze scenario, the person gets into a state of helplessness. He completely shuts down and withdraws from the discussion. He is almost like a deer who is caught in the headlights. The person is so startled that he cannot think.

The amygdala in our brain is constantly sensing situations which are unpleasant, ambiguous, dangerous, novel, or even uncertain. So when the amygdala senses a stressful situation or a potential danger, it triggers the adrenal glands to pump adrenaline and noradrenaline (also called norepinephrine) (Klein 2013). The immediate impact of this is that we become more alert and focussed on dealing with the existing situation. When the level of adrenaline and noradrenaline reaches a higher level, a third hormone, cortisol, is released. The impact of cortisol happens after some time, i.e. within minutes, while that of adrenaline and noradrenaline can be felt within seconds. The result of all these is that blood starts flowing from areas where it is not essential, such as skin and the digestive tract, to where it is needed, such as the muscles in your arms, legs, shoulders, eyes, ears, nose, etc. The impact of this is that we tend to breathe

DOI: 10.4324/9781003250517-22

faster. Our muscles become tense. We start to sweat. Our sight sharpens. Our mouths dry out. Our skin becomes pale. We become prepared both physically and psychologically to face the challenge.

When this happens, our mind bypasses the rational part of our brain and is in an attack mode. The automatic system of our brain takes charge of us, and the deliberate system goes offline. The impact of this on quality-improvement efforts is detrimental. The part of the brain that is needed most for building quality is not available. Just imagine, when a workplace has people who are defensive, they cannot suitably contribute towards building an organisation known for quality. The impact can be manifold when a large number of employees are in this state.

The typical outcomes of such defensiveness on employees are the following:

1 Employees feel disengaged.
2 Employees shun positivity and look at everything with a pessimistic view.
3 What surrounds us is fear.
4 They lose their ability to make the right choices.
5 Employees lose the ability to look at having a long-term view of things. They want to survive the current problem somehow.
6 People are not able to think creatively – a much-needed trait during problem-solving.
7 They don't enjoy what they are doing, so you cannot expect the best outcome.
8 They try to speed up things, which impacts accuracy.
9 There is a tendency to multitask, which takes away focus on what needs to be done.
10 Cognitive abilities and the ability to think and deliberate are harmed.

But it's important to understand what are the things that trigger defensiveness.

The work of former McKinsey consultant and behavioural science expert Caroline Webb (2016), in her book *How to Have a Good Day* (Macmillan 2016), tells us that defensiveness can be triggered by any of the following instances:

1 **Inclusion**

   •   When a person feels excluded from something

2 **Fairness**

   •   When a person perceives that someone has been unfair to him
   •   When a person feels that he has done a lot but is not receiving anything in return

3 **Respect**

   •   When a person is belittled in public
   •   When a person feels that he has not received recognition due to him
   •   When a person feel he is not listened to

4   Security

- When an event takes away resources that a person requires
- When there are uncertainties
- When the person does not receive what was promised to him

5   Purpose

- When something appears to be a violation of a person's personal values
- When a person thinks that what he is doing does not align with a larger purpose

6   Autonomy

- When someone is ordered to do something over which he has no control
- When someone has been presented with a fait accompli

7   Rest

- When the person is feeling exhausted or is rest deficient

8   Competence

- When the person feels less confident about his competence
- When the person feels that he would fail due to a competency deficit

Knowing the triggers will help us to know the causes of defensiveness. It clearly tells us what behaviours and actions should be avoided to prevent the creation of a defensive environment. From my three decades' experience in leading various organisations and catalysing many transformations, I have distilled key behaviours that should be demonstrated in a company conscious about quality. They are summarised in Table 21.1. I call them the 15 behaviours of highly effective leaders. This includes quality professionals and all other leaders in the company.

These 15 things, when practised, will create a positive environment in the organisation that spurs all employees to perform and give their best. They will also help to create a problem-solving culture, a much-needed element of a quality-focussed company. This is not going to be easy and will require awareness, and leaders would need to practise these things day in and day out.

Defensiveness in the workplace manifests in various forms. Here is the listing of behaviours that you may see:

- Blaming others
- Feeling hurt
- Rationalising
- Being accountability averse or not taking accountability

Table 21.1 15 behaviours of highly effective quality leaders

1	They make sure employees are involved and included in various initiatives.
2	They demonstrate fairness and transparency in all interactions.
3	They treat people with respect irrespective of context, work level, religion, and affiliations.
4	They ensure employees are listened to. They listen more than speak.
5	They sense and respond to the insecurities and uncertainties of employees.
6	They establish connections between an individual's work and the strategic objectives of the firm.
7	They explicitly communicate to employees the business case for all change efforts and make an emotional connection with them.
8	They never tell employees to do something that contradicts the organisational values or the employee's personal values.
9	They ensure employees always feel confident about their competence.
10	They do stretch their employees but don't do it so hard that they are overworked and get too few breaks.
11	They don't try to be the smartest person in the room.
12	They hire people smarter than them.
13	They set a good example by practising what they preach.
14	They have a pulse on the emotions of the team.
15	They hold people accountable.

- Shifting focus and diverting attention
- Withdrawing from discussions
- Justifying
- Not participating
- Going ballistic and being offensive
- Trying to control the other person
- Being pessimistic
- Prematurely leaving or walking out
- Being non-committal about actions
- Ignoring suggestions and ideas
- Making the problem or issue seem much smaller than it actually is
- Apologies are not genuine
- Not willing to listen
- You hear phrases such as "There he/she goes again", "Here we go again"
- Public displays of anger
- Excuses
- Daydreaming (people shun reality and go to the world where things are a bed of roses)
- Repression (people protect their self-image by rejecting thoughts that are unpleasant or would cause guilt or shame)

None of these help in the pursuit of quality and continuous improvement. To illustrate this point, let me share with you examples from the world of quality and continuous improvement:

- A set of accountants were working in a finance centre of excellence. They had been entrusted with the responsibility of doing some financial reporting using the International Financial Reporting Standards (IFRS). The team leader came and sarcastically told one member who had been struggling with elements of the IFRS that he doubted his ability to qualify as an accountant. He further told him that he was aghast that he was not aware of some IFRS basics. The team leader made this observation in front of all the other members. This was quite insulting for this employee. When the employee got back to work a few minutes later, he was not only unable to concentrate but just wanted to leave that place. However, he got to work and somehow completed what he had to do. But the team leader found the next morning that the work was a mess. Not only were there gaps in the IFRS, there were also issues with other analysis he had done the previous day that lacked substance. In his mind, the worker could not reconcile with the fact that someone had questioned his competency. He also felt belittled by what his boss had said in front of everyone.
- A company embarked on a multi-year customer experience transformation. This effort was led by a core team that had representatives from all functions of the enterprise. The journey began and all the necessary alignment happened among the team members. However, the leader seemed to be interested in only ideas from three people who were highly communicative and were also assertive. As a result, the other members started feeling excluded. They thought that their ideas were not valued. So two things started to happen. These individuals remained quiet in the meetings. They spoke only when they were nudged hard. Also, when it came to taking up accountability for implementation, these individuals seemed less interested. They not only missed timelines but also blamed others when things did happen as scheduled. It was not that these employees were incompetent; their behaviour was a result of not being included by the leader.
- During a meeting to discuss a quality-improvement project taking place in a manufacturing plant, the project leader stated that the maintenance department had employees who talked a lot but delivered less. This put the participant, who was from the maintenance department, on the defensive. He went on the offensive in the next phase of the meeting to demonstrate his capability and even question the intention of other teams. As a result, this meeting got derailed and what had to be done that day did not get done. Here, the leader had questioned a department's competence, which put this person on the offensive. Here, offensiveness was a demonstration of his defensiveness.

- A quality manager was sharing information about a customer complaint with all the divisional heads of a food company. He said that he had discussed the problem with the CEO of the company. According to him, the CEO was quite upset with the root causes that seemed to have emerged. He then indirectly started pointing fingers at the production department. This put the production manager on the back foot. He seemed to have been presented with a fait accompli. He went ballistic and asked how the quality manager could say that it was the fault of the production department. The production manager started saying that these problems were not due to the production team but because of the carelessness of the quality team. The rest of the meeting was squandered on blaming each other. The meeting ended with no concrete conclusion or action around the customer complaint.
- A quality team at a bearing manufacturer was trying to do a root-cause analysis of a chronic issue faced by the company. Just before they began working on this problem, the CEO told the quality team that if they were not able to solve the problem, they could lose their jobs. This put the entire team in a state of panic. They quickly huddled together to brainstorm the potential causes. Their faces had turned pale and worried. The quality leader who led the effort seemed to be in a state of shock. Despite using the required problem-solving tools, the team could not come up with the probable causes of the problem. Most of the members were also in a state of shock. Some of them were heard murmuring that they would not like to stay in a company which treated its employees so badly. Despite spending two full days on the problem, the team could not come up with concrete root causes. So next time you think of making a team defensive before they embark on solving a problem, think again.
- Arun Sharma was the COO of a food manufacturing company. He was known for his no-nonsense attitude and drive for results. He had recently joined this company with a mandate to turn around the operations. The business had been incurring losses, sales were down, and employees seemed to have lost direction. The operations function had a major role to play in embedding efficiency and ensuring quality products were delivered on time to customers. When the COO came to meet them and asked for their insights on how the business could be turned around, the head of operations started blaming the sales department. He proclaimed that the sales team had been ineffective in driving up volumes. He also mentioned how the operations team had been blamed in the past for business failures. This was an example of defensive behaviour. Instead of contributing to the future, the head of operations kept demonstrating a negative attitude.

While embarking on a quality-improvement journey, leaders should keep an eye on defensive behaviours that are summarised in Table 21.2. Immediate steps must be taken to arrest such behaviours.

Table 21.2 Defensive behaviours (Warner 2014)

- Trying to be correct always	- Belittling inputs from employees	- Agreeing too much	- Intellec tualising	- Being very critical
- Being judgemental	- Bragging about one's knowledge	- Delaying	- Constantly Interrupting	- Being sarcastic
- Jumping to quick conclusions	- Not taking accountability	- Indulging in self-denial	- Rejecting views of others	- Pointing the finger at people
- Showing disinterest	- Providing wrong information	- Becoming confused	- Being silent	- Trying to be too soft while speaking
- Feeling angry	- Speaking too fast	- Fumbling while speaking	- Arms folded across body	- Being agitated
- Showing obsessiveness	- Not making eye contact	- Selective listening	- Blaming others	- Putting on a grim demeanour

A company that wants to be known for quality and innovation cannot allow defensiveness to prevail in the company. If left unchecked, it can corrode the company and build a culture in which blame and lack of accountability are a way of life. To make this happen, this has to start from the board and top management. So what are some of the things that should be kept in mind which can prevent this from happening? Here are some ideas:

- Create a psychologically safe workplace in which employees feel comfortable speaking up. We have already discussed this in Lesson: 17.
- Provide emotional intelligence training to the employees. Enable them to realise their own defences and the consequences of their behaviour.
- Recognise why people are defensive. Understand why people behave the way they do. This could be due to one of the reasons which we have discussed.
- Teach leaders how to effectively communicate with defensive employees.
- When problems arise, investigate the process and context. Never blame the person.
- Reassure people, particularly those who are defensive due to insecurities.
- When you see defensive behaviour, address it head on. Have a separate conversation with the person on this matter.
- Train employees how to control their emotions and defensiveness.

Lesson: 22

Blind optimism during eruptions

Putting out a vision for quality is not easy. But it's definitely easier than executing it.

The journey of embedding quality in an enterprise is not always going to go as planned. Despite all the positive intentions and hard work, there could be incidences which could break the confidence of the leadership team. These could happen in myriad forms, and leaders have to be mentally ready. I call these incidences quality eruptions, or events that can have a detrimental impact on customers in myriad ways. These could be through issues pertaining to product quality, service quality, product features, product safety, technology, leadership, employee behaviour, employee attrition, health hazards, data privacy, cybersecurity, regulatory non-compliance, etc. These issues, if not handled well, can not only cause major financial loss but also impact the company's reputation. They can also result in regulatory embargos, fines, and the closure of businesses. Most importantly, they can impact customer goodwill, which may be hard to get back.

Quality eruptions are broadly of two types:

External Quality Eruptions

These are events that happen outside the company that have a detrimental impact on the final product or service promised to the customer. Examples of external quality eruptions could include the following:

- Customers becoming ill after eating at a prestigious fine-dining establishment
- Rampant mis-selling of insurance products to customers by an insurance company
- Car recalls due to issues with vehicle acceleration
- Mobile phones catching fire
- Customers being shocked by refrigerators

DOI: 10.4324/9781003250517-23

Internal Quality Eruptions

These are events that happen inside the company which, if not managed well, can negatively impact the final product or service quality. Examples of internal quality eruptions include the following:

- An unexpected increase in employee attrition
- Machines producing quality defects
- Pathogen contamination in an ice cream manufacturing plant

The following are a few examples of quality eruptions:

- Between 2009 and 2011, Toyota Motor Company recalled vehicles from around the world because the cars experienced unintended acceleration.
- In 2015, Nestle had to recall Maggi noodles from the Indian market because government laboratories found lead in them.
- In 2017, Samsung was forced to withdraw its Galaxy Note 7 phones due to explosions.

Each of these are critical moments in which the CEO, top management, and quality leader must not only manage the crisis but also know how to work through it without giving up.

This is where knowing the Stockdale Paradox helps. The concept of the Stockdale Paradox was popularised by Jim Collins (2001) in his book *Good to Great: Why Some Companies Make the Leap . . . and Others Don't*, first published in 2001. James Bond Stockdale was a vice admiral in the US Navy and was a senior officer held captive during the Vietnam War. His Skyhawk jet was shot down in North Vietnam on 9 September 1965. His aircraft was badly damaged, and he parachuted to a small village, where he was severely beaten and taken as a prisoner. He spent the next 7½ years as an American prisoner of war in Hoa Lo prison. He was routinely tortured there, and no medical attention was given to the leg which was disfigured when he was captured. Surviving the 7½ years was not easy, but he found ways and means to get through it. For example, he created an innovative way to communicate with other fellow prisoners by tapping on the concrete wall and even found a way to send letters to his wife.

As he told Jim Collins in the book *Good to Great* when asked on how he managed to cope during these trying years:

I never lost faith in the end of the story, I never doubted not only that I would get out, but also that I would prevail in the end and turn the experience into the defining event of my life, which, in retrospect, I would not trade.

On being asked by Collins on who did not make it out of Vietnam, Stockdale replied,

> Oh, that's easy, the optimists. Oh, they were the ones who said, "We're going to be out by Christmas". And Christmas would come, and Christmas would go. Then they'd say, "We're going to be out by Easter". And Easter would come, and Easter would go. And then Thanksgiving, and then it would be Christmas again. And they died of a broken heart.

Admiral Stockdale further added,

> This is a very important lesson. You must never confuse faith that you will prevail in the end – which you can never afford to lose – with the discipline to confront the most brutal facts of your current reality, whatever they might be.

How does this relate to a quality eruption?

Well, when there is a major quality problem, the CEO, entire top management, and even the quality leader should know how to survive this crisis. The first thing is that they have to shun pessimism. Despite all the efforts towards getting things back on the rails, if the leaders don't have psychological fortitude, they will find it difficult to come out of the crisis.

Even blind optimism will not work. That is the belief that we have used the right resources and strategies to get things back in shape, and things will happen within the planned dates. This may not work, because your planned vision for things may take more time than you had envisaged. If you fail to meet these deadlines a couple of times, you can get disillusioned and give up. Plus, there could be other issues that you may have to confront. What happens with optimism is that we set our sights on the outcomes and tend to overlook the current realities.

Optimism meets pragmatism

What really works is when optimism is laced with reality. This means, on the one hand, having a vision for the future, when things will get back on the rails and things will be normal. And on the other hand, be ready to brace for the days ahead when one could be hit with many after-effects of the quality eruptions, which could be things such as media outcry, court cases, warranty claims, regulatory audits, public scrutiny, and so on. Clearly, one must prepare oneself for an immediate future that could be arduous and know that the problem's resolution may take more time than envisaged. While this happens, never lose faith that at the end of the day, the problem will get resolved.

> ### Stockdale Paradox
>
> 1 Have a deep faith that you will be successful at the end and will come out of the quality eruption at the end.
> 2 Be ready to face the brutal facts due to the current reality.

It also means having the fanatical discipline to confront the brutal facts on a day-to-day basis. When an organisation is faced with a quality eruption of the magnitude we are talking about, it is suddenly inundated with myriad issues. This occurs as the organisation is scrutinised, and things that may have gone unnoticed previously come to light. Smaller issues also tend to be exaggerated. Fanatical discipline means working on a set number of issues every day until the problem is resolved. It means avoiding an approach wherein you work on 10 issues one day, and the next day, you don't do anything. It means having a regime for working towards resolving a fixed number of issues every day until the quality eruption is under control and you have won back the confidence of the customers. Don't try to be the hare. You need to have the unwavering faith of the tortoise so that, with consistent and focussed intensity, the quality issues are resolved.

When you confront the current adverse reality, you make realistic assessments of what's happening and then allocate resources to better face the challenge as it hits you. In the Stockdale Paradox, you adopt both positive (having faith that you will prevail at the end) and negative (accepting the brutal facts about the current reality) elements.

What this means to business is that it would be myopic to get carried away by the sunny and positive sides of an effort. What is also required is to understand the challenges of the now. It is accepting the negative associated with the current state while being positive about the future state.

The Stockdale Paradox can also be used to resolve chronic issues faced by a company. A company may have a great vision for the future, but it has to be ready to face the current realities. The following are some of the things that need to be done to balance optimism with reality in case of an external quality eruption.

The sunny aspects

- Craft a vision of the aspiration state that is being targeted to come out of the quality eruption.
- Communicate the vision to the entire organisation.
- Create a plan of action to achieve the vision.
- Create a detailed action plan to put the strategies into action.
- Ensure all relevant people are involved and held accountable for the execution.
- Form a task force and group of change leaders to work on this.
- Implement a strong communication strategy for both employees and the outside world.

The brutal reality

- Communicate transparently to all that the road forward is not going to be easy and there could be tough days ahead.
- Start planning for warranty claims, returns, and recalls.
- Prepare for the financial impact and how it will affect the business's profitability.
- Manage the company's reputation and what may appear in the media.
- Face the press and even disgruntled customers to confront the issue at hand.
- Be prepared to apologise to everyone who was affected by the quality eruption.
- Use strict discipline to review progress on a regular basis, ensuring that even minor issues are addressed.
- Be prepared for the possibility that a few things will not go as planned, and you may miss previously set deadlines.

The leaders of the organisation should have the patience, the mental fortitude, and the drive to go through the pain of resolving the current issues while forging ahead to achieve the vision.

It's critical that throughout the process, the CEO and top management should not lose faith and should make sure the employees don't lose faith. As they work on the eruption, they should realise that there are pains they will need to confront

The recipe for addressing a major quality problem comprises having faith that the problem will be resolved, along with confronting the unpalatable facts of the current situation.

Lessons from survival psychology

Research work done by John Leach, a survival psychologist, provides interesting insights into surviving a crisis. According to him, the reason some are not able to survive a crisis is that they develop extreme apathy, give up hope, and relinquish the will to live, and die, despite the lack of obvious physical causes. This is also called give-up-itis.

There are five stages to give-up-itis. It begins with social withdrawal, followed by a stage of profound apathy. In the third stage, the person loses his willpower and ability to act decisively. In the fourth stage, the person no longer feels pain, thirst, or hunger. The fifth and last stage is just before death when a person seems to have had a miraculous recovery when some goal-directed behaviour returns, but the goal itself becomes the relinquishing of life (Leach 2018). In the case of a quality eruption, the last two stages may not happen, but if you see the first three symptoms of social withdrawal, apathy, and not being able to act decisively, it indicates giving up and not being willing to fight the crisis.

John Leach (1994) makes interesting observations on adaptation:

> During the period of adaptation there is a slight initial decomposition of a victim's psychology. There is a breaking of the links of his previously learned behaviour. Once broken, the survivor's behaviour can be adapted and rebuilt to better fit the new environment. Initially, there is a natural reluctance to believe that the old environment has been torn away during the period of impact and consequently denial, crying, anger, and weakness are frequent reactions. The period of recoil follows, which is a further breakdown in the psychological bonds shown by despair, grief, depression, and so on. Only once the victim is through this period can new survival behaviours be developed.

Boris Groysberg and Robin Abrahams (2020) of Harvard Business School say:

> Adaptation is breaking and unlearning, followed by consolidation, during which the new circumstances – though they may be unwanted and hostile – are accepted as "real", and the survivor begins to function again.

Clearly, the Stockdale Paradox resonates with the research of John Leach (2011), who found that people who survive disasters are able to regain cognitive function quickly after the event, assess their new environment accurately, and take goal-directed action to survive within it.

Lesson: 23

Communicating visually

Visual communication is a critical element of a quality-improvement journey. We use it for communicating, engaging, evoking emotions, and making people take relevant actions.

In a world where the attention spans of people are getting shorter, it becomes extremely important to make sure what we put up for consumption is easily understood and people are able to take the required action.

The human brain processes information in images. It takes time to read and comprehend a paragraph. The characters in written text must be recognised and pieced together into words, then sentences – all before being processed for meaning (Savikhin 2013). Instead, a single image can convey the same information within a short time. It encapsulates many words in one image. After all, our brain processes visual images 60,000 times faster than text (3M Research 1997). And let's not forget that 90% of the information transmitted to the brain is visual. Researchers at MIT have found that the human brain can process entire images that the eye sees for as little as 13 milliseconds (Trafton 2014).

A Xerox study found it could increase attention span and recall by 82% (Xerox Whitepaper 2017). Another Quicksprout report found that content with relevant images gets 94% more views (The Ultimate Guide to Creating Visually Appealing Content 2021).

Practitioners of Lean Manufacturing emphasise the role visual management plays in its adoption. In a digital world, visual communication can take many forms, such as workplace visual boards, videos, posters, infographics, data visualisation, comics, photographs, screenshots, etc.

However, those involved in quality improvement need to know the finer nuances of visual communication and the psychology behind it.

Here are a few things that you need to keep in mind:

Make it contextual

What is very important in visual communication is to make the message contextual. This means it should relate to the people who are reading it and their day-to-day work. So if you are making a post for a credit card back office, don't

DOI: 10.4324/9781003250517-24

give examples or even images that are from a manufacturing shop floor. You have to make sure the image represents credit card operations, and the words/language should match those used by the credit card operations team. To make it happen, you first profile the audience, the language they understand, and their current workplace challenges. Your goal should be to link the visual communication to their day-to-day trials and tribulations in the language that they understand. Language has two dimensions. On one hand, it should be in the lingua franca of the company. On the other hand, it should use the technical terms relevant to that type of operation.

Let it be jargon free

Any message that you design should be bereft of jargon. It should be easy to understand so that the audience easily understands it without much thought. Don't clutter it with information. Let the key messages stand out. In psychology, there is something called "cognitive ease". It is the ease with which information gets processed in one's mind. Cognitive ease decides how positive or negative we feel about it. When information is difficult to process, people may not feel good about it and not adopt it for the required purpose. Too much information builds distrust and apathy towards the topic in which you are trying to engage them. It can result in people reverting to the status quo (The Chemistry of Communication 2016).

Hence, if you are putting up a visual communication for quality improvement, keep the following in mind:

- Limit the number of words.
- Use images. This will help the audience to process the information better.
- Use active voice over passive voice.
- Use easy-to-read fonts.
- Avoid cluttering the page with data and complex diagrams.

Use pictures

The need for images and pictures in visual communication has been mentioned. But as it is said, a picture is sometimes equal to a thousand words.

In psychology, there is something called the picture superiority effect. According to this, we tend to remember pictures and images more than words. McBride and Dosher (2002) found that "picture stimuli" embeds into memory twice, as both verbal code and an image. Words only generate a verbal code. Whatever image you use should be relevant to the context. The pictures should be such that they can viscerally connect with the employees. Don't use photos which have already been used. Authentic imagery taps into the passions and emotions of your audience by letting them see something of themselves, turning them into advocates of the story you're trying to tell (Newscred and Getty Images 2014).

Use character-based storytelling

Storytelling can be a powerful tool in visual communication. One of the approaches that I have found very effective is using charter-based storytelling. I know of a company which used a character called Qualix to communicate important messages of quality. Every week, there would be a comic-like, emotion-laden story on the company intranet where Qualix would do something or be a part of some act that would conclude with an important principle about quality. When the internal quality team did a survey with its employees, they all said that they looked forward to Qualix stories every week and found them more effective than bland messages being proclaimed by leaders of the enterprise.

Let it stand out

It's not easy to get the attention of the audience to your visual communication. This is where the principle of the distinctiveness effect can come handy. According to Waddill and McDaniel (1998), unusual information is generally recalled more readily than common information. While preparing visual communication for quality, include some image or data which gets the attention of employees. This has to be fairly unique so that the employees don't miss it (The Power of Visual Communication 2017).

For example, when communicating the importance of Six Sigma, companies use this information (see Figure 23.1), which gets the attention of the employees.

The other example is from an infant food company, which wanted to communicate the importance of hand washing to the workmen in the food processing plant. To share this, they created a poster of a small child in a hospital for having consumed contaminated milk.

Why 99.99% quality is not enough

- 119,760 income tax returns will be processed incorrectly this year.
- 144 incorrect medical procedures occur daily.
- 18 babies will be given to the wrong parents each day.
- 20,000 incorrect drug prescriptions will be written in the next 12 months.
- 56,700 checks will be deducted from the wrong bank accounts in the next hour.
- 567 pacemaker operations will be performed incorrectly this year.
- 69 malfunctioning ATMs will be installed in the next 12 months.

Figure 23.1 When 99% quality is not enough

Another example is that of a mobile phone company showing a picture of a mobile phone that has caught fire due to faulty circuitry.

However, it is critical to constantly redesign these visual communications, because they can cause fatigue and reduce employee engagement if the same ones are used over and over.

Involve the employees

To get traction with visual communication, let employees design it. When they are part of it, they will have a much greater sense of ownership. This is the reason that in Lean manufacturing, the workplace visual board is populated by employees. So if you are planning to create a poster, a video, an infographic, etc., reach out to the employees to see who would like to be a part of it. For example, if you are putting together an infographic on problem-solving and your employees don't have the wherewithal to design it, don't stop. Seek their advice on the content. Let them poke holes in it. Allow them to provide creative direction. However, if there are employees who can design the infographic, urge them to create prototypes that are then put before the rest of the organisation for their input. You can ask them to vote or just hold a meeting to discuss what needs to be changed.

Power of space

While preparing visual communication, don't use too many colours. Use contrast to highlight the content that is important. This is where we need to keep in mind the power of space in any design. By space, I mean the space between letters, images, figures, etc.

In psychology, there is a phenomenon called the isolation effect or the von Restorff effect. The study found that when participants were presented with a list of categorically similar items with one distinctive, isolated item on the list, memory of the item was improved (von Restorff 1933). So, if you examine a shopping list with one item highlighted in bright red, you are more likely to remember the highlighted item than any of the others. Similarly, in a list of words – pen, paper, pencil, table, gorilla, books, notebook, routine – gorilla will be remembered the most because it stands out against the other words in its meaning. We tend to remember things that are either placed in isolation or placed next to an alternative.

When we first see a visual communication design, we tend to make sense of the figure and the background. Important information should stand out from its environment. Hence, it's always good to keep a lot of empty space. By space I mean white space between figures/pictures and images in a design. When there is space, it gives your eye the freedom to navigate the content easily. It also increases legibility and readability. Space makes visual communication clutter free and easier to comprehend. It also helps to hold the attention of the readers as they navigate between pictures and words.

I use this principle in PowerPoint presentations. I let there be a lot of empty space in the background and use images in vibrant red.

Let space create contrast that guides the viewer's eye to what you want them to see.

Lesson: 24

Not-so-obvious tactics for solving problems

Problem-solving is an integral part of all business organisations. Companies spend a lot of money building capabilities in this domain. They put in place elements that help to build and sustain it – capability development, top management support, coaching, a structured approach, communication, rewards and recognition, performance management, and so on.

We have referred to problem-solving across the chapters in the book. In Lesson: 12, we looked at biases that need to be kept in mind.

However, beyond all these, there are things that are often not discussed but make a quiet contribution to enhancing the problem-solving capability of a team. The reason these don't get discussed is because people are not aware of them or don't consider them important. Here are five things that, when implemented properly, promote problem-solving.

Learn to get distracted

Problem-solving can be an intellectually draining exercise. Have we not seen instances when, despite all the focus on a problem, we are not able to get insights? We seem to be stuck, and the problem-solving effort does not seem to be moving anywhere. This is where distraction helps.

When your focus is on a single problem, your conscious mind is working on it. However, when you take a break and focus on completely unrelated matters, the unconscious mind continues to work on the primary issue even without your realising it. Later, when you retrain your attention to the problem, you are often surprised by your own fresh insights.

So, why does it happen? The answer lies in "incubation theory". What really happens is that when you take your focus off the problem and work on something completely unrelated, the mind is less constricted, and it finds associations which are often inaccessible when you are concentrating on that problem. Distraction also enhances your mood. So if you were feeling low during the problem-solving process, it helps to get back your mojo.

DOI: 10.4324/9781003250517-25

Hence, if you are solving problems, I recommend taking regular breaks and doing something completely different, whether it's watching a movie or going for a walk or creating a painting.

Keep an eye on team size

The size of the team involved in a problem-solving effort is critical. In our endeavour to be inclusive, we tend to put together a large team – which sometimes becomes a liability. A few years back, I was amazed to see a problem-solving team with 18 people. There was so much confusion. Not only did the project get delayed, but there were many differences among the team members.

When you think about team size for problem-solving, keep in mind the following.

The first one is Brook's Law, enunciated by Fred Brook in his 1975 book *The Mythical Man Month*. Brook's Law says, "Adding manpower to a late software project makes it later". So, avoid adding manpower.

The second is from Lawrence Putnam (Putnam and Myers 2003), another legendary figure in software development, who studied 491 projects at a large number of companies. He found that teams of three to seven people required 25% of the effort of groups of nine to twenty. Clearly, once the team size grew larger than eight people, it took a very long time to get things done.

The third is that you need to keep an eye on the communication channels in a project team. To find this, use the formula $n(n-1)/2$. So if your project team has six people, it has 15 channels. Similarly, an eight-person team will have 28 channels, and one with nine people will have 36!

A team is supposed to be a cohesive group in which each member needs to know what the other is doing. So if the number of channels is too big, it's a problem. Hence, my recommendation is that a core team for problem-solving should be small – ideally it should be seven plus/minus two (7 +/−2) (Sarkar 2021).

Walk as you work

If you are thinking about aligning with a senior leader or with a set of four to five people, try a walking meeting. The fresh air and sunlight energise the participants, improve their thinking, and boost their creativity. The best part of these meetings is that they are focussed, since people are walking so they tend to keep their answers shorter. Since the people walk together, it eliminates hierarchy which helps to remove potential hesitation. This, together with the outdoor environment, makes people relaxed and freer to discuss issues and challenges. I personally find these walking meetings to be great for aligning with senior leaders, helping to break down barriers, or bouncing around potential solutions. By the way, walking meetings were a favourite of Steve Jobs.

It matters how you sit down to discuss problems

Problem-solving is not a one-person job. It's best executed by a cross-functional team that works cohesively. A key but silent enabler for collaboration is how teams hold their meetings. For example, when people sit at right angles, it does not provide an opportunity for members to interact with each other. When teams sit in two rows facing each other, it creates an "us versus them" mindset. When teams sit in a row, the people in the centre tend to dominate and take more credit, while those at the end feel neglected. Instead, when teams sit in circles, it fosters collaboration, and members feel a greater sense of belonging. The beauty about circular seating is that since everyone sits at the same level and there is no head table, it eliminates hierarchy. They are more engaged and involved in the discussions and not afraid to speak their mind or issue challenges – which is essential for a problem-solving exercise.

The power of green

Greenery can work wonders for the creativity of a team. Research done by Dr Roger Ulrich found that people who work among live plants and flowers generate 15% more ideas (University Research Indicates Flowers and Plants Promote Innovation, Ideas 2021). Don't worry – you don't need to invest too much in this. Simply placing plants and flower pots in the workplace does the trick. It mimics a natural environment, and this enhances creativity and generates better problem-solving.

By the way, I have tried all of these and have seen a positive impact.

Taking employees on board

A successful quality journey requires the participation of employees. We have seen instances of quality-improvement efforts being launched with great fanfare, but they don't seem to get the required traction. One reason is that the employees aren't on board. They may show some interest in the beginning, but that slowly fades. The result is that quality improvement becomes the agenda of the quality leader, who runs around like a solitary reaper trying to push his agenda forward. We all know that a quality-improvement effort has to be owned by the entire enterprise. Everyone has to participate in it. The role of a quality leader is more like a catalyst. Quality has to be owned by line leaders. The delivery of the outcomes pertaining to quality needs to happen through these leaders and their team.

Quality professionals often struggle to get employees on board. To accomplish this, the quality leader requires influencing skills and political competence. The latter is about having a keen sense of who is with him on the journey and who is not, and taking proactive steps to address their concerns so that they join him. While leadership skills do play an important role here, there are lessons from psychology and behavioural economics which can come handy. Let's look at them.

Make them feel confident

Even if employees want to be a part of a quality journey, they hesitate because they do not know how to act. They don't have the required skills to catalyse or lead quality projects. It worries them that without the required capability, they could fail, and this may result in their looking bad in front of others. This is where you have to go all out to support them with relevant skills and train them on quality tools and techniques. This by itself may not be sufficient. You have to also assure them that you will handhold them in the initial days. You will also have to create a sort of help desk where they can reach out whenever they have queries. Your goal should be to guide them and make sure they can complete at least one quality project. This should give them sufficient confidence to take the agenda forward. When employees feel they will be supported in a quality journey, they will willingly participate.

DOI: 10.4324/9781003250517-26

Share what success looks like

Employees also don't come aboard a quality-improvement rollout because they are not clear on what it can deliver. When something is abstract, it becomes very difficult for human beings to go for it. This makes them indecisive, and they are unsure of the way forward. There are instances when quality programmes are conceptualised, but we don't do a good job of explaining to the employees what would be the outcome. Employees would like to know what good results look like and what types of benefits they can expect from the programme. There could also be conflict in their minds that the time and effort that they invest should not be squandered. They also have the fear of failure and the resulting shame and embarrassment. Failure, they believe, will impact their identity and put a question mark on their competence. Hence, it becomes important to share success stories with them. Talk about companies that have adopted quality practices and the benefits that they have reaped. Take them to visit a factory or an organisation where they can see the changes for themselves. Have them talk to the people at these companies. Let them see for themselves what quality can deliver. In particular, get them exposed to the impacts that these companies have reaped and how employees come on board. If visits are not possible, let them go through articles which talk about such successes. Another way could be to have them attend forums where professionals meet and discuss quality, how to embark, the associated trials and tribulations, pitfalls to be careful of, and the benefits that can be expected. All these are examples of social proof, where people tend to follow what others are doing. It removes their doubts and reinforces that the choice that they are going to make (quality improvement in this case) is the right thing to do.

Show them what to do and how to do it

Quite like monkeys, we humans like copying and aping what others do. When a child is growing up, we have seen how they copy the behaviours and actions of those around them. Let's talk about yoga here. For those who have not been initiated into yoga, it can be almost impossible to copy those complicated fitness postures and poses, pictures of which we may have seen somewhere. We want to do it but find it almost impossible. However, when someone demonstrates it to us step by step, the same posture that appeared almost impossible now appears doable. This is an example of learning by watching others do it. Eminent psychologist Albert Bandura (1977) called this phenomenon "observational learning". We learn by observing others. This consists of learning by observing and modelling what others do with respect to their behaviours and attitudes. Of course, the pre-requisites to make it happen are attention, retention, reproduction, and motivation. Through observational learning, even complicated stuff appears easy and doable. As a part of introducing quality practices to an enterprise and taking them on board, it's important to create a pilot location with the help of employees so that they can see for themselves what it takes to make things happen. Many things can be done here. For example, if you are introducing Lean thinking to an enterprise, it's a good idea to do a few "Lean Breakthrough" or "Kaizen Blitz" projects wherein a group of people not exposed to Lean can be brought together for five days and made to experience the steps required for Lean transformation (Sarkar 2016). They get to see for themselves how to go about Lean improvements. The other example is before rolling out an enterprisewide quality-improvement transformation, just create mini pilots with the help of employees.

This will not only teach the steps to the employees, but will also demonstrate to the company the promise and power of quality improvements.

Also, use videos or even YouTube channels to give a step-by-step rundown on what it takes to implement a quality-improvement programme. What is required here is to break the complexities into bite-sized steps so that employees understand and realise that they too can be a part of it. It's not as difficult as they think.

Make them see the future

In certain types of quality efforts, improvements may not be visible immediately. You have to do a lot of foundational work before benefits start to become visible. Take the example of business excellence models. You cannot expect to see the benefits immediately, and the challenge for the quality leader is what he does to get these employees and even the top management on board. The benefits don't come immediately, and it's hard to envision the future or the end state that may occur as a result of adoption of a quality approach. The reason employees have a reluctance to come on board in such cases is because the future is unclear. As we discussed in Lesson: 1, we humans tend to give less importance to something that will happen in the distant future. We tend to choose short-term gratification over long-term rewards (Dawnay and Shah 2005). When they are uncertain about the future, they either don't want to make a decision or they want to delay it. As a result, they don't come on board.

Hence, it becomes imperative to create a larger purpose which people want to be a part of. For example, my consulting firm was hired by a leading multilateral financial institution to enhance the team-effectiveness of their finance and budgeting functions. This was a multi-cultural team that was low on energy, highly siloed, and members kept quiet in the meetings. As a part of our assignment, we did a myriad of things, which included gathering their voices, understanding the workplace challenges, rolling out employee engagement initiatives, embedding new ways of working, and changing the behaviours of the leadership team. However, what accelerated the process and got employees on board, was that we worked with the team and put together a vision for the future. After a lot of deliberation and global benchmarking, the team came up with a vision to build a "world-class finance function". They also listed the 10 attributes of a world-class finance function, which included things such as knowledge work, digital tools, decision-making, client experience, metrics, controls, and talent. They also established how the work of each employee impacts the final outcome. They then embarked to make it happen. When engagement levels were measured every month, it was heartening to see the steep upward trend. This was a great example where a larger purpose had helped to take employees aboard an improvement journey. Employees are willing to be participants in an organisation's improvement journey if we involve them and they see a role in making a meaningful contribution to it.

Coax them to come out of the present

Another reason employees don't come on board is because they have a feeling that quality improvement is something that can wait. This is especially true when the benefits of a quality rollout are expected in the distant future. In psychology, there is a phenomenon called present bias. We discussed this briefly in Lesson: 1 and Lesson: 8. This is the tendency to overvalue the current instead of valuing the long term. When we have to choose between something that has an immediate benefit versus something that has a benefit in the future, we choose the former. For example, a person may prefer $20 today over receiving $30 tomorrow. So, when an employee has to choose between what he is doing now versus a quality-improvement programme whose benefit may be seen only in the long term, people tend to stay with the former. We somehow undermine the long term and go for what's in hand or on the horizon. Actually, there is no sense of urgency for a person to come on board, and he tends to defer the decision. What also happens here is that since the future is not concrete but the current is very visible and certain, he avoids joining a quality-improvement programme. After all, no human likes uncertainty, and there is no sense of urgency to come on board.

So, what should a quality leader do? He has to create a sense of urgency which pushes the employees to join the cause. There are many ways to do this. It could be through a burning-platform approach (also discussed briefly in Lesson: 8), in which employees are told that if they don't get involved in quality improvements, it could impact the survival of the company and hence their livelihood. But as Christina Gravert, a behavioural economist at the University of Copenhagen, mentioned in *The Financial Times,* getting people to fear something in order to change behaviour can only work in the very short term. It can be very exhausting to maintain in the long term, as it's an emotion (Hill 2021).

The other approach could be to let employees meet aggrieved customers and see for themselves why customers are unhappy and why there is a need to embark on quality improvement. It could also be exposing employees to bad news about the company, its product, its poor performance, its processes, or how customers experience the brand. We normally don't expose employees to bad news, thinking that they may not be able to handle it, and this may result in demotivation, employee exodus, or even a bad name for the company. However, if this bad news can be used constructively, it can galvanise the entire enterprise to come on board a quality-improvement programme. We have learned from John Kotter (2009) that creating a sense of urgency is a must in any form of change. As Constantinos Markides of London Business School mentioned in Andrew Hill's column in *The Financial Times*: "To create a more 'permanent sense of urgency,' chief executives should make the need for change positive and personal, and encourage their staff to feel emotionally committed to the necessary transformation". Not surprisingly, companies such as Toyota (Osono, Shimizu, and Takeuchi 2008) always let there be a sense of urgency to improve quality even if they already make world-class products. This is to make sure employees don't become complacent.

Create a context for FOMO

FOMO, or fear of missing out, is a psychological phenomenon in which a person has this feeling that others are experiencing something important and meaningful which he is missing out on. This uneasy feeling makes you think that others are doing something that is better than you or possessing something valuable which you don't have. This happens when you compare your life with those around you or those who matter in your life. In the case of a business organisation, this could be your colleagues in the company. In the workplace, FOMO can lead to dissatisfaction and employees feeling that they have been excluded from something they would like to be a part of. However, FOMO can be used intelligently to increase adoption of quality in a company.

So how do you create that context where employees have a feeling of FOMO as far as quality improvement is concerned? When beginning a quality journey, select a handful of individuals who are positive, change ready, can influence, and are always willing to try out new things. Take them through a structured 100-day programme wherein they understand the fundamentals of quality improvement by going through classroom sessions followed by hands-on work. These selected individuals would work on separate projects that focus on organisational issues that the company is facing. The quality leader has to make sure that teams work with each of these projects and they become successful. On completion of the projects, let these selected change leaders graduate as "certified quality catalysts" or "certified continuous-improvement champions" or whatever you may like to call them. What's critical here is to make sure that the projects are scoped in such a way that they can be completed within 90 to 100 days and also that the change leaders are supported very well as they execute the projects. After around 90 to 100 days, when the projects are done, hold an event to share the impact and let the CEO or someone from top management recognise these people through certificates. Once the projects are successful, those sponsoring them will become converts. Also, when other employees see the impact and then the subsequent recognition, they too will like to be a part of it. Their FOMO here can be used to take them on board. Other people would like to do similar projects, and that's where you will see them come on board in a quality journey. The mantra here is to select a few potential change leaders, help them to successfully complete a quality project, let the results speak for themselves, and have recognition around them.

I have successfully used this approach a couple of times with my clients, especially when they are starting their improvement journeys.

Make it resonate with what they value

When an insurance company embarked on an enterprisewide deployment of workplace organisation using the principles of 5S, there was a lot of resistance. This was because the quality leader pitched it as "workplace housekeeping". Many of the employees who were from leading business schools felt that an initiative around housekeeping was not what they had been hired for. They had gone to leading schools and universities to add value to the company and its performance, not for housekeeping. They felt that was the job of the housekeepers and the facilities team. Little did they know that 5S is a Japanese philosophy not just for workplace organisation but for enhancing workplace productivity and efficiency that has an impact on organisational performance (Sarkar 2006).

Then a consultant was brought in, and he suggested that it should be pitched in a way that appealed to the sense of identity of the employees. He suggested sharing the same 5S deployment effort as an initiative to enhance "workplace performance". He told the quality leader to emphasise that it was a simple approach that each person in the company could contribute to making the company better. He then linked the outcome of the rollout with customer response times, employee productivity, process lead times, and document retrieval times. The impact of this repositioning was such that many business leaders wanted to be a part of this programme. Now it appealed to their sense of identity (they were there to add value to the company and not do cleaning). It also resonated with what they all valued, which was workplace performance, because they saw metrics such as productivity, customer response times, etc. being positively impacted. Clearly tying quality-improvement efforts with individual or team identity and also what's of value to them can help in getting traction.

Make quality learning a default choice

Pushing quality on employees does not work. Instead, create an environment in which they willingly adopt practices that facilitate quality improvement. However, I recommend that as a part of the overall learning plan of each employee, make a few modules of quality a default option. The module should talk about the power of quality and how it positively impacts business performance. The module should talk about the promise of quality and how employees can contribute to its success.

The module could be delivered via e-learning/web-based learning or as a brief classroom session. This module should not be mandated, but it should be the default option, such that if the employee does not make a choice, he goes through the module. A default option is an option an individual gets if he does nothing. It is a pre-set course of action that goes into effect if nothing is specified by the decision-maker. As a result, a large number of people end up with that option, irrespective of whether they like it. For example, in certain countries, organ donation is an opt-out approach to organ donation called presumed consent. This means that if people don't want to donate their organs, they have to opt out. This has resulted in higher donation rates. We tend to opt for the path of least resistance, and hence highly favour the default option (World Economic Forum White Paper 2018). This pre-defined option will be followed by us until we change it.

What the default option does is provide an effective nudge when inertia and laziness guide choices. Default is one of the key elements of the choice architecture proposed by Richard Thaler, Cass R. Sunstein, and John P. Balz (2010). Choice architecture is about designing the context in such a way that people make decisions.

So in our case, when discussing the learning plan of an employee, let the module on quality be a default option. It will not be removed from the training list of an employee until he asks for it. This will ensure that a large population of employees will get an opportunity to get exposed to how quality enables business performance. Clearly, this can be a trigger for creating interest in quality improvements.

Make it hassle free

One important principle that psychology teaches us is that if you want people to do something, make it easy for them. Remove all the impediments that will prevent people from adopting the direction that you are proposing. Why do you think many of us love using Amazon? It's because of its one-click feature. A shopper does not need to manually add his billing and shipping information every time. Once he puts it on the Amazon website, it stays for good. So next time a shopper goes there, he does not have any hassle. With a single click, he had bought what he wanted.

This same principle has to be kept in mind while embarking on a quality journey. Make it easy for all employees to come on board. Go all out to remove friction. Here are some of the things that can be done to remove friction:

- Set up a help desk where employees can go with any questions about quality improvement.

- In the early stages of the quality journey, use quality practices (such as QC tools) that are easy to understand and produce good results.
- Be ready to provide mentoring support to those who want to explore the subject.
- Make information easily accessible. Give access to forums such as ASQ. com so that employees can explore the work of quality sitting at their desks.
- Adopt one problem–solving approach for the company.
- Persuade upper management to make quality a strategic priority.
- When someone expresses an interest in being a part of the quality projects, make sure their bosses are on board and willing to give them the time they need.

About the author

Debashis Sarkar is an educator and management consultant who believes behavioural science will play a critical role in business improvement efforts going forward.

He is the founder and managing partner of Proliferator Advisory & Consulting, which specialises in customer centricity, operational excellence, and workplace effectiveness. The firm has impacted clients in Asia, Africa, the Middle East, and Europe.

A quality-improvement pioneer, he is credited with having introduced Lean Management to service organisations in Asia in the early 2000s. He conceptualised the world's first blueprint for 5S implementation for service organisations. He successfully implemented this at ICICI Bank between 2003 and 2007. He also developed the world's first holistic approach for building a Lean service enterprise. He has also conceptualised improvement tools and tactics, which can be found in his books. He is currently focussed on applying behavioural science to business improvement and creating knowledge at their intersection.

He is the author of multiple books, which include *Little Big Things in Operational Excellence* (Sage, 2021), *How Can I Help You* (Penguin Random House, 2013), and *Lessons in Lean Management* (Amazon Westland, 2012).

He is invited the world over for keynotes, conferences, and workshops.

He is also a much-sought-after mentor for the C-suite and start-up founders.

A Fellow of the American Society for Quality, he has been awarded the Phil Crosby Medal in 2014 and the Simon Collier Award in 2020. He is also the recipient of the First Quality Champion Award in 2019 from the Quality Council of India – the highest award for quality given by the Indian government.

For more visit: https://debashissarkar.com or follow him on 🐦: @debashissarkar.

Bibliography

Adams, Sam. *War of Numbers: An Intelligence Memoir of the Vietnam War's Uncounted Enemy.* Lebanon, NH: Truth to Power, 2020.

"Amazon's Sixteen Leadership Principals". *Leadership Principals.* https://www.amazon.jobs/en/principles. Last Accessed: November 4, 2021.

Amrit, B. L. S. "Economic Survey Bats for Mixing Behavioural Economics, Indian Myth and Political Messaging". *The Wire*, 2019. https://thewire.in/economy/behavioural-economics-bjp-eocnomic-survey. Last Accessed: October 24, 2021.

Angier, N. "Blind to Change, Even as It Stares Us in the Face". *The New York Times*, April 1, 2008. www.nytimes.com/2008/04/01/science/01angi.html. Last Accessed: July 25, 2022.

Anzil, Fredrico. "Goodhart's Law". *Economicpoint.com.* https://economicpoint.com/goodharts-law. Last Accessed: July 26, 2021.

Arkes, H. R., & Blumer, C. "The Psychology of Sunk Costs". *Organizational Behavior and Human Decision Processes*, 35 (1985), 124–140.

Aronson, E., Willerman, B., & Floyd, J. "The Effect of a Pratfall on Increasing Interpersonal Appeal". *Psychonomic Science*, 69 (1966).

Bakshi, Sanjay. "Heard of Cobra Effect". *Economic Times*, 2017. https://economictimes.indiatimes.com/markets/stocks/news/heard-of-cobra-effect-be-careful-what-you-ask-for/articleshow/60866402.cms?from=mdr. Last Accessed: July 26, 2021.

Bandura, Albert, *Social Learning Theory.* Englewood Cliffs, NJ: Prentice Hall, 1977.

Basford, Tessa, & Schainger, Bill. "The Four Building Blocks of Change". *McKinsey Quarterly*, April 2016.

Beauchamp, Zack. "Jaren Kushner, Peter Navarro and Our Epidemic of Overconfidence". *vox.com*, April 7, 2020. https://www.vox.com/2020/4/7/21210282/coronavirus-trump-jared-kushner-peter-navarro-dunning-kruger. Last Accessed: October 25, 2021.

Berger, Warren. "Beyond a Company That Questions Everything". *Harvard Business Review*, April 30, 2014.

Berger, Warren. "The Power of 'Why?' and 'What If?'". *The New York Times*, July 2, 2016.

Best, Joel. "How to Lie with Coronavirus Statistics: Campbell's Law and Measuring the Effects of COVID-19". *Numeracy*, 14, no. 1 (2021), Article 6. https://doi.org/10.5038/1936-4660.14.1.1378.

Borness, Cate. "The Fearless Organization: Creating Psychological Safety in Workplace for Learning, Innovation and Growth". *Deloitte Insights.* https://www2.deloitte.com/au/en/blog/diversity-inclusion-blog/2019/fearless-organisation-creating-psychological-safety-in-workplace-for-learning-innovation-growth.html. Last Accessed: July 26, 2021.

"Brahma, Vishnu, Shiva". *Factsanddetails.com*. https://factsanddetails.com/world/cat55/sub354/item1353.html. Last Accessed: October 26, 2021.

Brendel, David. "Asking Open-Ended Questions Helps New Managers to Build Trust". *Harvard Business Review*, September 15, 2015.

Brooks, Alison Wood, Gino, Francesca, & Schweitzer, Maurice E. "Smart People Ask for (My) Advice: Seeking Advice Boosts Perceptions of Competence". *Management Science*, 61, no. 6 (June 2015), 1421–1435.

Brooks, F. P., Jr. *The Mythical Man-Month: Essays on Software Engineering*. Boston, MA: Addison-Wesley, (1975) 1995.

Buss, Dale. "CEO Guidelines for Speaking Out On Controversial Issues". *Chief Executive*, 2018. https://chiefexecutive.net/ceo-guidelines-controversial-issues/3/. Last Accessed: July 26, 2021.

Campbell, Donald T. "Assessing the Impact of Planned Social Change". *Evaluation and Program Planning*, 2, no. 1 (1979): 67–90.

Cardon, Nicolas, & Bribiescas, Francisco. "Respect For People: The Forgotten Principle in Lean Manufacturing Implementation". *European Scientific Journal*, 11, no. 13 (May 2015). ISSN:1857-7881 (Print); ISSN:1857-7431.

"The Carlyle Group Partners with Former Domino's CEO Patrick Doyle". *Globenweswire.com*. www.globenewswire.com/news-release/2019/09/04/1910667/0/en/The-Carlyle-Group-Partners-with-Former-Domino-s-CEO-Patrick-Doyle.html. Last Accessed: July 26, 2021.

Cassano, Jay. "The Science of Why You Should Spend Your Money on Experiences, Not Things". *Fast Company*, March 30, 2015. www.fastcompany.com/3043858/the-science-of-why-you-should-spend-your-money-on-experiences-not-thing.

Chabris, Christopher, & Simons, Daniel. *The Invisible Gorilla, and Other Ways Our Intuitions Deceive Us* (1st ed.). New York: Harmony, May 18, 2010.

The Chemistry of Communication. *PWC White Paper*, February 2016. www.pwc.com.au/pdf/2016-pwcs-creative-comms-the-chemistry-of-communication.pdf. Last Accessed: July 26, 2021.

Cherry, Kendra. "How Multitasking Affects Productivity and Brain Health". *Verywellmind.com*., 2021. www.verywellmind.com/multitasking-2795003. Last Accessed: July 26, 2021.

Cialdini, Robert. *Influence. The Psychology of Persuasion*. New York, NY: William Morrow e Company, 1984.

Cialdini, Robert. *Influence: Science and Practice*. Boston: Allyn and Bacon, 2008.

Collins, Jim. *Good to Great: Why Some Companies Make the Leap . . . And Others Don't*. New York: Harper Business, 2001.

Conner, Daryl R., *Managing at the Speed of Change: How Resilient Managers Succeed and Prosper Where Others Fail*. Toronto: Random House, 1993.

Courtney, Susan M., Petit, Laurent, Haxby, James V., & Ungerleider, Leslie G. "The Role of Prefrontal Cortex in Working Memory: Examining the Contents of Consciousness". *Philosophical Transaction of Royal: Society B, Royal Society Publishing*, 353 (1998), 1819–1828.

Coutu, Diana. *Leadership Lessons from Abraham Lincoln*. Boston: Harvard Business Review, April 2009.

Covey, Stephen, Merrill, A. Roger, & Merrill, Rebecca R. *First Things First: To Live, to Love, to Learn, to Leave a Legacy*. New York: Simon and Schuster, 1994.

Crockett, Zachary. "When Targets and Metrics Are Bad for Business". *The Hustle*, 2019. https://thehustle.co/Goodharts-Law. Last Accessed: July 26, 2021.

Csikszentmihalyi, Mihaly. *Flow: The Psychology of Optimal Experience*, 1990. https://www.researchgate.net/publication/224927532_Flow_The_Psychology_of_Optimal_Experience.

Csikszentmihalyi, Mihaly. *Finding Flow: The Psychology of Engagement with Everyday Life*. The Masterminds Series. New York: Basic Books, 1997.

Cukier, Kenneth, & Mayer-Schonberger, Viktor. "The Dictatorship of Data", *MIT Technology Review,* May 2013.

Daniel, J. *Siegel Mind: A Journey to the Heart of Being Human*. Norton Series on Interpersonal Neurobiology. New York: W.W. Norton & Co., 2016.

Dave, Sandeep. "Even Brahma, Vishnu, Mahesh Want You to Innovate: Check How!". *The RobinHoods.com.*, 2016. https://therodinhoods.com/post/even-brahma-vishnu-mahesh-want-you-to-innovate-check-how/. Last Accessed: July 26, 2021.

Dawnay, Emma, & Shah, Hetan. *Behavioural Economics: Seven Principles for Policy Makers*. London: New Economics Foundation, July 2005. www.neweconomics.org

Day, Matt, "Amazon Adds New Leadership Principles Days Before Jeff Bezos Steps Down", *Time,* July 1, 2021.

Delizonna, Laura. "High-Performing Teams Need Psychological Safety: Here's How to Create It". *Harvard Business Review*, August 2017.

Devega, Chauncey. "Our Dunning Kruger President: Trump's Arrogance and Ignorance Killing People". *Salon*, 2020. www.salon.com/2020/04/02/our-dunning-kruger-president-trumps-arrogance-and-ignorance-are-killing-people/. Last Accessed: July 26, 2021.

Doctor, Vikram. "Catchy Acronyms & Their Masters: How PM Modi Communicates". *The Times of India, Mumbai*, March 16, 2019.

Doll, Karen. *What Is Peak-End Theory? A Psychologist Explains How Our Memory Fools Us*, 2020. https://positivepsychology.com/what-is-peak-end-theory/. Last Accessed: July 26, 2021.

Dreyfuss, Emily. "Want to Make a Lie Seem True? Say It Again and Again and Again". *Wired.com.*, November, 2017. https://www.wired.com/2017/02/dont-believe-lies-just-people-repeat/. Last Accessed: October 25, 2021.

Duhigg, Charles. "What Google Learned From Its Quest to Build the Perfect Team". *The New York Times Magazine*, February 25, 2016.

Duica, Stefania. "Psychological Safety and Team Cohesions". *Todaysoftmag.com.*, 2019 www.todaysoftmag.com/article/1818/psychological-safety-and-team-cohesion. Last Accessed: July 26, 2021.

Dunning, David, "We Are All Confident Idiots". *Pacific Standard,* October 27, 2014. https://psmag.com/social-justice/confident-idiots-92793#.qhzfjntf7. Last Accessed: October 25, 2021.

Dunning, D., Johnson, K., Ehrlinger, J., & Kruger, J. "Why People Fail to Recognize Their Own Incompetence". *Current Directions in Psychological Science*, 12, no. 3 (2003): 83–87.

Easterlin, R. A. "Does Economic Growth Improve the Human Lot? Some Empirical Evidence (PDF)". In Paul A. David & Melvin W. Reder (Eds.), *Nations and Households in Economic Growth: Essays in Honor of Moses Abramovitz*. New York: Academic Press Inc., 1974.

Edmondson, A. "Psychological Safety and Learning Behavior in Work Teams". *Administrative Science Quarterly*, 44, no. 2 (1999), 350–383.

Edmondson, A. "Speaking up in the Operating Room: How Team Leaders Promote Learning in Interdisciplinary Action Team". *Journal of Management Studies*, 40, no. 6 (September 2003): 1419–1452.

Edmondson, Amy. "What Psychological Safety Not". *Quartz.com*. https://qz.com/work/1470164/what-is-psychological-safety/. Last Accessed: July 26, 2021.

Edmondson, A. C. *The Fearless Organisation: Creating Psychological Safety in the Workplace for Learning, Innovation, and Growth*. Hoboken, NJ: John Wiley & Sons, 2018.

Edmondson, A. C., Kramer, R. M., & Cook, K. S. "Psychological Safety, Trust, and Learning in Organizations: A Group-Level Lens". *Trust and Distrust in Organizations: Dilemmas and Approaches*, 12 (2004), 239–272.

Edmondson, Amy C., & Lei, Zhike. "Psychological Safety: The History, Renaissance, and Future of an Interpersonal Construct". *The Annual Review of Organizational Psychology and Organisational Behaviour*, 1, no. (2014), 23–43.

Ekman, Paul. *Emotions Revealed: Recognizing Faces and Feelings to Improve Communication and Emotional Life* (2nd ed.), Holt Paperbacks. New York, NY: Henry Holt and Co, March 20, 2007.

Elliot, A. J., & Friedman, R. "Approach-Avoidance: A Central Characteristic of Personal Goals". In B. R. Little, K. Salmela-Aro, & S. D. Phillips (Eds.), *Personal Project Pursuit: Goals, Actions, and Human Flourishing* (pp. 97–118). Mahwah, NJ: Lawrence Erlbaum Associates Publishers, 2007.

Elliot, A. J., Sheldon, K. M., & Church, Marcy A. "Avoidance Achievement Motivation: A Personal Goals Analysis". *Journal of Personality and Social Psychology*, 73 (1997), 171–185.

Eze, Patrick Ndubuisi. *Managing Emotions in Project Teams*. Thesis Towards Completion of MS in Project Management & Operational Development, KTH Royal Institute of Technology Industrial Engineering and Management, Sweden, 2017.

Federal Aviation Administration (FAA). *FAA Human Factors Awareness Course*. www.hf.faa.gov/webtraining/Intro/Intro1.htm. Last Accessed: September 6, 2012.

Fehlhaber, Kate. "Why a Bank Robber Thought of Covering Himself in Lemon Juice Would Help Him Get Away with It". *Quartz.com*., 2017. https://qz.com/986221/what-know-it-alls-dont-know-or-the-illusion-of-competence/. Last Accessed: July 26, 2021.

Fernam Street Blog. *Confirmation Bias and Power of Disconfirming Evidence*, 2021. https://fs.blog/2017/05/confirmation-bias/. Last Accessed: July 26, 2021.

Festinger, L., Schachter, S., & Back, K. "The Spatial Ecology of Group Formation". In L. Festinger, S. Schachter, & K. Back (Eds.), *Social Pressure in Informal Groups* (Chapter 4). Stanford, CA: Stanford University Press, 1950.

Frijda, Nico H. *The Law of Emotion* (1st ed.). New York: Psychology Press / Routledge, 2006.

Frimpong, A. Jemima, Myers, Christopher G., Sutcliffe, Kathleen M., & Lu-Myers, Yemeng. "When Healthcare Providers Look at Problems from Multiple Perspectives". *Harvard Business Review*, June 13, 2017.

Gächter, S., Orzen, H., Renner, E., & Starmer, C. "Are Experimental Economists Prone to Framing Effects? A Natural Field Experiment". *Journal of Economic Behavior & Organization*, 70 (2009), 443–446.

Gates, Bill. *The Road Ahead*. New York: Viking, 1995.

Gilovich, T. *How We Know What Isn't so: The Fallibility of Human Reason in Everyday Life*. New York: The Free Press, 1991. ISBN:0-02-911706-2. Summary.

Gilovich, T., Griffin, D. W., & Kahneman, D. (Eds.). *Heuristics and Biases: The Psychology of Intuitive Judgment*. New York: Cambridge University Press, 2002. ISBN:0-521-79679-2.

Gilovich, T., Keltner, D., & Nisbett, R. E. *Social Psychology*. New York: W.W. Norton, 2015. ISBN:0-393-97875-3.

Gilovich, Thomas, Kumar, Amit, & Jampol, Lily. "A Wonderful Life: Experiential Consumption and the Pursuit of Happiness". *Journal of Consumer Psychology* (2014). http://dx.doi.org/10.1016/j.jcps.2014.08.004

Gilovich, T., & Ross, L. *The Wisest One in the Room: How You Can Benefit from Social Psychology's Most Powerful Insights.* New York: Simon & Schuster, 2015. ISBN:978-1-4516-7754-6.

Goleman, D. *Emotional Intelligence: Why It Can Matter More Than IQ.* London: Bloomsbury Publishing Plc, 1995. ISBN:0-7475-2830-6.

Goleman, D., Boyatzis, R., & Mckee, A. *Primal Leadership: Learning to Lead with Emotional Intelligence.* Boston, MA: Harvard Business School Press, 2002.

Goldstein, D. G., & Gigerenzer, G. "Models of Ecological Rationality: The Recognition Heuristic". *Psychological Review,* 109, no. 1 (2002), 75–90.

Goldstein, Noah, Martin, Steve J., & Cialdini, Robert. *Yes! 50 Secrets from Science of Persuasion.* London and Great Britain: Profile Books, 2007.

Goodhart, C. A. E. "Problems of Monetary Management: The U.K. Experience". In *Papers in Monetary Economics* (Vol. I). Sydney: Reserve Bank of Australia, 1975.

Goodhart, C. A. E. "Problems of Monetary Management: The UK Experience". In *Monetary Theory and Practice.* London: Palgrave Macmillan, 1984.

Goodhart, C. A. E., & Crockett, A. D. "The Importance of Money". *Bank of England Quarterly Bulletin,* 10 (June 1970).

Green, Kevin, & Katie, Williamson. *Behavioural Change for Nature: A Behavioral Science Toolkit for Practitioners.* Rare, VA: Centre for Behavior and Environment, 2019.

Green, M. "Inattentional Blindness' and Conspicuity". *Visual Expert,* 2004. www.visualexpert.com/Resources/inattentionalblindness.html. Last Accessed July 25, 2021.

Grissinger, Matthew. "'Inattentional Blindness': What Captures Your Attention?". *P & T: A Peer-Reviewed Journal for Formulary Management,* 37, no. 10 (2012), 542–555.

Groysberg, Boris, & Abrahams, Robin. "What Stockdale Paradox Tells Us About Crisis Leadership". *Harvard Business School Working Knowledge,* Aug 17, 2020. https://hbswk.hbs.edu/item/what-the-stockdale-paradox-tells-us-about-crisis-leadership. Last Accessed: October 31, 2021.

Guszcza, James. "From Groupthink to Collective Intelligence: A Conversation with Cass Sunstein". *Deloitte Review,* 17 (2015).

He, Alison. "The Dunning-Kruger Effect: Why Incompetence Begets Confidence". *New York Times,* 2020. www.nytimes.com/2020/05/07/learning/the-dunning-kruger-effect-why-incompetence-begets-confidence.html. Last Accessed: July 26, 2021.

Hick, W. E. "On the Rate of Gain of Information (PDF)". *Quarterly Journal of Experimental Psychology,* 4, no. 1 (March 1, 1952): 11–26. doi:10.1080/17470215208416600.

Hill, Andrew. "It's Time to Extinguish the 'Burning Platform' for Good". *Financial Times,* June 8, 2021.

Hollingworth, Crawford, & Barker, Liz. "How to Debias Your Organisation". *Whitepaper from the Behavioural Architects,* 2020. https://www.thebearchitects.com/assets/uploads/ip/TBA%20Articles/How%20to%20Debias%20Your%20Organisation_C.pdf. Last Accessed: November 2, 2021.

Hood, Anthony C., Bachrach, Daniel G., Zivnuska, Suzanne, & Bendoly, Elliot. "Mediating Effects of Psychological Safety in the Relationship Between Team Affectivity and Transactive Memory Systems". *Journal of Organisational Behaviour,* 37, no. 3 (April 2016).

Husar, M. "Corporate Culture: Toyota's Secret, Competitive Advantage". *General Motors Internal Paper* (1991), 10–11.

Hyman, R. "Stimulus Information as a Determinant of Reaction Time". *Journal of Experimental Psychology*, 45, no. 3 (March 1953), 188–196. doi:10.1037/h0056940. PMID 13052851.

Indian Government's Economic Survey 2018–19, July 4, 2019. https://www.indiabudget.gov.in/budget2019-20/economicsurvey/doc/echapter.pdf.

Janis, I. L. *Victims of Groupthink: A Psychological Study of Foreign Policy Decisions and Fiascos'*. Boston: Houghton Mifflin, 1972. ISBN:0-395-14002-1.

Jhangiani, Rajiv, & Tarry, Hammong. *Principles of Social Psychology – 1st International Edition*. British Columbia, Canada: BCampus Open Education, 2014.

Johnson, E. J., & Goldstein, D. G. "Do Defaults Save Lives?" *Science*, 302 (2003), 1338–1339.

Jordan, Jennifer, & Sorell, Michael. "Why You Should Create a 'Shadow Board' of Younger Employees". *Harvard Business Review*, June 4, 2019.

Kahneman, D. "Maps of Bounded Rationality: Psychology for Behavioral Economics". *The American Economic Review*, 93 (2003), 1449–1475.

Kahneman, D. *Thinking, Fast and Slow*. New York: Macmillan, October 2011.

Kahneman, Daniel, Fredrickson, Barbara L., Schreiber, Charles A., & Redelmeier, Donald A. "When More Pain Is Preferred to Less: Adding a Better End". *Psychological Science,* 4, no. 6 (1993): 401–405.

Kahneman, D., & Frederick, S. "Representativeness Revisited: Attribute Substitution in Intuitive Judgment". In T. Gilovich, D. Griffin, & D. Kahneman (Eds.), *Heuristics of Intuitive Judgment: Extensions and Applications* (pp. 49–81). New York: Cambridge University Press, 2002.

Kahneman, D., & Lovallo, D. "Timid Choices and Bold Forecasts: A Cognitive Perspective on Risk Taking". *Management Science*, 39, no. 1 (1993), 17–31.

Kahneman, D., & Tversky, A. "Intuitive Prediction: Biases and Corrective Procedures". *TIMS, Studies in Management Science*, 12 (1979a), 313–327.

Kahneman, D., & Tversky, A. "Prospect Theory: An Analysis of Decision Under Risk". *Econometrica*, 47 (1979b), 263–291.

Kaplan, Robert, & Norton, David. *The Balanced Scorecard: Translating Strategy Into Action*. Boston: HBR Press, 1996.

King, J., & Slovic, P. "The Affect Heuristic in Early Judgments of Product Innovations". *Journal of Consumer Behaviour*, 13, no. 6 (2014), 411–428.

Klein, Sarah. "Norepinephrine: The Three Major Stress Hormones, Explained". *Huffington Post,* 2013. www.huffpost.com/entry/adrenaline-cortisol-stress-hormones_n_3112800. Last Accessed: July 26, 2021.

Kotter, John P. "Four Ways to Increase the Urgency Needed for Change". *Harvard Business Review*, April 15, 2009.

Kruger, J., & Dunning, D. "Unskilled and Unaware of It: How Difficulties in Recognizing One's Own Incompetence Lead to Inflated Self-Assessments". *Journal of Personality & Social Psychology*, 77, no. 6 (December 1999), 1121–1134.

Kruger, J., Wirtz, D., Van Boven, L., & Altermatt, T. W. "The Effort Heuristic". *Journal of Experimental Social Psychology*, 40, no. 1 (2004), 91–98.

Laundry, Lauren. "Why Emotional Intelligence in Important in Leadership". *Harvard Business School Online*, April 3, 2019. https://online.hbs.edu/blog/post/emotional-intelligence-in-leadership.

Leach John, *Survival Psychology*. New York: Palgrave Macmillan, 1994.

Leach John, "Survival Psychology: They Won't to Live". *The Psychologist,* 24 (January 2011). https://thepsychologist.bps.org.uk/volume-24/edition-1/survival-psychology-wont-live. Last Accessed: October 30, 2021.

Leach, John, "Give-Up-Itis: When People Just Give Up and Die". *TheConversation.com,* September 27, 2018. https://theconversation.com/give-up-itis-when-people-just-give-up-and-die-103727. Last Accessed: October 30, 2021.

LeDoux, J. "Rethinking the Emotional Brain". *Neuron,* 73, no. 4 (February 23, 2012), 633–676. https://pubmed.ncbi.nlm.nih.gov/22365542/. Last Accessed: July 26, 2021.

Lindgaard, G., & Dudek, C. *High Appeal Versus High Usability: Implications for User Satisfaction.* HF2002 Human Factors Conference, Melbourne, Australia, November 25–27, 2002.

Ludwig, Peter. "Objectivity's Blind-Spot: The Dunning-Kruger Effect". *Procractrination. com.,* 2021. https://procrastination.com/blog/31/objectivity-dunning-kruger-effect. Last Accessed: July 26, 2021.

Mahony, S. O. "Medicine and McNamara Fallacy". *Journal of Royal College of Medicines of Edinburgh,* 47, no. 3 (September 2017), 281–287.

Margolin, Emma, "Make America Great Again – Who Said It First?" *nbcnews.com,* September 9, 2016. https://www.nbcnews.com/politics/2016-election/make-america-great-again-who-said-it-first-n645716. Last Accessed: October 24, 2021.

Marsh, L. E., Kanngiesser, P., & Hood, B. "When and How Does Labour Lead to Love? The Ontogeny and Mechanisms of the IKEA Effect". *Cognition,* 170 (2018), 245–253.

Maurer, Robert. *One Small Step Can Change Your Life: The Kaizen Way.* New York: Workman Publishing Company; First Printing Edition, April 22, 2014.

Maze, Jonathan. "How Patrick Doyle Changed Domino's, and the Restaurant Industry". *Restaurantbusinessline.com.,* 2018. www.restaurantbusinessonline.com/leadership/how-patrick-doyle-changed-dominos-restaurant-industry. Last Accessed: July 26, 2021.

McBride, D. M., & Dosher, B. A. "A Comparison of Conscious and Automatic Memory Processes for Picture and Word Stimuli: A Process Dissociation Analysis". *Consciousness and Cognition,* 11 (2002), 423–460.

McGrath, Jane. "5 Failed McDonald's Menu Items". *howstuffworks.com,* 2008. https://money.howstuffworks.com/5-failed-mcdonalds-menu-items.htm#pt4. Last Accessed: October 25, 2021.

McKenzie, C. R., Liersch, M. J., & Finkelstein, S. R. "Recommendations Implicit in Policy Defaults". *Psychological Science,* 17, no. 5 (2006), 414–420.

Medhat, Sa'ad. "Is Your Business on a Burning Platform?" *Brite Innovation Review,* 2019. https://brite.nridigital.com/brite_spring19/is_your_business_on_a_burning_platform. Last Accessed: November 3, 2021.

Meyer, R. "Google's New Product Puts Peer Pressure to a Sunny Use". *The Atlantic,* June 12, 2017. www.theatlantic.com/technology/archive/2017/06/googles-new-product-puts-peer-pressure-to-a-sunny-use/529974/. Last Accessed: July 26, 2021.

Monahan, Kelly, Murphy, Timothy, & Johnson, Marcus. "Harmonizing Change: Developing More Effective Change Management Strategies". *Deloitte Review,* no. 19, 2016.

Moradzadeh, Linda, Bluementhal, Galit, & Wiseheart, Melody. "Musical Training, Bilingualism, and Executive Function: A Closer Look at Task Switching and Dual-Task Performance". *Cognitive Science,* 39, no. 5 (October 2014).

Morris, Jessica. *The Growing Problem of Treatment Waiting Times,* 2018. www.nuffieldtrust.org.uk/news-item/the-growing-problem-of-treatment-waiting-times. Last Accessed: July 26, 2021.

Mortimer, Gary, Mathmann, Frank, & Grimmer, Louisse. "The IKEA Effect: How We Value the Fruits of Our Labour Over Instant Gratification". *The Conversation, Australian Edition*, April 18, 2019.

Moses, John. "Get Action Instead of Indifference: Using Behavioral Economics Insights to Deliver Benefits Messages". *Benefits Quarterly*, third quarter (2013).

Mullainathan, Sendhil, & Thaler, Richard H., *Behavioral Economics*. MIT Department of Economics Working Paper No. 00–27, September 2000. SSRN. https://ssrn.com/abstract=245828 or http://dx.doi.org/10.2139/ssrn.245828.

Murali Shankarnarayanan Profile. 2019. https://nasscomhrsummit2019.sched.com/speaker/murali_shankarnarayanan.1zqngxk5. Last Accessed: July 26, 2021.

Nadler, A., Ellis, S., & Bar, I. "To Seek or not to Seek: The Relationship Between Help Seeking and Job Performance Evaluations as Moderated by Task-Relevant Expertise". *Journal of Applied Social Psychology*, 33, no. 1 (2003), 91–109. https://doi.org/10.1111/j.1559-1816.2003.tb02075.x. Last Accessed: July 26, 2021.

Neil, D. *What Is Flight or Fight Response*. www.thebodysoulconnection.com/Education-Center/fight.html. Last Accessed: July 26, 2021.

Newscred and Getty Images. "The Power of Visual Storytelling 4 Principles". 2014. https://view.ceros.com/newscred/the-four-principles/p/1. Last Accessed: October 30, 2021.

Norton, Michael I., Mochon, Daniel, & Ariely, Dan. "The IKEA Effect: When Labor Leads to Love". *Journal of Consumer Psychology*, 22, no. 3 (July 2012): 453–460.

O'Donoghue, Ted, & Rabin, Matthew. "Doing It Now or Later". *American Economic Review*, 89, no. (1) (1999), 103–124.

OECD. Tools and Ethics for Applied Behavioural Insights. *The Basic Toolkit*, 2019. www.oecd.org/gov/regulatory-policy/BASIC-Toolkit-web.pdf. Last Accessed: July 26, 2021.

Ophir, Eyal, Nass, Clifford, & Wagner, Anthony D. "Cognitive Control in Media Multitaskers". *Proceedings of the National Academy of Sciences*, 106 (2009): 15583–15587.

Oppland Mike. "8 Ways to Create Flow". *PositivePsychology.com*. https://positivepsychology.com/mihaly-csikszentmihalyis-flow/. Last Accessed: July 26, 2021.

Osman, M. et al. "Learning Lessons: How to Practice Nudging Around the World". *Journal of Risk Research* (2018), 1–9. http:/dx.doi.org/10.1080/13669877.2018.1517127.2018.

Osono, Emi, Shimizu, Norihiko, & Takeuchi, Hirotaka. *Extreme Toyota*. Hoboken, NJ: Wiley, 2008.

Patrick, V. M., Chun, H. H., & MacInnis, D. J. "Affective Forecasting and Self-Control: Why Anticipating Pride Wins Over Anticipating Shame in a Self- Regulation Context". *Journal of Consumer Psychology*, 19, no. 3 (2009), 537–545.

Perrigo, Billy. "Get Brexit Done: The 3 Words That Helped Boris Johnson Win Britain's 2019 Election". *Time*, 2020. https://time.com/5749478/get-brexit-done-slogan-uk-election/. Last Accessed: July 26, 2021.

Petter, Olivia. "Multitasking Inhibits Productivity, Research Claims". *The Independent*, March 13, 2018.

Philip, Lijee, & Vijayraghavan, Kala. "Mahindra Group Follows Management Practice of Shadow Boards". *The Economic Times,* July 15, 2015. https://economictimes.indiatimes.com/news/company/corporate-trends/mahindra-group-follows-management-practice-of-shadow-boards/articleshow/6169552.cms. Last Accessed: November 4, 2021.

Plumer, B. "Solar Power Is Contagious: Installing Panels Often Means Your Neighbors Will Too". *Vox*, April 1, 2015. www.vox.com/2014/10/24/7059995/solar-power-is-contagious-neighbor-effects-panels-installation. Last Accessed: July 25, 2021.

Plutchik, Robert. "The Nature of Emotions". *American Scientist*, 89, no. 4 (July–August 2001), 344–350. www.jstor.org/stable/27857503?seq=1%25252523page_scan_tab_contents. Last Accessed: July 26, 2021.

Poundstone, William. *Head in the Cloud*. New York: Little, Brown, Spark, June 2017.

The Power of Visual Communication. *PWC White Paper*, April 2017. www.pwc.com.au/the-difference/the-power-of-visual-communication-apr17.pdf. Last Accessed: July 26, 2021.

Putnam, L., & Myers, W. *Five Core Metrics: The Intelligence Behind Successful Software Management*. New York, NY: Dorset House, 2003.

3M Research. "Polishing Your Presentation". *3M Meeting Network*, 1997. https://web.archive.org/web/20001102203936/http%3A//3m.com/meetingnetwork/files/meeting guide_pres.pdf, Last Accessed: October 30, 2021.

Resnick, Brian. "An Expert on Human Blind Spots Gives Advice on How to Think". *Vox.com*, June 26, 2019. www.vox.com/science-and-health/2019/1/31/18200497/dunning-kruger-effect-explained-trump.

Robson, David. "Constantly Late with Work – Blame Planning Fallacy". *BBC.com*, November 16, 2019. www.bbc.com/worklife/article/20191104-constantly-late-with-work-blame-the-planning-fallacy. Last Accessed: July 26, 2021.

Rodamar, Jeffery, "There Ought To Be a Law! Campbell Versus Goodhart". *significance magazine.com*, December 2018.

Rosenzweig, P. *The Halo Effect: . . . and the Eight Other Business Delusions That Deceive Managers*. New York: Free Press, 2007 (2009).

Rubinstein, J. S., Meyer, D. E., & Evans, J. E. "Executive Control of Cognitive Process in Task Switching". *The Journal of Experimental Psychology: Human Perception and Performance*, 27, no. 4 (August 2001), 763–797.

Samson, A. "A Simple Change That Could Help Everyone Drink Less". *Psychology Today*, February 25, 2014. www.psychologytoday.com/blog/consumed/201402/simple-change-could-help-everyone-drink-less. Last Accessed: July 25, 2021.

Samson, A., & Ramani, P. "Finding the Right Nudge for Your Clients". *Investment News*, August 27, 2018. www.investmentnews.com/article/20180827/BLOG09/180829939/finding-the-right-nudge-for-your-clients. Last Accessed: July 25, 2021.

Sarkar, Debashis. *5S for Service Organizations and Offices – A Lean Look at Improvements*. Milwaukee: ASQ Press, 2006. ISBN: 978-0-87389-677-1.

Sarkar, Debashis. *Lean for Service Organizations and Offices: A Holistic Approach for Achieving Operational Excellence and Improvements*. Milwaukee: ASQ Press, 2007. ISBN-13: 978-0873897242.

Sarkar, Debashis. *Building a Lean Service Organisation – Reflections of a Lean Management Practitioner*. New York: Productivity Press, 2016. ISBN:9781498779593.

Sarkar, Debashis. *The Little Big Things in Operational Excellence*. New York: Sage Publications. September 2021. ISBN:9789354790065.

Sarstedt, M., Neubert, D., & Barth, K. "The IKEA Effect: A Conceptual Replication". *Journal of Marketing Behavior*, 2, no. 4 (2017), 307–312.

Savikhin, Anya C. "The Application of Visual Analytics to Financial Decision-Making and Risk Management: Notes from Behavioural Economics". *Financial Analysis and Risk Management* (2013), 99–114.

Schindler, S., & Pfattheicher, S. "The Frame of the Game: Loss-Framing Increases Dishonest Behavior". *Journal of Experimental Social Psychology*, 69 (2017), 172–177.

Shah, A. K., & Oppenheimer, D. M. "Heuristics Made Easy: An Effort-Reduction Framework". *Psychological Bulletin*, 134, no. 2 (2008), 207–222.

Shapiro, Aaron. "The Next Big Thing in Design? Less Choice". *The FastCompany*, April 4, 2015.

Shiv, Baba, & Fedorikhin, Alexander. "Spontaneous Versus Controlled Influences of Stimulus-Based Affect on Choice Behavior". *Organizational Behavior and Human Decision Processes*, 87 (2002): 342–370. http://dx.doi.org/10.1006/obhd.2001.2977.

Siebert, Horst. *Der Kobra-Effekt: Wie man Irrwege der Wirtschaftspolitik vermeidet (in German)*. Munich: Deutsche Verlags-Anstalt, 2001. ISBN:3-421-05562-9.

Sloane, Paul. *The Leader's Guide to Lateral Thinking Skills: Unlocking the Creativity & Innovation in You and Your Team* (2nd ed.). London: Kogan Page, September 3, 2006.

Sloane, Paul. *How to be a Brilliant Thinker: Exercise Your Mind and Find Creative Solutions* (1st ed.). London: Kogan Page, January 3, 2010.

Slovic, P., & Corrigan, B. *Behavioral Problems of Adhering to a Decision Policy*. Talk Presented at The Institute for Quantitative Research in Finance, Napa, CA, May 1, 1973.

Slovic, P., Finucane, M. L., Peters, E., & MacGregor, D. G. "The Affect Heuristic". In T. Gilovich, D. Griffin, & D. Kahneman (Eds.), *Heuristics and Biases: The Psychology of Intuitive Judgment* (pp. 397–420). New York: Cambridge University Press, 2002.

Smith, Emily Esfahani. "Your Flaws Are Probably More Attractive Than You Think They Are". *The Atlantic*, January 9, 2019.

Sunstein, C., & Hastie, Reid. *Wiser: Getting Beyond Groupthink the Make Groups Smarter* (pp. 44–45). Boston: Harvard Business Review Press, 2015.

Sutton, Robert, & Rao, Huggy. *Scaling Up Excellence*. New York: Random House, 2014.

Sweis, B. M., Abram, S. V., Schmidt, B. J., Seeland, K. D., MacDonald, A. W., Thomas, M. J., & Redish, A. D. "Sensitivity to 'Sunk Costs' in Mice, Rats, and Humans". *Science*, 361, no. 6398 (2018), 178–181.

Taylor, Bill. "How Domino's Pizza Reinvented Itself". *Harvard Business Review*, November 28, 2016. https://hbr.org/2016/11/how-dominos-pizza-reinvented-itself. Last Accessed: July 27, 2021.

TED Talk. *Mihaly Csikszentmihalyi – Flow*, 2004. www.ted.com/talks/mihaly_csikszentmihalyi_flow_the_secret_to_happiness?language=en. Last Accessed: July 26, 2021.

Thaler, Richard, *Misbehaving: The Making of Behavioral Economics*. New York: W. W. Norton & Company, May 2015.

Thaler, Richard H., & Sunstein, Cass R. *Nudge: Improving Decisions About Health, Wealth, and Happiness*. New Haven: Yale University Press, April 2008.

Thaler, Richard H., Sunstein, Cass R., & Balz, John P. "Choice Architecture", April 2, 2010. SSRN: https://ssrn.com/abstract=1583509 or http://dx.doi.org/10.2139/ssrn.1583509

Times of India News Item. "Take Road to Growth: Shun ABCD Culture". *Times of India*, December 30, 2014. https://timesofindia.indiatimes.com/business/india-business/Take-ROAD-to-growth-shun-ABCD-culture-Modi/articleshow/45683269.cms. Last Accessed: October 24, 2021.

Trafton, Anne. "In the Blink of an Eye". *MIT News*, 2014. https://news.mit.edu/2014/in-the-blink-of-an-eye-0116. Last Accessed: July 26, 2021.

Turner, J. R., & Müller, R. "Co-Operation on Projects Between the Project Owner as Principal and the Project Manager as Agent". *European Management Journal*, 22, no. 3 (2004), 327–336.

"The Ultimate Guide to Creating Visually Appealing Content". *Quicksprout.com. Blog.* www.quicksprout.com/the-ultimate-guide-to-creating-visually-appealing-content/. Last Accessed: July 26, 2021.

"University Research Indicates Flowers and Plants Promote Innovation, Ideas", based on study by Ulrich, Roger S., & Varni, James. "The Impact of Flowers and Plants on Workplace Productivity". https://greenplantsforgreenbuildings.org/wp-content/uploads/2015/01/TAMUresearch.pdf. Last Accessed: November 1, 2021.

von Restorff, Hedwig. "Über die Wirkung von Bereichsbildungen im Spurenfeld" [The Effects of Field Formation in the Trace Field]. *Psychologische Forschung* [*Psychological Research*] (in German), 18, no. 1 (1933), 299–342. doi:10.1007/BF02409636.

Waddill, P., & McDaniel, M. "Distinctiveness Effects in Recall". *Memory and Cognition*, 26, no. 1 (1998), 108–120. http://link.springer.com/article/10.3758/ BF03211374. Last Accessed: November 2, 2016.

Wang, M., Rieger, M. O., & Hens, T. "The Impact of Culture on Loss Aversion". *Journal of Behavioral Decision Making*, 30, no. 2 (2017), 270–281.

Warner, Jon. *Dealing with Defensive Employee Behaviour.* 2014. http://blog.readytomanage.com/dealing-with-defensive-employee-behavior/. Last Accessed: July 26, 2021.

Webb, Caroline. *How to have a Good Day.* London: Macmillan, 2016. ISBN 978-1-4472-7651-7

West, R. F., Toplak, M. E., & Stanovich, K. E. "Heuristics and Biases as Measures of Critical Thinking: Associations with Cognitive Ability and Thinking Dispositions". *Journal of Educational Psychology*, 100, no. 4 (2008), 930–941.

Whyte, W. H., Jr. "Groupthink". *Fortune* (March 1952), 114–117, 142, 146.

Windsor, Matt. "Psychological Safety Is Secret to Workplace Success". *UAB Reporter*, 2019. www.uab.edu/reporter/resources/learning-development/item/8770-psychological-safety-is-the-secret-to-workplace-success. Last Accessed: July 26, 2021.

World Economic Forum White Paper. *Behavioural Strategies to Strengthen Health Programmes and Policies*, March 2018. http://www3.weforum.org/docs/WEF_35662_WP_Behavioural_Strategies_to_Strengthen_Health_Programmes_Policies.pdf. Last Accessed: July 26, 2021.

Xerox Whitepaper. *20 Ways to Share Color Knowledge.* 2017. www.office.xerox.com/latest/COLFS-02UA.PDF. Last Accessed: July 26, 2021.

Yablonski, Jab. "The Psychology of Design". *Alistapart.com.*, 2018 https://alistapart.com/article/psychology-of-design/. Last Accessed: July 26, 2021.

Yankelovich, Daniel. *Corporate Priorities: A Continuing Study of the New Demands on Business.* Stanford, CT: Daniel Yankelovich Inc., 1972.

Zajonc, Robert. "Attitudinal Effects of Mere Exposure". *Journal of Personality and Social Psychology*, 9 (1968).

Index

Note: Page numbers in *italics* indicate a figure and page numbers in **bold** indicate a table on the corresponding page. Page numbers followed by "n" indicate a note.

ABCD approach 52–55; A=Attention 52–53; B=Beliefs 53; C=Choice 53–54; D=Determination 54–55; defaults 54
Abrahams, Robin 150
accurate self-assessment 64
achievement 64
acronyms 27–28
action, in gaining commitment 19
Adams, Sam 134
adaptability 64
adherence to processes 125
affect heuristics 107
anchoring bias 77–78
Angier, Natalie 124
anticipatory design, using 89–90
approach goal 130
Ariely, Dan 96
Aronson, Elliot 4
articles 60
ascertain step, to frame a message **30**
attention 52–53
audience 101
authenticity 101
authority 9
autonomy 140
availability bias 56, 76–77
availability heuristics 107
avoidance goal 130
Ayushman Bharat (being blessed with long life) 26

Balanced Scorecard 134
balancing skills with challenge 69–71
Balz, John P 165
Bandura, Albert 160
bandwagon effect, avoiding 49–50

Barker, Liz 77
Beck, Aaron 3
behavioural economics 2–3
behavioural science mantras for change 56–57
belief perseverance 75–76
beliefs 53
Bharatiya Janata Party (BJP) 22
biases 43, 55–56, 108–109
biases in problem-solving 75–83; anchoring bias 77–78; availability bias 76–77; belief perseverance 75–76; cognitive bias versus heuristics **76**; confirmation bias 76; motivated reasoning 78; planning fallacy 78–79; rewards 78; sunk cost fallacy 79–80; unpredictable unplanned events 78; *see also* groupthink
blogs 60
Blumenthal, Galit 87
boredom 125
bounded rationality 2
bounded self-interest 2
bounded willpower 2
Boyatzis, R. 63
Brendel, David 121
Broadbent, Donald 3
Brook, Fred 157
Brooks, Alison Wood 14
Brook's Law 157
Brown, Roger 4
building bonds 65
business case: for quality improvement 10; solidifying 7–11

Campbell, Donald T. 133
Campbell's Law 133–135

capacity 125
cause analysis 62
Certified Customer Experience Catalyst (CXC) 69
Certified Lean Service Catalyst (CLSC) 69
Certified Master Black Belt 69
Certified Quality Manager (CQM) 69
Chabris, Christopher 123
change, intricacies of 48–57; autonomy need 52; availability bias 56; bandwagon effect, avoiding 49–50; behavioural science mantras for 56–57; biases 55–56; communicating the change 55; confirmation bias 56; groupthink 56; growth need 52; improvement and personal goals mismatch, managing 49; loss aversion 56; meaning need 52; needs 52; positive emotions, evoking 48–49; present bias 56; role modelling 50–51; show and not tell 51–52; see also ABCD approach
change blindness 123
change catalyst 65
character-based storytelling, using 153
charter, signing 21
choice 53–54
Chun, H. H. 49
Church, Marcy 131
Cialdini, Robert B. 8, 13, 20, 23
Clifton Strength assessment 47n1
Cobra Effect 134
codify step, to frame a message 30
cognitive bias 43, 56–57
cognitive misers 106
cognitive overload, minimising 84–91; anticipatory design, using 89–90; distraction, shutting from 88; Hindu pantheon in 90–91; metrics refresh 89; multitasking, stopping 86–87; prefrontal cortex in 85; prioritisation, educating employees on 88–89; re-design work 87; unnecessary tasks, removing 89
Collins, Jim 146
commitment, gaining 19–24; asking small questions 19–20; charter, signing, making people to 21; public commitment, securing 20–21; small contribution, importance 23–24; us-versus-them approach 22–23
communicating visually 151–155; character-based storytelling, using 153; getting audience attention 153–154; involving employees 154; jargon free 152; making the message contextual 151–152; pictures use 152–153; power of space 154–155; storytelling 153
communication: data to avoid 31–32; importance 65–66; improvement, questions in 122; for quality improvement 29–30, 30, 30; through framing 28–31; ways to 31
competence 14, 17, 140
complaint clarity 101
comprehend step, to frame a message 30
confirmation bias 43–46, 56, 76; in problem-solving 45; quality-improvement efforts 44
Conner, Daryl 48
continuous improvement 4–6, 34, 42–43
contrast 124
Cooper, Deb 14
corporate social responsibility (CSR) 55
countermeasures deployment 62
Covey, Stephen 88, 130
Csikszentmihalyi, Mihaly 4, 68–69, 74
C-suite 11
Cukier, Kenneth 136
culturally relevant names, using 26–27
customers: and halo effect 106–107; obsession 95
customer service 101
customer solution design 92–97; customer solutions (Rule 3) 95; customer's context, understanding (Rule 4) 95–96; giving a sense of control (Rule 2) 93–94; making customer labour to value something more (Rule 5) 96–97; rules for 92–97; thinking in terms of experience (Rule 1) 92–93

Darwin, Charles 39, 121
data inundation, disadvantages 39–40
data limitations 5
default option 165
defaults 54
defensive behaviours 143, **144**
defensive employees 138–144
determine step, to frame a message 30
developing others 65
Dichter, Ernest 96
distraction: removing 71–73; shutting from 88; in solving problems 156–157
Dosher, B. A. 152
Doyle, Patrick 96–97
Drucker, Peter 132
Dudek, C. 106

Dunning, D. 36–37
Dunning-Kruger effect 36, 38

Easterlin, Richard Ainley 92
Edmondson, Amy 110–111
Eisenhower, Dwight 88
Eisenhower matrix 88
Ekman, Paul 4, 61
e-learning/web-based learning 165
Elliot, Andrew 131
emotional intelligence (EQ) 63–64
emotional self-awareness 64
emotional self-control 64
emotions 61–67; activity roster in place
    66–67; cause analysis 62; comfort and
    the need to control 66; communication,
    importance 65–66; countermeasures
    deployment 62; *Emotions Revealed* 61; in
    the initial stages 62; installing measures
    to sustain the project benefits 63; interest
    in the project 65; kaleidoscope of, being
    aware of 62–63; managing, ability to
    63–65; perception of progress 65–66;
    role of 61–67; trust 65
empathy 64
employees 138–144, 154; *see also* defensive
    employees
employees on board, taking 159–166;
    FOMO, creating a context for 163–164;
    making employees confident 159; making
    it hassle free 165–166; making quality
    learning a default choice 164–165;
    present bias, coming out of 162–163;
    seeing the future 161–162; sharing in
    160; showing the ways 160–161; values
    attached, understanding 164
enterprise might 102
eruptions, blind optimism during
    145–150; brutal reality 149; optimism
    meets pragmatism 147–148; survival
    psychology 149–150
European Foundation for Quality
    Management (EFQM) 70
Evans, Jeffrey 86
expectation 124
experience 9
expertise and competence 9
external customers 17
external quality eruptions 145

facts, overlooking of 42–47; belief system
    44; bias 43

fairness 139
familiarity, power of 58–60
Fast Company 89
*Fearless Organisation: Creating Psychological
    Safety in the Workplace for Learning,
    Innovation and Growth, The* 111
fear of missing out (FOMO) 163–164
feedback 73
feelings 62
Festinger, Leon 3
First Thing First 88
Flow: The Psychology of Optimal Experience
    68, 74
Four Sigma levels 51
Frederickson, Barbara 17
Frijda, Nico 61
fundamental attribution error 33–34

Gächter, Simon 8
Gates, Bill 41
Gilovich, Thomas 92
Gino, Francesca 14
give-up-itis 149
goals, measurements, and targets 130–137;
    Campbell's Law 133–135; data in 136;
    Goodhart's Law 132; McNamara Fallacy
    135–137; reframing of quality goals 131,
    132; *see also* SMART goals
Goldstein, Noah 23
Goleman, D. 63, 65
Goodhart's Law 132
*Good to Great: Why Some Companies Make
    the Leap . . . and Others Don't* 146
Gravert, Christina 162
Gray, Asa 40
Gray's Manual of Botany 40
Green, Marc 124
Grissinger, Matthew 124
groupthink 56, 80–83
Groysberg, Boris 150

halo effect 103–109; bias, ways to avoid
    108–109; customers and 106–107; good
    ideas 105; in performance appraisal 105;
    psychology behind 106; quality team
    105; in survey questionnaires 105
hearts and minds, engaging 68–74;
    distractions, removing 71–73; feedback
    73; mental state, challenge and skill level
    of 69, **70**; performance objectives **72**; in
    quality objectives 71; sense of control 73
Henry, Tod 10

heuristics **76**, 106–107; *see also* affect
   heuristics; availability heuristics;
   representative heuristics
Hick, William Edmund 85
Hick–Hyman Law 85
Hill, Andrew 163
Hollingworth, Crawford 77
Hood, Anthony 115
Hood, B. 96
Hooker, Joseph Dalton 40
hospitals 126
Howden, Tim 22
How to Have a Good Day 139
Huxley, Thomas 40
Hyman, Ray 85

Ikea Effect 96
improvement goals 49
inattentional blindness 123
inclusion 139
incubation theory 156
Indian Institute of Technology (IIT)
   schools 104
influence 65
Influence 8
Influence: Science and Practice 20
Influence: The Psychology of Persuasion 13
initiative 64
inspirational leadership 65
intention, in gaining commitment 19
internal customers 17
internal quality eruptions 146
International Financial Reporting Standards
   (IFRS) 142
intranet 60
investment, in gaining commitment 19
Invisible Gorillas 123–129; managing
   127– 128; opportunity in 128–129; reasons
   for 124–125; *see also* quality improvement
isolation effect 154

Jan Dhan Yojana (money of the people) 27
Janis, Irvin 81
jargon free communication 152
jigsaw classroom 4
Jobs, Steve 22, 157
Johnson, Lyndon 135

Kahneman, Daniel 3, 7, 17, 78, 95
Kaizen Blitz 63
Kanngiesser, P. 96
Kaplan, Robert S 134

Kaul, Satish 13
Kennedy, John F 135
key performance indicators (KPIs) 134
Kotter, John 163
Kruger, J. 36–37

Land, Edwin H. 121
Law of Emotions, The 61
Leach, John 149–150
leadership principles 95
leaders mindful behaviours in 116–117
Lean Breakthrough 49, 63
Lean method 39
Lean Sigma effort 42–43
Lewin, Kurt 4
Lindgaard, G. 106
little changes, importance 23–24
Liu, Simon 45
loss aversion 7, 56
Lyell, Charles 39

MacInnis, D. J. 49
Malcolm Baldrige model 70
Marsh, L. E. 96
Martin, John 103
Martin, Steve 23
Maurer, Robert 20
Mayer-Schönberger, Viktor 136
Mazon, Adolph 42–43
McBride, D. M. 152
McDaniel, M. 153
Mckee, A. 63
McLean Burger 28
McNamara, Robert 135
McNamara Fallacy 135–137
measurements 130–137
mental state in terms of challenge level and
   skill level 70
mental workload 125
messaging, power of 25–32; acronyms
   27–28; communication through framing
   28–31; culturally relevant names, using
   26–27; short/simple messages 25–26;
   slogans 25–26
metrics refresh 89
Meyer, David 86
Meyer, R. 55
Milgram, Stanley 3
Miller, George Armitage 84
*Misbehaving: The Making of Behavioral
   Economics* 3
Mochon, Daniel 96

Modi, Narendra 22, 27
moods 62
Moradzadeh, Linda 87
morale sag 102
Morris, Jessica 133
Moses, John 32n1
motivated reasoning 78
Moze, Andy 103
muda (Japanese for waste) 84
Mullainathan, Sendhil 2, 6n1
Müller, R. 65
multitasking, stopping 86–87
mura (Japanese for unevenness) 84
muri (Japanese for unreasonableness) 84
Myers Briggs Type Indicator 113
Mythical Man Month, The 157

Namamai Gange (I pray to Ganga) 26
Nass, Clifford 86
negative emotions 48
networking and power of familiarity 59
Norton, David 134
Norton, Michael 96
Nudge 3
numbers 9

objective, in gaining commitment 19
observational learning 160
O'Donoghue, Ted 9
*One Small Step Can Change Your Life: The
    Kaizen Way* 20
open-ended questions, power of 119–122;
    see also questions
Ophir, Eyal 86
optimism 64, 147–148
organisational awareness 65
Organisation for Economic Co-operation
    and Development (OECD) 52
*On the Origin of Species by Means of Natural
    Selection* 39
overconfidence, disadvantages 39–40

past successes 40–41
Patrick, V. M. 49
Pavlov, Ivan 1
Peak-End Rule 17
people 33–35
personal goals 49
pictures use in communication 152–153
planning fallacy 78–79
Planning Poker software system 50
Plumer, B. 55

Plutchik, Robert 61
positive emotions: creating 17–18; evoking
    48–49
power of green 158
power of reciprocity 13–14
power of space 154–155
pragmatism 147–148
pratfall effect 14
present bias 56, 162–163
press queries 102
*Primal Leadership: Learning to Lead with
    Emotional Intelligence* 63
prioritisation, educating employees on
    88–89
problems, questions in 121
problem solving 5, 45, 75–83, 126–127,
    156–158; *see also* biases in problem-
    solving
Project Aristotle 110
propinquity effect 15
Prospect Theory 3
psychological push 99–100
psychological safety 110–118; by asking
    questions 114; blaming people, avoiding
    117–118; building 110–118; creating
    shadow boards 115; by embracing
    positivity 115–116; employees to hold
    fellow employees accountable 113;
    employees voice, encouraging 112;
    leaders mindful behaviours in 116–117;
    meeting beyond the workplace 115;
    nudging people for improvement 114;
    roles and responsibilities 117; shared
    purpose in, creating 111–112; teams
    urged to embrace vulnerability 113; trust
    versus 111, **112**; working ways for 117
psychology, defining 1
public commitment, securing 20–21
purpose 19, 140
Putnam, Lawrence 157

quality: clear objectives around 71; as a
    concept 22; external quality eruptions
    145; goals, reframing of 131, **132**;
    internal quality eruptions 146; leaders
    behaviours 140, **141**; learning
    164–165
quality experts 36–41; continuous-
    improvement and 39; data inundation,
    disadvantages 39–40; overconfidence,
    disadvantages 39–40; past successes 40–41;
    what they need to know 36–41

quality improvement 4–6, 8, 125–127;
   adherence to processes 125; beyond
   technical solutions 5; business case for
   10; data limitations 5; eight cardinal rules
   for 127–128; hospitals 126; humans,
   as irrational 5; people as hearts of 4–5;
   problem-solving 126–127; problem-
   solving, importance 5; training and
   practise 126; uncommon events 125–126
quality issues, making them known 98–102;
   about humiliation 100; focus 99; intention,
   articulating 99; psychological push 99–100;
   sense of urgency 100–102; transparency,
   embedding 100
questions 119–120; benefit of 119–120;
   in communication improvement 122;
   in influencing 120–121; in problem
   solving 121; prevent us from becoming
   complacent 120

Rabin, Matthew 9
Rao, Huggy 22
reciprocity 13–14
re-design work 87
relationship management 64–65
relationships, cementing 12–18; being
   in touch 15–16; being vulnerable,
   advantages 14–15; competence,
   establishing 14, 17; delivering promises
   16; positive memories, creating 17–18;
   power of reciprocity 13–14; reliability,
   demonstrating 16–17; trust in 16
relevance 124
reliability, demonstrating 16–17
repetition and power of familiarity 59
representative heuristics 107
respect 139
rest 140
rewards 78
role modelling 50–51
Rubinstein, Joshua 86

Scaling Up Excellence 22
Schacter, Daniel 4
Schiller, Robert J. 4
Schweitzer, Maurice E. 14
scrutiny 102
security 140
Seibert, Horst 134
self-awareness 64
self-confidence 64
self-management 64

Seligman, Martin 4
sense of control 73
sense of urgency 100–102
service 65
shadow boards 115
Shapiro, Aaron 89
shared purpose, creating 111–112
Sheldon, K M 131
Shiller, Robert 3
short messages, importance 25–26
similarity 9
Simons, Daniel 123
simple messages, importance 25–26
Six Sigma Black Belt 70
Six Sigma method 39, 77, 153
Skinner, BF 4
slogans, importance 25–26
Slovic, Paul 40
small contribution, importance 23–24
SMART goals 130
social awareness 64–65
social media 101
social proof 8
solving problems *see* problem solving
stamps of approval 9
state step, to frame a message **30**
Stockdale Paradox 146–148, 150
storytelling 153
strategic business unit (SBU) 104
sunk cost fallacy 79–80
Sunstein, Cass R. 165
survival psychology 149–150
Sutton, Robert 22

targets 130–137
team size in problem solving 157
teamwork and collaboration 65
Thaler, Richard 2–4, 165
Thinking, Fast and Slow 3, 78
Thorndike, Edward 103
traditional economics 2
training and practise 126
transparency 64, 100
trust 16, 111, **112**
Turner, J. R. 65
Tversky, Amos 3, 7, 78

Ulrich, Roger 158
uncertainty 9
uncommon events 125–126
understand step, to frame a message **30**
Unnati (advancement) 27

unnecessary tasks, removing 89
unpredictable unplanned events 78
us-versus-them approach 22–23

Victims of Groupthink: A Psychological Study of Foreign Policy Decisions and Fiascos 81
Visual Expert.com 124
von Restorff effect 154
vulnerability; teams urged to embrace 113; uses 14–15

Waddill, P. 153
Wagner, Anthony 86
walking meeting 157
War of Numbers: An Intelligence Memoir of the Vietnam War's Uncounted Enemy 134
Webb, Caroline 139

Wheeler, McArthur 36
Whyte, William H, Jr 81
Wiseheart, Melody 87
Wong, Pinser 45–46
working memory 85
working ways 117
workplace, meeting beyond 115
Wundt, Wilhelm 1

Yankelovitch, Daniel 135
Yes! 50 Secrets from the Science of Persuasion 23

Zajonc, Robert 4, 58
Zanuck, Darry 117
zero defects 10, 128
Zero Defect Zero Effect (ZED) 27
Zimbardo, Philip 4